THE
smArt
Canadian
Wealth-
Builder

*Stepping Stones
to Financial
Independence*

Cover: Goodall Design, Victoria, BC

Note for Librarians: A cataloguing record for this book is available from Library and Archives Canada at:
www.collectionscanada.ca/amicus/index-e.html

Third Printing 2013
Fourth Printing (with Full Update) 2014
Fifth Printing (Second Edition) 2015
Printed in Canada by Friesens

ISBN: 978-0-9865790-0-4

Cufflands Publishing
9711 Second Street
Sidney, BC
V8L 3C3

www.canadianwealthbuilder.ca
www.dolezalconsultants.ca
pdolezal@smartcanadianwealthbuilder.ca

....

Other Books *by* Peter Dolezal

The Naked Homeowner

The Naked Traveller

peter dolezal

NOTICE TO READERS ....

This book is intended for Canadians as a tool for broadening their knowledge of the many issues important to successful wealth-creation.

It is not intended for, nor should it be used by readers as a guide to specific investments.

Readers are urged to make specific investment decisions only *after* consulting with a qualified financial advisor, and *after* taking into account their individual circumstances.

What Readers Have Said .....

"Many Canadians mishandle their financial affairs, creating unnecessary stress and dependencies, simply due to lack of knowledge. Peter Dolezal explains the basics of personal financial planning in very clear terms. Everyone from novice to the financially-aware can benefit greatly. This book is a must-read for all."

Bryan Wilson, Chief Financial Officer

....

"*The Wealthy Barber* started the trend. Peter Dolezal's book has pushed the envelope to a new level; full of contemporary easy-to-read-and-understand examples and TIPS. I have long felt, as a former university professor, that nothing is more important in a curriculum than financial literacy concepts. This book fills the bill – and then some. These are the lessons of life!"

G. Lorne Firman, Labour Lawyer

....

"Peter Dolezal takes the reader on an easy-to-read-and-understand journey by defining all of the concepts covered in a well-organized, plain-language approach to building financial health and wealth. Reading it yourself will be very rewarding, but giving it to your children will be priceless!"

Bruce Clow
Human Resources Executive, and Past Trustee
Public Service Pension Plan

....

"This is such an important subject which has largely been ignored. Congratulations on identifying the need and then doing something about it. Your book is both practical and, most importantly, understandable. I wish I had had something like this in my younger years."

Claude G. Heywood, Deputy Minister of Labour (Retired),
Province of British Columbia

....

"As a retired educator and Principal, I am impressed with the book's common sense practices that point the way to long-term financial security, both for young adults, and for their parents and grandparents."

William Smith, BPE, MA

....

"Congratulations, Peter! Your simple and straightforward explanation of difficult financial concepts provides a great roadmap to wealth-creation and its management for all ages. I'd love to see your book incorporated into the life skills program in all high schools."

Allan Crawshaw, IT Executive

....

"For young adults and those of us who find financial material desperately 'dry', this book is an invitation to an excellent, easy, instructional and informational read! The 120 TIPS are a great guide for persons of all ages."

Mary-Lynn Hyndman, Operating Theatre Nurse

....

"A challenge to educators! Use Peter's book in your high school or college business class. Teach to his wealth-accumulation TIPS. Do the math activities he suggests to let students see how growth works. Both teacher and student will be the wiser and richer for it!"

Sandra Jaques, Educator

....

"This book should be required reading for all who wish to learn to manage their money with a view to accumulating wealth."

Richard Keogh, M.D., Radiologist

....

"I wish I had had a family member share this crucial information with me when I was young. It would have saved me a lot of time and effort over the years. Lucky grandkids indeed, to receive this smart guidance while still young adults!"

Christina Issmer, Dental Hygienist

....

"I really enjoyed pondering the possibilities, both personally and educationally, that this book offers. The style of writing is easy to follow and inviting to all age groups. The content offers much latitude for entry into the subject of personal financial management. I highly recommend this book to my own grown kids and suggest that everyone would profit from reading it!"

J. L. Shaw-Ringham, Educator

....

Contents

Financial Planning

Understanding Pensions

The Entrepreneur

Miscellany – More Money Management

Final Wisdom

INTRODUCTION
. . . .

Jenny and Kevin are the two oldest of our five grandchildren. Jenny, at twenty, is attending community college. Kevin is nearing high school graduation. Neither has yet settled on a specific career path.

Both Jenny and Kevin have always been intrigued by Grandma's and my retirement lifestyle. To them, we seem to live better than many other couples, even when both partners are still working full-time. They often try to figure out how we manage to be so comfortable financially.

Guidance counselors at the high schools and colleges are available to help Kevin, Jenny, and their classmates sort out their career interests. A huge gap exists however, throughout the education system. It has not yet begun to address students' needs for an understanding of personal financial management and wealth-creation.

Failure to equip our youth with at least the basics of financial literacy, does not serve society well. Graduates leave school poorly-equipped to manage their incomes once they enter the *real world* of employment. At best, this basic life-skill deficiency becomes a drag on their efforts at future wealth-creation, and their ultimate financial independence. At worst, it increases their risk of drifting into irresponsible financial behaviour.

Youth is smart. Generally they understand the basic concept – the better their education level, the greater their opportunity for a quality lifestyle, which they equate to making more money. No one teaches young adults however, how to develop even a simple financial plan, or how to save, spend and invest wisely, as their career progresses.

As a consequence, many of us are left to develop our money-management skills the hard way – through personal trial and error. For many, this leads to an early, and at times lasting debt-trap, with potentially severe consequences for their and their family's future well-being.

Having had a lifelong passion and interest in all aspects of financial planning and investment, I jumped at the chance, when Jenny's and Kevin's curiosity became evident, to share my enthusiasm and knowledge with them.

The format I suggested was simple. Working around their school and part-time work schedules, we could get together at my home, for a series of Saturday afternoon discussions. I would share with them, in a simple yet comprehensive manner, my experiences, with lessons learned over forty years, and my own efforts at wealth-creation.

To my surprise and delight, both Jenny and Kevin embraced the idea, especially after I made *THE OFFER* – if they were interested enough to sit through the entire series of Saturday discussions, Grandma and I would stake them to $1,000 each. With their new-found knowledge, they could invest this wisely, adding to their existing, very modest investment account.

....

We three enjoyed our project immensely. Because I love writing, I told Jenny and Kevin to relax as we talked, without taking notes, since my plan was to write a book capturing the essence of our chats.

This book is a summary of those Saturday sessions.

It serves as a practical guide for a relatively safe, and predictable path to personal wealth-creation and long-term financial independence.

The contents will provide not only all our grandchildren, but also Canadians of all ages, with a reference point for lifelong use.

At the outset, I emphasized to Jenny and Kevin that our discussions were not intended to make them experts in all matters related to the principles of financial management, financial planning and investment. Nor is this book so intended.

My purpose instead, is to provide a sufficient basic understanding of these subjects, so that they, or you, the reader, could act knowledgeably, and perhaps independently, in a prudent, and financially beneficial manner.

This book is not meant to replace the need for an *independent financial planner* or *advisor*, whose services can be invaluable as you navigate your way toward a financially stress-free retirement.

The key conclusions reached in our discussions are highlighted in the form of easy-to-understand **TIPS**. Taken together, these **TIPS** are the framework that Canadians can adopt to greatly enhance their ability to build their own net-worth and ultimately, to achieve financial independence.

Because few of us have been exposed to formal lessons in the basics of financial literacy, it is my hope that this book will prove beneficial to a cross-section of Canadians of all ages. Hopefully you, the reader, will benefit personally, but also, will emerge better equipped to provide guidance to your own children and grandchildren.

....

Throughout this book, I have often used the masculine, singular form in making specific points. This is done simply for the sake of convenience. I hope that the many female readers will accept that no sexist bias is intended.

....

Read on. Eavesdrop on a chat between a wise old goat and two voracious youngsters who, eager to evolve into financially-savvy adults, are convinced that they too, will achieve financial independence – probably a lot sooner than their grandparents.

THE
FOUNDATION

. . . .

CHAPTER ONE

BREAKING THE ICE –
The First Saturday

"Well, Grandpa, here we are," enthused Kevin, as he and older sister Jenny joined me for our first Saturday discussion on wealth-creation. "I can't wait to find out how we can become rich!"

"Kevin, don't be a nerd! Money isn't everything!"

"You know, Jenny, you're absolutely right. There *is* much more to life than money. But would you agree with me that whenever the money you earn from your part-time job runs short, you're more stressed and less happy than when you receive that pay cheque every second Thursday? Don't you feel more comfortable and independent when you're not scraping together loonies and toonies to put gas in your car?"

"I guess what you're saying, Grandpa, is that we need enough money to be able to meet our daily needs comfortably," acknowledged Jenny.

"Told you, Jenny," said Kevin. "It all boils down to having lots of money."

"You're both partly correct. Earning enough money is important. And because you both intend to pursue some form of higher education which will give you a good start up the career-ladder, I expect you'll do well in that regard.

You may not be aware that with the Canadian population shifting dramatically toward a higher proportion of retirees, landing a good job for a hard-working, well-educated individual, should not be too difficult in the next several decades."

....

"The unfortunate reality however, is that many Canadians *do* make good money all their working life, yet they never really achieve financial independence. Often in fact, they have to really tighten their belts when they retire. Why do you think that is?"

"They don't know how to save," offered Kevin.

"They don't know how to invest their money," added Jenny.

"You're both on the right track. And here's my first tip for you."

TIP #1..... **The total income earned in one's working life is much less important to wealth-creation, than how one uses the money earned.**

....

"Knowing how to *save* money and how to *invest* wisely are only two elements of how one uses his disposable income. We'll deal with both of these in detail, later in our discussions. But first, what do you think are other factors important to our smart use of money?"

"Don't fritter your money away," suggested Kevin.

"You're absolutely right, Kevin! Before we even consider savings and investment ideas, every one of us, at any age and income level, should be shrewd in how we *spend* the money we earn. Can either of you think of any examples of the *smart* use of one's disposable income?"

"What do you mean by disposable income, Grandpa?" asked Kevin.

"Good question, Kevin. I'll try to define any new terms we come across."

> *DISPOSABLE INCOME is the money actually deposited in one's bank account. It is the amount left over, after an employer subtracts income taxes, pension contributions, insurance costs, union dues, employment insurance contributions, or any other required deductions. It is the amount of money that is actually spendable.*

"Oh – well, in answer to your question, I've been with you when you were buying expensive or multiple items, and I've seen you, often successfully, negotiate the asking price," offered Kevin.

"Right again, Kevin! I learned that tactic from watching my father when I was young. I often squirmed when I was with him and saw the lengths to which he carried his negotiations. I'm a bit more conservative in my approach, but I do instinctively look for any *reasonable* opportunity to negotiate a purchase. You've seen a few examples, but here are some for Jenny's benefit:

- Each year, when I order eight hanging baskets from my favourite nursery, I search out the owner and routinely receive a significant price reduction.

- When booking a hotel room, especially for multiple nights, I always check out the best online price, but then I go a step further. I use the 1-800 number for the hotel and speak to the reservations manager, to ask for his best price. Very often, I'll get a discount that beats any online deal.

- Even when buying appliances that are on sale, or expensive electronic items, I'll ask for the department manager and try to negotiate a further discount. Often I'm successful.

These are just a few examples. Individually, they seem to amount to very little. But over the last forty years, when most people would not even think of trying, I have saved tens of thousands of dollars by negotiating purchases.

The key of course, is to be *reasonable* and *polite* when asking for price consideration. Although you may not always be successful, you definitely won't be if you don't try.

Can you think of other smart ways to limit your spending?"

"I guess you should not only negotiate, but shop around first, and compare alternatives that may be available," suggested Jenny. "I know Mom uses coupons, and watches for sales, or she'll get a great discount because something has a scratch or a dent."

"Right, Jenny! There are many examples I could give you, from furnishing a home, to car-buying, and even to choosing the lowest-fee bank accounts. But perhaps the most significant ones you're likely to encounter over the course of your life are:

- When buying a home, the effort you invest in really looking around, comparing options, and looking for *best value*, even before negotiating price, can save you many thousands of dollars on each purchase.

- Perhaps even more important, shopping around for the best-value mortgage, whether for your first home, or the renewal of a current mortgage, can save you *tens of thousands* of dollars over the life of your mortgage.

Both of these scenarios have such a huge potential impact on the growth of your long-term net-worth, that we'll spend more time discussing each in a later session.

Always keep in mind this next tip."

TIP #2..... **There is no easier way to stretch disposable income, and indirectly, to add to *net-worth*, than to minimize the cost of planned expenditures right at the time of purchase.**

"I'll be referring to *net-worth* often, so I'd better explain what I mean by that. In simple terms:

> **NET WORTH is a measure of wealth. It is the total of all your cash, savings, real estate market value, vehicles, financial or other investments (YOUR ASSETS), less any money owed by you (YOUR LIABILITIES).**

If the total amount of your assets exceeds the total of your *liabilities*, you have a *positive net-worth*.

The fundamental objective of wealth-creation is to increase net-worth. Your ultimate aim is to keep increasing your assets, while reducing your liabilities toward zero."

....

"Since we're talking about net-worth, can you guess what the median net-worth of young Canadians, say at age twenty, might be?"

"Not much, if they're anything like me," quipped Jenny.

"You're right, Jenny, and that's normal at your age. In their early twenties many people may well have student-loan liabilities, minimal income and very few assets. This often results in a *negative* net-worth at this stage of their life.

This is not necessarily a bad thing. If ever there were a good reason for debt, it's a student loan to upgrade one's education. An investment in post-secondary education of any type, should pay off big time.

Canada's **Money Sense** magazine quoted a *People Patterns Consulting* statistic showing as of September, 2009, the following distribution of net-worth, by age group, for Canadian households:

	Average	Median
Under 35	$100,000	$ 25,000
35 to 44	$325,000	$145,000
45 to 54	$490,000	$245,000
55 to 64	$670,000	$420,000
65 Plus	$505,000	$315,000

The *median* net-worth numbers are more representative of reality. The *average* figures are skewed upward by relatively few, very wealthy households.

The reduction in net-worth after age 65 is due primarily to retirees beginning to draw down their accumulated wealth once employment income disappears.

Today, these may seem to you like fairly high numbers. However, as our discussions continue, I'll share with you how, relatively easily, you can each *far* exceed these levels of net-worth by the time you reach these age groupings."

"I knew you'd show us how to get rich!" enthused Kevin, still focused on being a millionaire.

....

"Well, I've heard that a million dollars is no longer enough to retire on – that inflation has eroded its value so much that it isn't such a great number to aim for," Jenny commented. "Is this true?"

"Good observation, Jenny. I've often heard the same. But let's put that one-million-dollar figure into perspective.

Do you know that only about 9% of all Canadian families have a net-worth of more than $1 million? Moreover, most of that select group are over age 60, with a significant portion of their net-worth comprised of the equity built up in the value of their home.

Yet, many other retired Canadians live very comfortably, even with modest net-worth.

The reason is that net-worth is only *one* major element of one's retirement standard of living. The *other* component, perhaps more important, is the combined retirement pension and investment income that the retiree receives on a regular basis. We'll delve further into investments and pensions in our future discussions.

So, Jenny, one million dollars in net-worth is still a *very* big number. Proof of that is in the fact that this goal has *not* been attained by more than 90% of all Canadian families.

I believe I'll be able to show how you can each not only achieve, but even beat that number, *if* you determine it to be a reasonable target. It's premature at this stage however, to start speculating what *your target* should be. You simply don't have all the information you need at this early stage in our discussions."

"So, Grandpa, what's next?" asked Kevin.

"Well, now that you understand the concept of *net-worth* and the interaction of *assets* and *liabilities*, you'll probably understand intuitively, that if we don't control the *liabilities*, or debts that we accumulate, we'll have less money to invest. We therefore undermine our ability to increase net-worth."

"Seems to me we just have to figure out the difference between what we want and what we need," commented Kevin.

"You're on the right track, Kevin.

This is so important, I'd like to spend a bit of time chatting about the whole concept of **debt** and its role, not only in your lives, but in the lives of all Canadians."

CHAPTER TWO

. . . .

OUR CULTURE OF DEBT

"This is such an important part of our discussion, what say we take a quick break before we carry on?"

"Great idea!" echoed both Jenny and Kevin, as they headed for the kitchen. Soon they were back, eager and attentive.

"First a little background, to help you better understand how debt, its availability and importance, have evolved over the past decades.

In their day, Grandma's and my parents, and their parents, had few problems with debt. Why do you think this was so?"

"Maybe they were smarter than we are today," offered Kevin.

"You may be onto something, Kevin. However, it really *was* much easier for them to be smart in the use of debt, simply because credit was generally harder to come by, and often non-existent. If you had the cash, you bought what you wanted. If you didn't have the cash, you did without until you had saved sufficient funds."

. . . .

"*Credit cards* were a fledgling novelty in the 60's and only became mainstream in the 70's. As profitability of credit card companies grew, their numbers exploded. More and more consumers began to succumb to the 'Buy now – Pay later' philosophy.

Before long, most *males* could qualify for a credit card. Grandma remembers that early on, a woman could *not* have a card issued in her own name. She could have a card, but it bore her husband's name. He however, was responsible for the charges.

Early qualification rules soon eased drastically. I remember bizarre examples in which credit cards were approved and issued in the name of a dog. Before long, people rushed to obtain multiple cards, for many different purposes. Credit became as easy as signing your name on a slip of paper in almost any store. Suddenly you could enjoy instant gratification – ownership of almost anything covered by your credit card spending limit. If you stayed reasonably current on your minimum payments, your card limit would be increased, often automatically, providing even more credit.

Department store credit cards also began to proliferate. Special discounts on a new cardholder's first purchase lured many to sign up. Eager shoppers filled their purses and wallets with numerous charge cards from stores like Eaton's, Woodwards, Simpson Sears, and countless others. You've probably noticed some of these offers, even today."

"They're very difficult to ignore," observed Jenny. "They even offer loyalty programs that earn points you can apply to future purchases."

"You're right, Jenny. It's all part of the lure to get customers to spend more and to return to *their* store.

Furniture and appliance stores joined the parade, with tempting offerings of debt. Irresistible offers of 'no-money-down, no-interest and no-payments-for-12-months' and even longer, attracted more buyers. The public could now buy expensive items instantly, not having to worry about payments until many months later, at actual interest rates often approaching 30%.

North American automobile manufacturers, desperate to stem their market-share losses to foreign auto makers, began offering zero-down, zero-interest, new-car purchase deals."

"With a deal like that, I can see why so many of my friends are tempted," Kevin added.

"And as you've heard on the news in the past several years, mortgages, usually the typical homeowner's largest debt obligation, began to be packaged so attractively, that even marginal, U.S. 'sub-prime' borrowers were encouraged to try for the brass ring of home ownership.

A SUB-PRIME MORTGAGE is a mortgage issued to a borrower whose income level and credit history make it highly unlikely that he will be able to meet future repayment obligations on a regular basis.

The mortgage is 'sub-prime' in the sense that it is a much riskier loan from the perspective of a lender.

For several years, even in Canada, it was possible to buy a home with zero down and a 40-year mortgage. Fortunately for prospective borrowers, the income and credit qualification requirements remained stringent. As a result, Canadians were not caught up in sub-prime lending.

The consequences of years of sub-prime lending in the U.S. on the other hand, were catastrophic, and cascaded quickly throughout the world's economy in 2008 and 2009.

The root cause of the economic crises facing governments world-wide by 2009, may have been the irresponsible overuse of credit by a relatively small proportion of the U.S. population. However, the problem was greatly magnified by lax government oversight of the mortgage, banking and insurance industries, and by the greed of associated corporations. Companies packaged their products, and granted credit in a fashion designed to *lure* consumers, including those who clearly could not afford it."

"If the professionals can't be more on the ball than that, Grandpa, how on earth is the ordinary person supposed to be smart?" exclaimed Jenny.

"Well, Jenny, I think that governments, bankers, and others have learned a tough lesson as well. Hopefully, more prudent lending practices and regulatory oversight will become the norm in the future. But the onus must always be on ourselves as individuals, to resist unaffordable temptations."

....

"That's just a bit of history, to help you understand how personal credit evolved and grew, for both better and worse.

Today, we Canadians, and our American neighbours, live in an almost inescapable *culture of debt*. Our governments, at all levels, carry huge debts on our behalf. We, as individuals, are continually urged, by both our government and by the many enterprises looking to profit from our consumerism, to increase our spending.

Federal governments issue monthly reports on the spending activity of their citizens. The first sign of a general decline in personal spending is reported with great trepidation, as a potential indicator of an emerging recession. The concern is understandable, since some 70% of the Gross Domestic Product (GDP) of both the U.S. and Canada is dependent on the personal spending of their citizens.

GROSS DOMESTIC PRODUCT is the total of all goods and services produced by an economy.

This increased pressure on more and more personal spending works for the economy and for most consumers, *if* disposable incomes increase proportionately. Unfortunately in recent years, disposable incomes have stagnated, and savings have dropped to near zero."

....

"For much of the first decade of this century, we lived in a fools' paradise. We watched our real estate and financial investments soar with no seeming end in sight. Confident and excited by our growing net-worth, our credit card use boomed, and with it, massive credit-card and other debt.

17

Because homeowners' equity increased as house values rose dramatically, refinancing a mortgage to fund a vacation, home renovation, or car purchase became a habit for many. In effect, many treated the equity in their home as a personal ATM machine. Refinancing could often be arranged in a matter of days. Savings disappeared, debt levels increased, yet we felt wealthier.

As you heard and read, in late 2008 and 2009 reality hit home. Stock markets plummeted as did real estate values. In Canada these drops were dramatic; in the U.S. they were catastrophic. Although much tougher banking and mortgage regulations protected Canadians from the real estate meltdowns and bank crises of the United States, we were not totally immune.

With the combination of the U.S., our largest trading partner, in a downward economic spiral, and our global economic interconnections, Canadian stock market indices plummeted some 50% in the nine-month period beginning mid-2008. During the same period, Canadian real estate prices dropped about 10% nationally. In the more severely hit U.S. real estate market, average home prices dropped by more than 30%.

With these severe declines, the net-worth of North American families shrank dramatically. Debt burdens became more onerous. No longer able to maintain unaffordable lifestyles simply by increasing debt through mortgage refinancing, some 10% of U.S. mortgage holders had fallen into delinquency or foreclosure by early 2009. Home equity values of Canadians also shrank, but the rate of defaulting mortgage payments remained at less than 0.5%, thanks to Canada's more stringent lending rules."

FORECLOSURE is the legal process used by a mortgage lender to gain title to a home on which the owners had failed to make payments for a specified period of time.

"How could this have happened to so many people in the U.S.?" wondered Jenny. "Weren't they just following their dream of home ownership rather than paying rent?"

"Good observation, Jenny. It's great to follow one's dream, but only after it becomes affordable.

Between the late 1990's and 2006, many U.S. mortgages were issued to homeowners with a restricted ability to repay their loan, based on what we in Canada would consider to be normal lending criteria. As house prices began to soften in 2006, delinquencies soared and foreclosures followed."

....

"Securities which were backed with sub-prime mortgages, and which were widely held by financial firms in many countries, lost much of their value. This resulted in major write-downs of capital assets by many banks and other financial institutions. Major banks world-wide were threatened with collapse.

Credit tightened everywhere. Government bailouts and stimulus packages, funded by huge deficits, were quickly crafted in a semi-coordinated, world-wide effort to prevent the deterioration of a global recession into a full-blown depression.

Our culture of debt, particularly in the U.S., had clearly gone beyond the bounds of reason. The wealth of millions of individuals, corporations, and countries became severely impaired."

"It boggles the mind that the situation could even be allowed to happen," exclaimed Kevin.

"Yes, Kevin. You're right. It became a near catastrophe world-wide. The frightening vulnerability of even the most careful investors became evident. Learning from this harsh experience, many investors would never again strive to recover and build wealth, without *first* examining much more critically than they had in the past, traditional definitions of *risk*. We'll deal with risk more extensively later in our discussions.

So severe was the shock that many North Americans of all ages began to severely restrain their spending. Once again, they began to save a few dollars. This trend however, served to slow the economy even more, and in the short term, added to the problem.

The next TIP will now make sense to you."

TIP #3..... The ever-increasing spending of its citizens contributes significantly to the growth of a country's economy. However, if such increases are powered primarily by increased *debt* rather than higher incomes or savings, the euphoria can soon turn to disaster for many individuals, and into a recession for the nation.

In North America a RECESSION is considered to be present, if the nation's GDP declines for two consecutive quarters.

....

"Grandpa, what's the difference between a recession and a depression?" asked Kevin.

"A *recession* is an occasional downturn in an economy. It is *not* reasonable to expect that any economy can continue to grow uninterrupted for decades on end. Various national and international events will periodically combine to cause a pause, or even a downturn in economic activity.

A *depression* on the other hand, is a very severe and prolonged economic downturn, lasting for many years. It is characterized by chronic unemployment at extremely high levels, by falling wages, and by a major, extended meltdown in stock market values.

Since the 1929 Great Depression, which lasted four years, the world has experienced fourteen *recessions*, almost all of which lasted less than twelve months. The good news is that the world has not experienced a *depression* since 1929. With lessons learned in the subsequent decade by both government and business, a

repeat event is most unlikely, but certainly not impossible, as
warning flags demonstrated in the 2008–2009 recession period."

....

"As we have just discussed, the major economic problems of 2008
and 2009 were caused by the *overuse of credit* by some. As a result,
lending rules and regulations have tightened. Credit for many
individuals and corporations is not quite as easy to come by today,
as it was before 2008.

For those with a ***good credit rating***, ample credit is still available.
As such, it remains a huge temptation, which too many of us do
not handle well.

Credit is a useful and necessary tool for vibrant, growing economies.
For individuals, credit is virtually a necessity in our modern way
of life. It simply is not realistic for example, to expect families to
save the full $390,000 price of an average home in Canada, before
becoming a homeowner.

The challenge for all of us, is to utilize debt strategically, to *our*
best advantage. We want to ensure that its use does not become
an unacceptable *drag* on our efforts to increase our net-worth and
eventually, to achieve financial independence.

No sooner do Canadians reach adulthood at age nineteen, than
they are bombarded with offers of credit cards, and numerous
other debt instruments."

"Yes, I know," interjected Jenny. "I can't believe how many offers to
sign up for various cards have been showing up in my mailbox."

"Not surprising, Jenny. You'll see more and more of these once you
begin full-time work and start building your credit rating."

"Excuse me, Grandpa, but what exactly do you mean by 'credit
rating'?" asked Kevin.

A CREDIT RATING is a broadly-accepted report card of an individual's credit worthiness, based on his handling of all previously-incurred debt obligations, usually during the previous six years.

"If your credit rating is good, you'll be eligible for more credit, and at lower interest rates, than someone whose rating is poor."

"Grandpa, how would I know what my credit rating is?" asked Jenny.

"Good question, Jenny. These days, almost everything can be done online, even checking your credit rating. Just google **Canadian Credit Rating**, select a provider like **Equifax**, pay a small fee, and receive your report online."

> TIP #4..... **The wise use of credit is a key element in net-worth growth. Good credit leads to lower interest costs on necessary borrowing, such as for a home mortgage. This in turn allows loans to be paid off more quickly, thereby accelerating wealth-creation.**

"Before we can learn to effectively manage the various forms of credit available to us, it's important to understand how significantly *debt drag* can impact our efforts at wealth-creation."

CHAPTER THREE

· ·

THE DEBT DRAG

"Kevin, why do you think I use the term *debt drag* when I refer to debt?"

"I guess because debt is like an anchor. It weighs down your chances of increasing your net-worth," replied Kevin.

"Well put, Kevin! And it's not only a drag on net-worth growth. For many of us, debt can become an overwhelming weight on our and our family's shoulders. If excessive and uncontrolled, the burden can lead to personal bankruptcy, poor health, and even family break-up. This leads me to the next tip."

> **TIP #5.....** **The most important cornerstone of any plan for wealth creation is the early, continuous, and passionate effort to manage, and as quickly as possible, eliminate debt of any kind.**

"By making this a regular practice, you'll limit and more quickly eliminate the *debt drag* on your efforts at wealth-creation."

"That sure seems like common sense," agreed Kevin.

"Well today, it might seem like common sense to you, Kevin. I hope it will always be so. However, the temptation for so many, at any age, is instant gratification. Buying something today, and paying for it in the future, often overrides common sense."

"Hmmm…Remember the thirty bucks you just borrowed from me to fill up your car, Jenny?" teased Kevin.

"I'm assuming *that's* an interest-free debt. But listen to this statistic:

2009 data shows that, aside from interest paid on mortgages, the average Canadian family spends 6.3% of its after-tax income on interest on various loan obligations. Since many Canadians have zero debt, the average percentage is actually much higher for those who do carry debts."

....

"You'll be shocked to learn that in a typical year, having decided there is no other solution to their debt problems, almost 100,000 Canadians declare *personal bankruptcy*. This may seem like an easy solution to wiping out debt. It is not. Bankruptcy involves the total loss of all significant assets, as well as a credit rating that is destroyed for seven years.

It's eye-opening to learn that the average debt of those declaring bankruptcy is around $35,000. Such a sum is easy to rack up using only three or four credit cards."

"Wow!" exclaimed Kevin. "That's a huge number of people going broke every year."

"You're right, Kevin. Every one of those unfortunate individuals, regardless of age when they declare bankruptcy, has to start rebuilding assets from scratch. Very few are likely to bounce back enough to enjoy a comfortable retirement."

....

"You've both been lucky to grow up knowing all of your great-grandparents. Let me focus for a moment on two of them – my parents. What you may not have known is that during their working lives, their family income while comfortable, was certainly not much above that of the average Canadian family. Yet they managed to accumulate a very substantial net-worth, and a good income in their retirement years. So how do you think they achieved this?"

"Well, earlier you pointed out that credit wasn't as easily available for your parents and grandparents, so maybe, it's because they had little debt during their working lives," replied Jenny.

"You're absolutely right, Jenny! But my parents, like most others, *did* require a mortgage loan to buy their house. The difference though was that unlike many others, they kept increasing their payments until their mortgage was paid off in only nine years instead of the usual twenty-five."

"Wouldn't they have had to pay big penalties when they fast-tracked their mortgage loan repayments?" asked Kevin.

"Not really. Most mortgages allow penalty-free payment acceleration and even an annual lump-sum repayment of 10 to 15% of the outstanding loan balance.

Once their house loan was paid off, my parents began investing their savings in rental properties and financial investments. By the time they retired at age 60, their net-worth, combined with pension and investment incomes, allowed them to live more lavishly. But content with their lifestyle, they chose not to. They actually *added* to their net-worth, even in retirement."

"That's sure something!" exclaimed Jenny. "But I'm not sure I inherited their frugal genes."

"My parents never bought an automobile unless they paid cash for it. If they had saved only $3,000, that was the most they would spend on a vehicle. Only after they retired, did they finally buy their first new car.

When they eventually acquired a credit card the year they retired, they used it strictly as a convenience. They *never* spent one nickel in credit card interest payments. In short, except for their mortgage, they had no *drag* on their wealth-creation efforts."

"Wow, that's pretty awesome, to go through life with so little debt, and still be able to live as they wanted. I know they were very generous to our family as we got older," commented Kevin.

"Yes, it is awesome, Kevin. I'm not necessarily suggesting that either of you emulate your great-grandparents in avoiding debt at any cost, but it's useful to see that my parents had an intuitive understanding of how severely debt can hamper efforts to achieve financial independence."

....

"Let me give you an example of the significance of debt, as a drag on wealth-creation.

Assume your neighbour is living in an *average* Canadian household. In 2014 this family had a total outstanding debt amounting to $1.63 for every $1 of disposable income. At first glance, this number may seem quite modest. But remember that the *average* calculation lumps in those who have no debt at all. It includes some 60% of Canadian families who have paid off their mortgages. It does, however, give us a figure to work with.

This *average* family's wealth accumulation is not only impaired by the money they owe, but also, by the *compounding interest* cost of carrying their debt until it is paid off. This generally, more than doubles the total amount eventually repaid."

COMPOUND INTEREST ON DEBT is the repeating interest paid on every single dollar of debt, until that dollar is paid off.

"Since we're talking about debt, have either of you heard the expressions *good debt* or *bad debt*?"

"I have," offered Jenny. "But I wouldn't want to explain to anyone what it means."

"No problem, Jenny. It may be worth a few minutes to understand exactly what people *do* mean when they use these expressions."

CHAPTER FOUR

GOOD DEBT vs. BAD DEBT

"From time to time we hear about *good debt* and *bad debt*. Each is associated with a different category of debt.

It may be easiest to list the main types of debt, and the interest cost that each typically attracts. To make it simpler, let's discuss them in descending order, starting with those with the highest *average* annual interest rate charges, as they were reported by **Money Sense** magazine in its October, 2008 issue:

- Department store credit card - 28.8% interest
- Bank credit card - 19.9% interest
- Personal loan (unsecured) - 10.9% interest
- Car loan (48-month) - 7.9% interest
- Home equity loan - 6.8% interest
- Line of credit (secured) - 6.7% interest
- Mortgage (posted 5-year fixed-rate) - 6.4% interest
- Mortgage (posted variable-rate) - 4.7% interest

Not listed, but also useful to include is *Student Loan Debt* – interest-free while studying, then repayable at around prime rate.

These *average* interest charges may vary from time to time, in response to fluctuating economic conditions; however the differentials will remain roughly the same.

More frightening than even the extremely high department store credit costs, are the *Payday Loans* offered by various *Money Marts* which can be found in most communities. Their annualized interest charges are off the scale, and should be avoided like the plague.

For the individual who is really serious about creating wealth, none of these forms of debt should be considered *good debt*.

I prefer to view this list as starting with the *least acceptable* form of debt, and ending with the *most acceptable* – a mortgage, or a student loan.

This brings me to the next, very important tip."

TIP #6..... **The only truly GOOD DEBT is NO DEBT at all. However, some debt, such as loans for education and home mortgages, falls into the ACCEPTABLE DEBT category.**

"Why do you think I refer to education loans and home mortgages as *acceptable* forms of debt?"

"Probably, because those loans result in something with a lasting benefit," ventured Jenny. "In a way, aren't they sort of an investment?"

"That's right, Jenny. An *education loan* is an investment in your future career and potential earning power. The odds are very high that your higher income over your working life will far exceed the amount of your loan, even with the cost of interest added in.

The *Canadian Millennium Scholarship Foundation* released a report in 2009. It compared the *lifetime (40-year) earning statistics* of individuals with *post-secondary* education, to those with high-school diplomas only. The figures indicate the total earnings *over-and-above* those of the average high-school graduate:

- Trades Graduate: $231,000 (BC); $453,000 (Alberta)
- Community College Graduate: $394,000 (national average)

- Bachelor's Degree: $746,000
                                     (national average)

- Post-Graduate Degree: $1.17 million
                                     (national average)

Perhaps as important as the economic benefits of post-secondary education however, is the greater job satisfaction that one can expect from careers that require post-secondary credentials.

Fortunately in Canada, the government has established a tax-efficient education savings program, the *Registered Education Savings Plan (RESP)*. More and more parents are wisely taking advantage of this opportunity to help their children with the ever-increasing cost of post-secondary education. We'll discuss this *RESP* vehicle in greater detail later in our chats.

Nevertheless, despite the availability of RESPs, about half the students enrolled in post-secondary programs end up graduating with an average student-loan debt of more than $27,000. As the premium in earnings demonstrates, even with such a significant debt, there are few investments an individual can make that produce a better return throughout his working life."

....

"In the case of a *home mortgage*, this too, despite the interest costs, is a good investment. Why do you think that's so?"

"Well, like you're always saying, you have to live somewhere, and over time, house prices do go up in value," suggested Kevin.

"Right again, Kevin! Despite the unusual downward price adjustments of 2008 and 2009, home values over the years have proven to produce one of the best increases in value of any investment one could have made. Furthermore, as you've also heard me say, when you eventually sell your home, any profit you make is totally *tax-free*. The increase in home-value is one of the very few tax-free gains available to Canadians.

And as you and I say, Kevin, you *do* have to live somewhere. Wouldn't you rather be paying down your own mortgage, than paying rent, and through it, your landlord's mortgage?

All this is not to say, once you have it, that you should be totally relaxed about your student loan or mortgage debt. In later discussions, I'll show you how tremendously beneficial it is for you to *accelerate* debt repayment – not only the higher-interest credit card or department store debt, but also mortgages."

....

"Let me make one more point worth noting. Except for a loan which permits you to invest in your education or your home, almost any other kind of debt you incur will go toward the purchase of a *depreciating asset*."

A DEPRECIATING ASSET is one that steadily decreases in value after you buy it.

"Whether you buy a car, a flat-screen TV, furniture or appliances, the day you take it home, it will already be worth less than you paid. It is a depreciating asset. Most purchases we make have a built-in obsolescence, and with time, they go down in value.

We can't change the fact of depreciating value. But, if we buy these items with money we have managed to *save*, they are a good way to reward ourselves for our hard work and saving ethic.

Consider however, what happens if we *borrow* the money to buy a depreciating item. At the same time that the value of our car for example, is decreasing, we are paying substantially more than the purchase price. The *interest* cost on the loan adds to the original price. Let's be more specific:

Let's say you buy a new car for $30,000, including all taxes. The bank lends you the full amount for a 5-year period, at an interest rate of 8%. At $560 per month you will, after five years, have paid *off your car. The total cost? $33,630. The car's value at the end of five years? You'll be lucky if it's worth $10,000!"*

....

"To drive home the point, a more dramatic example may be the impact of borrowed funds on for example, a one-week vacation to Hawaii:

You charge the $5,000 cost to your credit card. You enjoy your vacation tremendously, then return home. In just seven days, your borrowed 'investment' of $5,000 is gone. All you have left are happy memories and awesome photos. You are now faced with paying for them, possibly over a number of years, at an interest rate often approaching 20%. You could eventually end up paying more than $7,000 for that $5,000 trip!"

"Wow! That's crazy," exclaimed Jenny.

"Sure is," added Kevin. "But it's easy to understand the temptation."

"I know you can guess the next useful tip."

TIP #7..... **Except in situations of family emergency, one should, *IF* debt is required to finance the purchase, make every effort to avoid buying a depreciating asset.**

....

"Here's a question for you. If someone were to offer you a 30% return on your money, with absolutely no risk and no tax consequences, what would you think?

Before you answer, let me first tell you that $1,000 invested at 30% over three years would be worth $2,197 at the end of that period. That's how significant a 30% return is."

"You mean you could more than double your money in just three years?" Jenny exclaimed. "I'd sure be tempted to jump at that," she added.

"I'd wonder what the scam is," added Kevin. "No one just gives money away like that!"

"Most of us would react with the same scepticism as you. In the real world, achieving a 30% return-on-investment is normally a *very* difficult thing to do.

Yet consider this. Anyone carrying department store debt with its typical 30% interest rate, has exactly that opportunity. Simply by paying off the monthly balance and thereby avoiding interest charges, he will be saving tax-free, the equivalent of the annual 30% interest on the full amount of his purchases.

The sad reality for many of us is that paying off in full, a significant monthly balance, is easier said than done. Once we have a substantial debt, coming up with a lump sum to pay it off is very difficult, unless we fortuitously come into an inheritance, win a lottery, or most likely, refinance the high-interest debt with lower-interest, but potentially longer-term debt.

The surest way of avoiding this 30% annual interest-cost penalty, is to avoid the debt in the first place, or to pay it off in full, before any interest is charged.

This leads nicely into the next useful tip."

TIP #8..... **With the major exception of mortgages and education loans, it is wisest to avoid incurring credit charges which *cannot* be paid off in full, before interest charges begin to accrue.**

....

"This is a good time to call it quits for today. We've covered a lot of ground in our first session. Mainly, we've discussed a few ways to best-manage and minimize the *liability*, or debt side, of our wealth-building efforts.

Because I've dwelt at length on this subject, I don't want you to get the idea that debt is always to be avoided at any cost. What I do want to emphasize however, is that we all need to be aware of how to use and manage debt prudently, even to our advantage.

As a matter of fact, at our next get-together, I'm going to suggest a number of ways in which *smart use of debt* can add significantly to our ability to create wealth."

....

"If next Saturday afternoon suits you, I'll buy you lunch at my favourite little place around the corner; then we can come back here and add another layer to your knowledge of successful wealth-creation."

"I'll go for that," said Kevin. "I'm itching to get to where you show us how to become millionaires!"

"Me too," enthused Jenny. "A million would do me nicely in my old age, but preferably much sooner!"

"I'll enjoy explaining how you can actually achieve that, *if* it's really what you decide to set as an objective. But I think you'll be surprised to learn over the next few Saturdays, that a net-worth target of one million dollars may not be the objective you want. You may end up choosing to set your sights much higher!"

"Who would think it? Thanks Grandpa," echoed Jenny and Kevin. "See you next Saturday around noon."

CHAPTER FIVE

SMART USE OF CREDIT

"Well, here we are – our second Saturday. Now that we've had a good lunch, are you both ready to get back to examining more pieces of the wealth-building puzzle? Do either of you have any questions as a result of our discussions last week?"

"Near the end of last week's meeting, Grandpa, you mentioned that there are actually some *smart* ways to use credit, which might help us create wealth even faster," said Jenny. "Are you going to tell us about some of these?"

"Sure, Jenny. Let's start there today.

Remember, we talked about education loans and home mortgages as two obvious examples of the *acceptable* use of debt. This was because these loans represent investments that, over the longer term, are almost a sure thing. They provide great returns – the first, through better careers and salaries; the second, through increased home-equity value. Both have great potential to actually help us increase our net-worth.

We also agreed that any other type of debt, for the purchase of a *depreciating* asset, is generally, not a good idea.

"But, Grandpa, what about credit cards?" asked Jenny. "It's pretty hard to stay away from using at least one."

"You're right, Jenny. Credit cards have become a necessary fact of life. Virtually every adult has at least one card. It's often impossible to make travel arrangements, or hotel or car rental reservations, without a credit card.

There's nothing wrong with credit cards, as long as we follow some basic rules to minimize their cost and optimize their value to us.

Let's spend a few minutes talking about this important subject."

CREDIT CARDS

"First off, there are many *types* of credit card available. We have to be careful in choosing the one which best meets our personal needs. Because a specific card may offer an enticing lure such as a very low interest-rate for the first six months, we shouldn't automatically apply for it. We should shop around and compare all options.

If a consumer has any intention of regularly carrying a balance-owing on a card, the most important element of choice for him, is to select the card that offers the lowest ongoing interest rate.

However, as you've heard me say several times, the *smart* credit card user will carry a balance on his card only in an absolute emergency situation.

In fact, the last numbers I saw indicated that about 60% of Canadians pay off their monthly credit card balances *in full*. Unfortunately, that leaves about 40% who do not, thereby incurring high interest costs. Here's a real-life example:

The **Brash** *family owes on average, a* **$10,000** *total monthly balance on various credit cards. Since their income is sufficient, they have chosen to enjoy life and continue to carry this average balance throughout their 40-year working life. They usually make only the minimum monthly payments that are required.*

The consequence of their decision, is that after 40 years they will have paid, assuming a typical 19% credit card interest charge, a total of **$76,000** *in interest charges alone.*

Put another way, this $76,000 is greater than the annual, after-tax income of an average Canadian family. This means that the **Brash** *family would need to spend more than a full year of its career earnings, simply to pay the **interest** on their various cards!"*

"Wow, you'd have to be awfully dense to do that!" exclaimed Kevin.

"Perhaps 'poorly informed' would be the better term, Kevin. Many credit card users simply don't realize that the impact can be so huge. They rationalize that if they can afford the minimum monthly payment, that's all they need to worry about. They may pay the monthly minimum required, but then charge at least as much again later in the month, effectively making no difference in their total indebtedness."

....

"Now let's look at the slightly more savvy **Banks** family:

*Their wake-up call came when their credit card debt reached **$10,000**. They decided to stop charging anything further, vowing to pay off the whole amount. They decided to do so as painlessly as possible by paying only the specified minimum monthly payments, at 3% of outstanding balance. With each payment, their minimum monthly payment slowly dropped as the outstanding balance-owing slowly reduced.*

Can either of you hazard a guess at how long, following their plan, it would take the Banks family to pay off the $10,000?"

"At least five years?" ventured Jenny.

"You'll be shocked to learn that it would actually take **287 months**, or almost 24 years, for this family to pay off the full $10,000. The total interest they would have paid out would be $10,948. Can you imagine spending almost $21,000 to pay off $10,000?"

"Now I understand why credit card companies are so successful. But I don't think the **Banks** family is much smarter than the **Brash** family," suggested Kevin. "What if they had paid a bit more, say $350 *every* month, instead of only the $300 minimum initially required? How much would that have lowered their total interest cost?"

"By setting and keeping their monthly payments at $350, and sticking to their plan to not add new charges, their $10,000 debt would have been repaid in 39 months. They would still have paid a substantial total interest cost of $3,417, resulting in a total repayment of $13,417."

> **TIP #9.....** **If you absolutely cannot pay off your total credit card balance in any month, pay off as much as you can, over-and-above the minimum required, in order to reduce the balance owing as quickly as possible.**

"Studies have shown that those who cannot pay the full amount owing, tend to pay only the minimum required on their monthly statement. Credit card companies love this tendency.

We need only remember the **Banks** family. By paying only the minimum monthly amounts required, it took almost 24 years to liquidate their $10,000 debt. The only winner in this scenario was the credit card company which received almost $11,000 in interest payments."

....

"To avoid complications in managing total monthly credit card expenditures, the next tip is also important."

> **TIP #10.....** **Credit card use is best limited to one or two cards only, for better overview and control of spending.**

"That makes sense," agreed Jenny. "I can't imagine juggling a whole bunch of credit cards like I sometimes see when shoppers open their wallet."

"You'll be amazed at the latest statistic which shows that in Canada, about 68 million bank credit cards are in circulation – more than three cards for every adult in the country. If we add department store and other retail charge cards, the number of cards per person increases dramatically."

....

"If you, Jenny and Kevin, make it a practice to always fall into the group of Canadians who *never pay interest on their cards*, you will have taken one of the most important steps along your path to wealth-creation.

You will have achieved not only a *good credit rating*, but also zero *credit card drag* on your effort at increasing your net-worth.

You'll be using your credit cards exactly as the smart consumer should – as a short-term convenience to *you*, at zero cost."

RETAIL STORE CARDS

"All of our conclusions about the smart use of credit cards are even more critical when we opt to incur credit at department stores, and other retail outlets that issue their own, in-store 'charge' cards.

These businesses generally charge even more interest than credit cards issued by financial institutions. That's why such a large number are so keen to offer you that 10% off your first purchase, if you sign up for their card. Competition for your credit business is fierce and it's everywhere. Many further encourage your loyalty and spending with extra in-store 'bonus' or 'reward' points if you charge your purchase to their card.

Here's an interesting fact. A recent study showed that about half of those who open a department store credit account just before Christmas, are still one year later, paying off the balance from those initial purchases.

The next tip will help eliminate this retail card risk."

> TIP #11..... There is little logic to owning a higher-interest retail store card if you already have an all-purpose credit card. Almost every business will accept a credit card when a customer wishes to charge a purchase.

THE LURE:
'BUY NOW! ZERO-PAYMENT, ZERO-INTEREST'

"I'm sure neither of you can have missed the ongoing bombardment of TV, radio, and print ads offering furniture, appliances, new roofs, and home renovations, with zero-down, zero-interest, and zero-payments for a year or more, all in order to attract customers."

"Sure, we see those on TV all the time," replied Jenny. "They actually sound like a good deal to me."

"They're meant to sound good, Jenny. And those tactics *do* work. Many shoppers take advantage of them, often with disastrous results. Let's explore why.

First of all, when you decide to go for one of these special credit deals, the basic *list price* of the item may actually be set higher than if you were opting to pay by cash or credit card.

Furthermore, when you sign up for this special credit purchase, you will usually be charged an initial 'service fee' of $30 or more."

"So they're advertising a 'zero-interest' deal, but it's really costing you money?" inquired Kevin.

"Absolutely, Kevin. What these various fees add up to, is really an indirect and hefty form of interest charge.

But the most shocking cost comes if you fail to pay the full balance owing *before* the interest-free period is over. In the fine print of the credit document that you initially signed, you will find that the interest rate *after* the free period ends, is astronomical – often approaching 30%. Usually too, the interest charges will be applied retroactively, back to the day you took the items home!"

....

"But, Grandpa, I remember our mom getting all new windows installed a few years ago. They had a zero-interest offer, and I think you told her it was a good deal. Isn't that what you said?" inquired Jenny.

"You're right, Jenny. I did advise her to go ahead, but the situation was not typical. The company was offering a fully-competitive price on their windows, at zero-interest for one year, but with twelve equal payments to pay off the debt *within that year*.

Although she didn't have the funds to pay the full amount up front, your mother was certain that she could afford the $600 monthly payment for twelve months. She also knew that she had the discipline to make each payment on time. I agreed that for her, it was a good opportunity. She smartly gave the company twelve post-dated cheques as soon as the installation was completed. One year later, her windows were fully paid, interest-free.

However, had your mom failed to pay the full balance-owing within the year, a very high interest charge would have started ticking away and adding up fast.

It's unfortunate. Many of us lack your mom's financial self-discipline in following through on a time-sensitive, interest-free repayment opportunity."

TIP #12..... 'Interest-free', deferred-payment options should be used only if the purchaser has the financial ability and the discipline, to repay the purchase price in full, *before* the interest-free period expires.

"I think I've just figured out another important tip," mused Kevin.

"And that would be?"

> **TIP #13.....** **Carefully read over *all* the fine print in any contract you're thinking of signing.**

"That's certainly a relevant tip, Kevin. Thanks for suggesting it."

LEVERAGE

"Another major type of debt that is often used, is also frequently misused. It's called *leverage*. Let me explain what I mean by that term."

> *LEVERAGE is used to describe the use of someone else's money (a loan), to enable an individual to invest a greater sum than would be possible solely through his personal savings.*

"Generally those who use leverage borrow a sum of money and invest the proceeds in financial, real estate, or other investments. They do this in the belief that the investment will produce more income, or go up in value, or both, by more than the interest cost of the loan."

"But, Grandpa, isn't that what you do when you take out a mortgage?" asked Jenny.

"Yes, Jenny. When we take out a mortgage loan for our condo or house, that's essentially what we're doing. We've already agreed that as long as we can clearly afford to make the monthly payments, this is usually a very smart thing to do. We buy our home primarily to meet our need to live in a comfortable place of our own. But also, we realize that homes have proven to be an excellent, tax-free investment over time.

Where the use of leverage gets more dicey, is when we borrow money and invest it for example, in the stock market. Any idea why this might be more risky?"

"Maybe because stocks can crash, like they did late last year," offered Kevin.

"Crash is exactly what they did, Kevin. Remember, we talked about the sub-prime borrower meltdown in the U.S., all the bank problems, and the many other issues that flowed from that? Stock markets plummeted in the second half of 2008, and continued their downward spiral in early 2009."

"But, Grandpa, didn't house prices drop as well?" asked Jenny.

"Yes, Jenny, they did, but not nearly as dramatically as the stock market. Just to give you a feel for the difference, the *Canadian S&P/TSX Index* dropped by more than 50% in the nine-month period commencing in mid-2008, but house prices across Canada dropped, on average, by only about 10%."

THE S&P/TSX INDEX (Standard & Poor/Toronto Stock Exchange Index) is the main Canadian yardstick which tracks the market-value movement of the Toronto Stock Exchange.

....

"We can say that borrowing for a home purchase represents a completely different level of risk than borrowing to make a financial investment, such as in the stock market. A key reason is that real estate markets tend to be much *less volatile* than stock markets."

"Can these up-and-down cycles in stock and real estate markets be predicted, Grandpa?" asked Jenny.

"Unfortunately, Jenny, no one has come up with an effective crystal ball to accurately predict a market cycle for *any* investment, whether in real estate or the stock market.

But…with our home, as long as we can afford our monthly payments, it really doesn't matter whether today's value is higher or lower than in the recent past. We're confident that over time, its value *will* go up. Our net-worth will grow, not only as a result of that increase in value, but also, as a result of the mortgage loan-reduction that occurs with each payment we make. In the meantime, we enjoy the security of living in our *own* home.

If however, we *borrow* to invest in the stock market, we incur an *extra* obligation, over and above our normal living costs. We *must* make monthly interest payments to service the loan. The cost is not always just dollars and cents. We remain relaxed and happy if we see our stocks going up; but if they drop, we're bound to get anxious and even stressed.

The downside risk of an *investment loan* may be *partly* offset at tax-time. We can write off the interest cost if the loan was used *outside* an RRSP for most financial investments, including stock purchases. Interest on *rental-property* investment loans also qualifies. In Canada however, interest on a *personal* home mortgage is not a permitted tax deduction. Interestingly, it *is* allowed in the U.S.

Despite the potential tax benefit flowing from interest-cost deductibility on various investment loans, leverage remains a *very risky* use of credit. Generally, it should be utilized by investors *only* when *both* of the following exist:

- a very strong tolerance for risk; and

- the leveraged investment represents only a small percentage of the investor's net-worth."

TIP #14….. Leverage should be used as a tool for financial investments, *only* if the investor can comfortably handle not only the repayment obligations, but also the prospect of a significant loss on the investment.

"If borrowing for investments causes you to worry and lose sleep, it's probably the wrong thing for you to do."

"So what you're saying, Grandpa," clarified Jenny, "is that borrowing to buy your own condo or house is a smart use of credit because you need some place to live anyway. But borrowing to invest in the stock market is much riskier, because you could lose your shirt on the investment, and still have to pay off your full loan?"

"Well put, Jenny. The use of leverage for financial investments *may* be an excellent tool for some high-net-worth individuals, but for the average Canadian like you and me, it should generally be avoided."

....

"But, Grandpa, you said that Great-Grandma and Great-Grandpa added substantially to their net-worth by investing in rental properties. How does that make sense given what you just said? Didn't they have to borrow to be able to do this?"

"A really good observation, Kevin! Did you notice though that when I talk about careful use of leverage, I usually add 'for financial investments'?

What my parents always believed was that if you could save enough for the down payment on an investment property, and if the rent you received from your tenants could comfortably pay off the mortgage and other costs, why not go for it. And they were correct. Not only were their tenants paying off the mortgage, but as with their own home, the value of their investment properties was reasonably certain, over time, to increase."

> TIP #15..... Owning a carefully-chosen investment property on which the rent carries the mortgage and other costs, is often an excellent means to increase net-worth over time.

"But, Grandpa, you're adding to your debt by having a mortgage on your own home *and* another on the investment property! Doesn't that contradict our basic rule of reducing all debts so that our net-worth can grow?" asked Jenny.

"Not really, Jenny. With an investment property, the debt is being reduced for you by your tenants. Over time, the value of your asset is very likely to increase. The widening difference between the increasing value of your asset, and the decreasing loan obligation, represents the growth in your net-worth.

Don't get me wrong. Buying an investment property takes a lot of forethought. It should not be entered into lightly.

It's likely to become a realistic option only *after* your own mortgage and other loans are substantially repaid. It *is* worth considering under the right circumstances. We'll delve into this subject in more detail when we discuss specific investment options."

CREDIT COUNSELLING

"By the time some of us catch on to the horrendous pitfalls of too much debt, we may be so far over our head that we need the assistance of a credit-counselling organization.

These organizations, particularly those that operate on a not-for-profit basis, can be very useful in helping renegotiate interest rates and total debts owing. They can also assist with consolidation of many different debts into one. If successful, these steps can allow the debtor to handle payment obligations in a reasonable and organized manner.

Banks and other creditors are often willing to renegotiate their loans, particularly if the alternative is the debtor's bankruptcy, under which the creditor may receive zero.

A distinct advantage of these organizations is that after an agreement with creditors is reached, the debtor may be able to make only one pre-determined monthly payment to the counselling organization; it in turn allocates the agreed proportion to each creditor.

Once this process is successfully put in motion, it will stop the barrage of calls from debt collectors, *and* lift a huge burden off the shoulders of the harried debtor."

www.creditcounsellingcanada.ca includes a directory of credit counselling agencies, by location.

....

"Ultimately of course, if the debts are truly overwhelming, the only practical option may be **bankruptcy**.

While this option may sound appealing at first glance, it results in severe and long-lasting consequences. It should really be a last resort, if all else has failed.

After at least nine months, bankruptcy can wipe the debt-slate clean. It will also however, have substantially absorbed most assets owned by the individual, above a basic allowable value.

After a bankruptcy, borrowing of any kind will be extremely difficult for at least seven years. Even if a loan is available, the interest rates will be extremely high. For a long time, bankruptcy may well impair one's ability to buy a home."

....

"Regardless of whether a debtor ultimately solves his problem on his own, *or* with the help of a credit counselling agency, *or* through bankruptcy, the resolution does not by itself change the behaviour that led to the massive debt problem in the first place.

The only sure way of avoiding a repeat of the debt problem, is for the individual to avoid further debt like the plague. *Force-fitting his spending to his disposable income,* except in the most extreme emergencies, is the only assured solution for the future."

CONCLUSIONS ON CREDIT

"I hope this discussion helps you understand that debt in itself is not necessarily bad. If we strategically use what we've identified as *acceptable* debt, and if we focus on minimizing its cost and duration, it can actually work to our advantage in building our wealth.

Credit in today's society *is* necessary. As I mentioned earlier, without its availability and use we could not:

- rent a car;
- reserve a hotel room;
- make an airline reservation; or
- make purchases online."

"I guess we'd have to start carrying huge wads of cash to make our purchases, Grandpa," quipped Jenny.

"You know, Jenny, that's actually what billions of people throughout the world still have to do when making purchases. Many don't have a bank account, and haven't even heard of a credit card.

If we do *not* make use of credit, it can work against us. We cannot establish a *credit rating.* Without a credit rating, we will have difficulty borrowing for a major purchase such as a house, for which a loan is nearly always necessary. Without that solid credit history, a mortgage will be either unavailable, or extremely expensive."

TIP #16..... Credit is a useful *tool,* but only if used prudently. It should always be used in a manner that minimizes both interest rates and the duration of the debt incurred.

CHAPTER SIX
....

HOME OWNERSHIP

"We touched on some of the benefits of home ownership earlier in our discussions, but a few points are worth emphasizing."

OWNERSHIP vs. RENT

"Sometimes we hear debates about whether it's better to own or to rent. Let's examine the main reasons favouring *ownership*:

Non-Economic Reasons

- Pride of ownership;
- Decision-making freedom over *your* property;
- Certainty of tenure. Nobody can evict you.

Economic Reasons

- Increased ownership, or *equity* value, as you pay down your mortgage;
- Tax-free equity growth as home value increases;
- Ease of future upgrade to a higher-value home – increased equity will often generate the larger down payment required;
- Disciplined net-worth growth – paying off a mortgage is similar to a forced savings plan. Your monthly payment is automatic."

"Grandpa, I understand the reasons for paying down the mortgage as soon as possible. But what I don't get, is how much can we expect our home value to go up, and over what period of time?" asked Kevin.

"Well, Kevin, from year to year it's difficult to make an accurate prediction. But a 2007 *Re/Max* study showed that in the previous 25 years, the average home in Canada had increased in value by 264%.

The average Canadian home price in 1981 was approximately $80,000. The average price 25 years later in 2006, had risen to about $299,000.

If in 1981, the average buyer had a down payment of 25% ($20,000), this is what his situation would have been in 2006:

- Assuming he had a 25-year amortization (loan repayment period) on his mortgage, his home would now be mortgage-free.

- The difference between his original $20,000 down payment and his 2006 home-value would be $279,000.

- This gain in value on the original down payment represents a compounded annual rate-of-return of 11.4% – all of it tax-free!"

"But, Grandpa," interjected Kevin, "don't you have to take into account all those monthly payments he had to make for 25 years to pay off the mortgage?"

"I can see you're really paying attention, Kevin! You're right about the payments, but remember, the owner had to live somewhere during those 25 years. Had he rented instead, his monthly rent wouldn't have been much different than the mortgage payments. The key difference is that with rent payments, at the end of 25 years he would have had nothing to show for them."

"And the landlord would probably be burning *his* mortgage papers," quipped Jenny.

"To be absolutely accurate, we should say that the *combined effect* of paying off the mortgage *and* market-value increases, allowed the owner's net-worth to grow by $279,000 over those 25 years."

"That makes sense," replied Kevin.

....

"Here's an example that will drive the point home even further, Kevin. With a 25% down payment in 1993, your mom purchased your house for $207,000. Today, the house is worth about $550,000, and your mom's mortgage is almost paid off. This is because she *accelerated* her monthly payments as much as she could afford over the past 16 years.

Had she instead rented a similar house, she would have paid a rent roughly equal to her mortgage payments. She certainly wouldn't have been able to save very much after making such large rent payments. So by purchasing the house, she has managed to add almost $500,000 to her net-worth, in just 16 years."

"You've convinced me, Grandpa," said Jenny. "After graduation, I can't wait to buy a condo and start decorating as soon as I can afford it."

"Yeah, me too!" exclaimed Kevin. "And, Grandpa, I'll take you along when I'm buying, so you can get them to throw a wide-screen TV into the deal."

> TIP #17..... **Owning one's home is one of the most tax-efficient and least-risky ways of achieving significant, long-term, net-worth growth.**

CHAPTER SEVEN

MORTGAGES

"While we all agree that owning a home is a great long-term means of increasing our net-worth, we still have to be careful in our search for the right mortgage.

That mortgage will very likely be the largest single debt we will ever incur. So it makes sense to understand the basics about mortgages, and how to achieve best-value on the one we eventually choose."

"Grandpa, what exactly is a mortgage?" asked Jenny.

"Good question Jenny."

A MORTGAGE is the pledging of a property to a lender as security for a home purchase loan.

"The mortgage itself is not a debt — it is the contractual evidence of a debt.

If you as a borrower (mortgagee) fail to live up to the payment obligations to which you have agreed in the mortgage document, the lender can foreclose on your home, gain title to it, sell it, and attempt to recover the full value of his loan, along with any overdue obligation, such as interest."

"Not a situation I'd ever want to become familiar with," commented Kevin.

"Grandpa, I've heard that some people have a second mortgage. What's that?" asked Jenny.

"On occasion, a situation will arise where the borrower cannot qualify for the full amount he needs by means of a *first mortgage*. He may then try to secure a *second mortgage*. Since a second mortgage ranks in priority behind a first, it represents a higher level of risk for the lender. As a result, the interest rate on a second mortgage will be much higher than on a first mortgage."

TIP #18..... **Because of their very high interest cost, second mortgages are best avoided by the average borrower.**

"Before we talk further about mortgages, let's be sure we understand a few key terms:"

CONVENTIONAL MORTGAGE:	*A mortgage that does not exceed 80% of the purchase price of a property.*
HIGH-RATIO MORTGAGE:	*A mortgage which exceeds 80% of the purchase price of a property.*
AMORTIZATION PERIOD:	*The number of years that it would take for specified payments to pay off a mortgage.*
MORTGAGE TERM:	*The number of years over which an agreed interest rate is applied.*
FIXED-RATE MORTGAGE:	*A mortgage for which the interest rate is fixed for a specified period of time.*
VARIABLE-RATE MORTGAGE:	*A mortgage on which the interest rate floats up or down, relative to the prime rate.*

53

"Wow, this sounds complicated, but I *think* I understand," commented Jenny. "Grandpa, once I have a full-time job, how much of a down payment would I need to save up for my first condo, before I could qualify for a mortgage?"

THE FIRST-TIME BUYER

"Ideally, Jenny, you should try to have saved-up at least 20% of the value of the property. This would make you eligible for a *conventional mortgage.* 20% is an important number, because if you meet or exceed it, banks and other lenders will grant you a mortgage without requiring you to buy *high-ratio* mortgage insurance, which is very expensive.

Realistically though, very few first-time buyers like yourselves can save up for example, the $40,000 which would be needed for a 20% down payment on a $200,000 condo.

In the future, once you've owned that first condo for a few years, it's quite likely that you'll eventually decide to upgrade to a higher-value home. The increase in your condo's value will probably give you the 20% down payment required on that next, but more expensive purchase. As a result, your future mortgages will be considered as 'conventional'. You will no longer need the 'high-ratio' mortgage insurance."

"So as I understand it, you're saying that once I own my first place for a while, it should get easier for future moves. The biggest challenge I guess, will be to get my foot in that first door," quipped Jenny.

....

"Fortunately for people like you, Jenny, Canadian mortgage lending rules allow purchasers with as little as 5% down, or $10,000 in our $200,000 condo example, to *potentially* qualify for a mortgage.

Any mortgage which is granted with a down payment of between 5 and 20% of the purchase price, is considered a higher-risk, *high-ratio* mortgage. High-ratio mortgage insurance is required to protect the lender, in the event that the borrower defaults on his payment obligations. Such insurance however, will add several thousand dollars to the total amount of your mortgage loan."

....

"Did you notice that I said purchasers can *'potentially'* qualify for a mortgage? No matter how large the down payment, lenders will always want proof that the mortgage holder's income and *other* debt obligations, will allow him to make the regular monthly mortgage payments required.

Most lenders have two key yardsticks that they use:

- *The total sum of monthly mortgage payments, plus estimated property taxes, plus one-half of any strata payments, plus utility costs, cannot exceed 32% of the borrower's gross monthly income. This is referred to as the* **Gross Debt Service Ratio (GDS)***;*

and

- *All of the above costs, PLUS the monthly total of all the borrower's other debt payments, such as a vehicle loan and credit card debt, generally cannot exceed 40% of gross income. This is known as the* **Total Debt Service Ratio (TDS)***.*

And don't ask me why only half the strata fee is used. It's been that way as long as I can remember.

Normally, to qualify for a mortgage loan, you'll be required to meet both of these criteria.

Although it's wise to choose the shortest *amortization period* which you can manage, you are *permitted* to choose one stretching as long as 25 years. The longer the amortization period, the lower your monthly payments, and the easier it will be for you to meet these two ratio tests."

....

"Grandpa, this gives new meaning to the term 'crash course' – so many new rules and words!" exclaimed Kevin.

"You're right, Kevin. It isn't easy at first. But keep in mind that Grandma and I don't live in a gold bubble; we've made our share of unwise financial decisions. As a result, we've learned that it's worth the effort for you to gain this understanding *early* in life, if it helps you avoid future pitfalls.

Let's slow down and use an actual example. It'll help you better get the hang of what all this means.

You've completed your education. You've been working for a year in your first full-time job, which pays you $4,000 a month (your gross income). Your grandma has given you $5,000 to help with a down payment, and you've managed to save another $5,000 yourself.

*With a total down payment of $10,000, the most you can pay for a condo at this point in time is $200,000. Remember, that's because you **must** have a minimum of 5% down.*

Before even beginning your search for the perfect place to buy, you visit both a mortgage broker and your Bank, to get an idea of the interest rates available. You also need to confirm that you meet all the other lending criteria. You determine that the mortgage broker can get you the best deal. He lays out the following facts:

- *A 5-year term, fixed-rate loan is available at 5%. Amortized over 25 years, your $190,000 loan would cost you $1,105 per month. When the broker adds the estimated property taxes, utilities, and one-half the estimated strata fee to these payments, he informs you that you will qualify for the mortgage. Your GDS ratio will be about 32% – right at your eligibility limit.*

- *When the mortgage broker looks at your only other debt obligation, he adds in your $250 monthly car payment. He needs to determine if you fit under the maximum 40% TDS ratio within which his lender likes to stay. Luckily, the number works out to 34%, so you do qualify.*

*One last test that the lender will use before extending you a loan of any kind, will be to check your **credit-rating**. Fortunately, you have always met your payment obligations on time. You now enjoy excellent credit.*

*You receive a **pre-approval** for a maximum mortgage loan of $190,000. You are now confident that if you find a suitable condo within your $200,000 price range, you will have access to the necessary financing."*

....

"If I were this first-time buyer, it seems like I would barely qualify for my mortgage," observed Kevin. "Shouldn't I wait another year or two, save some more cash, and then be able to qualify more easily, maybe for an even higher-priced, better unit?"

"You may be right, Kevin. Whenever you, or anyone else just barely qualify for a mortgage, you should be extremely careful before proceeding. What if illness or some other circumstance interrupts or reduces your pay cheque? How would you meet all your monthly payments?

And here's something else to think about, Kevin, which reinforces the point you just made. Say Jenny or you were to buy the condo and proceed with the mortgage in our example. To finalize the purchase, you would need *another* several thousand dollars in addition to your down payment.

Provincial and federal governments waive for first-time buyers, *some* taxes associated with home purchases. But you will still need to pay your lawyer or notary, as well as for the cost of a property-value appraisal required by your lender. Also, before committing to a specific purchase, you as a prudent buyer, should hire a home inspector to ensure no ugly surprises. All these costs add up. Nor do these figures include any expenses involved in furnishing your new home.

So yes, you are probably right, Kevin. Although you *could* manage to proceed in our example, it *may* be wiser in this instance, to wait a year or so, and build up your savings before wading into such a major financial obligation.

Temptation however, lurks everywhere. While waiting longer and trying to save more, you would also need to ensure that you don't add to your monthly debt obligations, and that you maintain your good credit-rating. It would be a shame to save enough for a higher down payment, only to fail to qualify for a mortgage solely because you lost sight of other qualification criteria that lenders use."

....

"So, Grandpa, how about this to make that first purchase easier? I get together with a friend, and we buy that first condo together. That way we split all the costs 50/50 and have much less trouble qualifying, income-wise, for a really good two-bedroom unit. Can people do that?" inquired Jenny.

"That's a great idea, Jenny! And quite a few home buyers arc doing exactly that. There are as always, some cautions:

- One needs to be very sure about the longer-term compatibility of the partnership. This arrangement is not the same as sharing a rental unit. This is in fact a *legal partnership*. It is much harder to escape if for instance, the two end up getting on one another's nerves, or one partner encounters financial difficulties, decides to move to another community, or plans to marry.

- It would be necessary to draw up a legal agreement, spelling out the details of how, and when one can buy out the other, and how the future price is to be established.

The arrangement *could* be less risky if close relatives get together on a joint purchase. Maybe you and Kevin could be partners in your first condo."

"No way, Grandpa! You must be kidding," exclaimed Kevin. "I'm planning to get my own place."

"Grandpa, if it's several individuals or a couple who want to buy a home together, would the lender allow them to add their *total* incomes together, so they could more easily qualify for a mortgage?" asked Jenny.

"Absolutely, Jenny. The lender uses the *total gross income of the household* in his calculation. But keep in mind – he would also tally the total household *debt* in calculating the *Total Debt Service Ratio (TDS)*."

....

> TIP #19..... For most of us, a very beneficial strategy for *long-term* wealth creation, is to purchase our first home before age thirty, and to pay off our mortgage as quickly as possible.

"Most of us *can* achieve this dream of early home-ownership. To do so however, we need to:

- Achieve a sufficient, steady income stream;
- Carefully limit the level of debt-obligations;
- Maintain a good credit-rating;
- Save a minimum 5% down payment.

As we form personal partnerships and family units, incomes tend to rise, and if debts are kept under control, it becomes easier to qualify for a mortgage."

SELECTION OF AMORTIZATION PERIOD

"Let's look at how the selection of various amortization periods affects the total interest amount paid over the life of a loan.

*This time we'll use a mortgage of **$300,000**. This a fairly typical requirement for many Canadian home buyers, in their early years of family formation.*

*Let's assume this is the purchaser's first home. The best rate he has found for the **5-year**, **fixed-rate** mortgage which he prefers, is 5%. His family income is sufficient to qualify for either the **20-year** amortization with its higher monthly payments, or the **25-year** amortization with somewhat lower payments.*

The choice of amortization period in this case is therefore strictly up to the borrower. Which should he choose? The numbers tell the tale:

	25-Year Amortization	20-Year Amortization
Original Loan Amount	*$300,000*	*$300,000*
Monthly Payments	*$1,745*	*$1,971*
Total Payments Over Life of Mortgage	*$524,000*	*$473,040*

*For the privilege of reducing his monthly payments by $226, this borrower would pay an **extra** $51,000 in interest, before his mortgage is finally paid off 25 years later.*

In this example we assume that after each 5-year mortgage term, the borrower is able to renew his mortgage on the same terms for each subsequent 5-year period, until the loan is fully repaid."

"Wow, Grandpa, both of these amounts are huge!" exclaimed

Kevin. "It's unbelievable that even at what seems such a low interest rate, a $300,000 mortgage loan can end up costing almost twice as much by the time it's paid off."

"Unfortunately, Kevin, the numbers don't lie. And they *are* staggering. This leads me to two more tips."

> TIP #20..... Increasing mortgage payments whenever possible, is one of the best investments a borrower can make. The amortization period of the mortgage will be shortened, and the interest costs avoided will be dramatic.

> TIP #21..... Because of the huge long-term impact of interest costs, selecting the best-value mortgage is usually more important to one's future economic welfare, than negotiating the best-possible purchase price on the property.

....

"And here I always thought that getting the best-possible deal on a condo or house was the most important!" exclaimed Jenny. "So aside from picking the shortest amortization period that I can afford, Grandpa, how do I make sure that I'm getting the best possible mortgage deal?"

"Another great question, Jenny. The most important thing to remember is to **shop around** for a mortgage. By all means go to your Bank or Credit Union and check for their best deal, but *always*, check with one or two Mortgage Brokers as well.

Mortgage Brokers in Canada arrange more than 35% of all mortgages. This number is growing fast. The reason? Each broker typically deals with some twenty to thirty *lenders* all over Canada. Brokers are therefore able to *shop* for the best possible deal among all of their lenders.

Banks, on the other hand, tend to set for all their branches, a mortgage interest-rate which generally will be much higher. *If you are one of their preferred customers, they may negotiate the rate down toward the rate that a mortgage broker can get you.* Often though, they will not fully match the Broker.

A difference in your mortgage rate of as little as 1% will have a huge impact on the amount of your monthly payments, and consequently, on the total interest you end up paying on the mortgage loan.

Again, let's return to our real-life example – the $300,000 mortgage:

The best interest-rate available from your Bank, on a 5-year term, fixed-rate mortgage, is 6%. A Mortgage Broker can provide the same mortgage for 5%. Both are amortized over 25 years. You'll be amazed at the difference."

	5% Interest Rate (Broker)	*6% Interest Rate (Bank)*
Monthly Payments	*$1,745*	*$1,919*
Total Payments Over the 60-month Term	*$104,700*	*$115,140*

"In lowering his interest rate by just 1%, the borrower has saved himself a total of *$10,440* over the *5-year term* of his mortgage!"

"I'm convinced. You can bet *I'll* shop around for my mortgage, once I'm in the market," exclaimed Kevin. "On that one-percent difference in interest rates, I could buy a set of wheels with the money I save over five years!"

"What's even more amazing is how few of us, of all ages, understand the significance and impact of these huge costs which can result from the differences in both interest-rate and amortization period. The dollars involved are simply too big to ignore, yet many of us do just that.

Over the years, I've encountered many individuals who missed opportunities to compare options. They automatically signed up for their first or renewal mortgage at their Bank's posted rate. Little did they realize that paying the posted rate was like paying full list-price on a vehicle!

From an early age, we learn to *negotiate* the price of a vehicle. Many of us however, fail to do the same for a mortgage, where the impact of our negotiations is much more important to our economic well-being."

TIP #22..... Whether arranging a mortgage for the first time, or renewing an existing one, a borrower should *always* compare the best rates offered by an independent Mortgage Broker, Bank or Credit Union.

MORTGAGE OPTIONS

"In all our examples, we've been using 5-year fixed-rate mortgages. It's important however, to understand that many other options exist in the marketplace."

Term of Mortgage

"Generally, mortgages are available for contract terms ranging from month-to-month, to ten years.

Month-to-month mortgages typically are **open mortgages** which can be paid off, in part or in total, without penalty, at the borrower's discretion, at any time of his choosing.

Because the rates on open mortgages are far higher than the rates on other mortgages, we won't dwell on them. An open mortgage may be useful if within a few months, the borrower expects to come into an inheritance, or otherwise acquire a large sum of money, and plans to pay off his mortgage at that time. The high short-term premium in interest rates *may* then be worth the extra flexibility.

Other than the open mortgage, two other key options are available:

- **The Fixed-Rate Mortgage**: This will be familiar from our examples. These mortgages guarantee, for whichever term selected, a fixed rate of interest. You know precisely, your monthly payments for the entire mortgage term.

  Historically, *most* borrowers opting for a fixed-rate mortgage choose either a 3-year, or a 5-year term.

- **The Variable-Rate Mortgage**: With this mortgage, the interest-rate floats up or down relative to *prime rate*. If for example, your variable-rate mortgage is set at the Bank prime rate plus 1%, then for the term of your mortgage, your interest rate will always be 1% *above* the periodically-changing prime rate.

PRIME RATE is the lending rate that commercial banks charge their most credit-worthy borrowers, such as large blue-chip corporations. It is a benchmark rate, usually posted at the same level by all major lending institutions.

Although the amount of interest paid with a variable-rate mortgage will vary, the monthly payments usually do not change. Instead, whenever rates drop, the lender will apply a greater portion of the monthly payment to *principal* and less to interest. When rates increase, more of the monthly payment will be applied to *interest* and less to principal.

Effectively, with a variable-rate mortgage, the amortization *period* slides slightly, up or down, as rates change. Over the long term, the repayment period decreases when rates drop, and lengthens when rates go up."

....

"Which is better, Grandpa? A variable-rate mortgage, or a fixed-rate one?" asked Kevin.

"That's a difficult question to answer, Kevin. It really depends on each individual's level of *risk tolerance*.

With a *fixed-rate* you'll have no surprises during the entire term of your mortgage. For that reason, many prefer that extra comfort level.

Here's an interesting fact: A recent study showed that over the last fifty years, those who held *variable-rate mortgages* paid *less* interest about 89% of the time, than those who consistently held fixed-rate mortgages. When Grandma and I had a mortgage, we always had a variable-rate one, because we were aware of that advantage.

The current situation has changed somewhat. Until 2008, it was normal for lenders to offer variable-rate mortgages at 0.5 to 1.0% **below** prime rate. Since the economic setbacks of 2008 and 2009 however, variable-rate mortgages were offered **at** or **over** prime rate. Clearly, their historical advantage had shrunk substantially."

> TIP #23..... When securing a mortgage, always consider both fixed-rate and variable-rate mortgages. Select the one most compatible with your comfort level and tolerance for risk.

....

"We've covered a lot of ground this afternoon. I know it's a heavy topic, but hopefully you can now appreciate the huge impact of mortgages on your efforts at wealth-creation. Mortgages are almost unavoidable during your working life. But, if you are smart in the way you research and select them, you can significantly accelerate their liquidation. This will result in more rapid growth of your net-worth, and ultimately, the timing of your financial independence."

> TIP #24..... The sooner a borrower pays off his mortgage, the sooner he reduces the liability side of his net-worth statement, and the sooner his net-worth will increase.

"It's been an eye-opening session, Grandpa, but I think for the first few mortgages I'll be picking your brain a lot, to make sure I don't do something stupid," mused Jenny.

"And I'll be more than happy to help you, Jenny. You'll be surprised however, at how easily both you and Kevin will catch on, particularly if you read over the summary of our discussions. Remember? I intend to write it all up in book form.

And.... if you want even more detail, not only on mortgages, but also on the best-value techniques for buying or selling your home, you can always reread your copy of my book, ***The Naked Homeowner***. A quick read of that before buying or selling, whether for the first or the tenth time, would benefit you or any of your friends.

Remember, Canadians move on average, about every six years. Most of those moves involve both the sale and purchase of a home. That means for you, that over your 40-year working life, you may actually enter into a dozen or more buy-and-sell transactions. The total value of all those transactions may well exceed *several million dollars*.

Since all those home purchases and sales have such a huge impact on your eventual financial independence, I think you now know how and why achieving *best-value* on every deal you make, and on every mortgage you negotiate, can literally add several hundred thousand dollars to your net-worth."

"What an incredible difference. Using my smarts can clearly get me my millionaire status sooner! You can bet I'm going to really focus on achieving best-value in both of these areas," enthused Kevin. "I may even do better than you have, Grandpa!"

"Sounds like a plan!" agreed Jenny.

"So.... next Saturday? Same time?"

"Sure, Grandpa. And I'm hoping that you're offering lunch first, like today?" prompted Kevin.

"Thanks, Grandpa. See you next Saturday," added Jenny.

CHAPTER EIGHT

THE SAVING CHALLENGE

"Well, here we are again. We've covered a lot of topics and new terminology. So far, our focus has been on minimizing spending, and the management and control of debt, whether at age twenty or sixty-five.

The techniques we've discussed are particularly important for young people like yourselves. It's at your age that spending and debt-management habits are established – for better or worse. These early tendencies generally become ingrained, often becoming a lifelong habit.

If these initial habits are poor, the *wealth-drag* that we talked about earlier will probably become a major negative factor for the individual, impairing his efforts at wealth-creation throughout his whole life."

....

"So, what then, do you two think should be our next logical subject for discussion?"

"I hope we're ready to talk about, other than through home ownership, how *else* to grow our net-worth," suggested Kevin. "Like maybe, how to *invest* our money?"

"We're moving in that direction, Kevin. But we're not quite ready yet to discuss investing strategies. What do we need to have first, before we can invest?"

"Well, you can't invest if you don't have anything *to* invest. So I guess we need to be able to save money," suggested Jenny.

"Absolutely right, Jenny! Throughout our life, one of the biggest challenges we all face, no matter how much or how little we earn, is how to put money aside on a regular basis, in order to be able to make investments, and to increase our personal wealth over the long term.

You both know, despite the good part-time jobs you each hold, how very difficult it is to have any money left over at month-end."

"You want to believe it!" exclaimed Jenny. "I often have to ask Mom for a few dollars to tide me over 'til my next pay cheque."

"And you would think that saving money would get easier once you have a full-time job. Guess what? It really doesn't. Do you know why?"

"I guess because you're no longer living at home. You have rent or a mortgage to pay, you own a car and have to pay for it, and other things like that," offered Kevin.

"Hey, Kevin, I'm shocked that buying food wasn't at the top of your list!" quipped Jenny.

"You're right, Kevin. And let's not forget another major factor. Once you have a full-time job, taxes and other deductions will be taken off each pay cheque.

As a student with part-time work, you pretty much avoid income taxes. With tuition and book costs added to your normal personal tax credits, you can each make approximately $15,000 annually before having to pay taxes.

That great tax *holiday* ends however, when you enter the work-force full-time. Even with your first full-time job, you're likely to pay hundreds of dollars each month to the tax man.

Don't forget either, those work-related costs such as transportation, parking, clothing, tools for a trade, and so on. All these costs will need to be covered out of that take-home pay."

....

"So today, let's look at how we can, throughout our working life, use different techniques to save a great deal of money. Only once we know how to do that, will it make sense to look at various investment strategies."

"Yeah, well, I need either a genie in a lamp or some other magic that helps me save – and the sooner the better!" muttered Jenny. "I certainly haven't stumbled across any magic solutions so far."

"Let's hope that by the end of this afternoon, you'll agree that practical techniques for saving money do exist, and even better, that they aren't particularly difficult to implement, even for you, Jenny, with your near-empty wallet."

SAVING SMART

"So the key question is, what do we have to do, to be able to save money on a regular basis?"

"I'd probably have to stop doing just about everything that's fun," grumbled Jenny.

"Actually, Jenny, you've already been doing some very smart things for a while.

We've previously touched on a few simple techniques that you're already using, but to make you feel better, they're worth repeating:

- Shop around. Negotiate price whenever possible. If you want to be even more thrifty, try this. After successfully negotiating the price on a significant purchase, transfer the equivalent of what you saved into your savings account. You'll be amazed at how fast your savings will grow!

- Avoid interest charges on any type of credit card. Pay off the full balance every month. Every dollar of interest you pay is one less dollar that you can save. Remind yourself how much better off you are, by always force-fitting your spending to your *actual* disposable income.

Here are a few other ideas that can produce surprising results:

- What if you were to stop spending your loonies and toonies? Every day instead, you throw them in a large jar. At the end of the year, you roll it all up, and voila! You'll deposit perhaps $1,000 in your travel or Christmas shopping account! Try it out. It works and it's an easy way to save.

- As long as you don't plan to pay interest on your credit card, select the card that offers an *incentive* of most value to you. If you like to travel, select the card with the best frequent-flyer mileage plan. If you prefer a cash rebate, select the card that offers the best percentage refund on your total charges.

You two know that Grandma and I love to travel. By enrolling in for us, the best possible frequent-flyer program, and combining it with a credit card that earns points in the same plan, almost every fourth flight we take is virtually free!

Jenny and Kevin, **we live in a consumer society**. There are always expenditures we must make. But look for every opportunity to make those expenditures produce the greatest benefit for you. Any savings you can achieve by using your smarts in what, when, and how you purchase, will put the savings into *your* pocket."

"It all makes perfect sense while we're talking about it, Grandpa," commented Jenny. "But even if I do *buy smart*, how do I get ahead of the game, and make sure at the end of the month, that I can actually save a few dollars, let alone a significant amount of money?"

"Great observation, Jenny! Believe it or not, there is a relatively straightforward solution."

SAVE FIRST

"Back in the early 90's, David Chilton wrote a very popular book titled *'The Wealthy Barber'*. It was about exactly what the title implies – how an ordinary barber managed to become very wealthy. I highly recommend this book as a great additional read for both of you.

In his book, the author hit on the simplest, and probably only technique that works consistently, in saving significant sums of money. He called it *Pay Yourself First*.

Let me clarify what the author meant by this term.

Jenny, even today as a struggling student, your part-time work gives you a pay cheque every two weeks, of about $400. Am I right?"

"Close enough, Grandpa," replied Jenny.

"OK. Let me ask you something. If the job paid $380 instead of $400, could you get by?"

"Well I guess I could, if that's all I was earning. Why do you ask?"

"Because we're talking about only 5%, or $20 of the $400 that you now earn every two weeks. And you've agreed that if you did not have that extra $20, you would get by somehow.

This hits on the very principle, that if applied throughout your working life, can make you very wealthy."

"Now we're getting to what I want to hear," said Kevin. "But exactly what do you mean, Grandpa? I'm not sure I'm clear on this magic principle."

"The *Pay Yourself First* concept is exactly what Jenny just agreed she could do, even as a student on a very limited income. She agreed that she could take $20 – that's 5%, out of her modest pay cheque, and squirrel it away, pretending she had not earned it.

To make it even easier, Jenny could arrange to have her Bank every two weeks automatically transfer that $20 to a savings account. By the time she finishes college three years from now, her total savings, with earned interest, would be approaching $2,000."

"Wow! That's pretty good for a starving college student," exclaimed Kevin.

"You're right, Kevin. And remember, the key to building net-worth is being able to *save money*, whether for a down payment on a first home, or to invest in other wealth-creating instruments that we'll talk about at a later session."

....

"One other thing is crucial, if your savings effort is to pay off and lead to wealth-creation. What would you guess that is?"

"Keeping your hands off that savings account. But as it grows in value, this can become more and more challenging, I would think," offered Jenny.

"Absolutely, Jenny. No doubt about it. It can be very tempting to raid this growing nest-egg. But you'll succeed in letting it accumulate if, right from the start, you *force* yourself to apply a bit of smart self-discipline, while still rewarding yourself. For example:

- Have two separate savings accounts. The first is your **Wealth-Creation Account**. You simply do *not* tap into it, except in the most extreme emergency.

  Think of this as your *'Save It and Forget It'* account.

  The second savings account can be a *'just for me'* one you use to save up for new camping gear, a Mexican vacation, or some such.

- Access your **Wealth-Creation Account** only once it has reached the level you set as your objective when you set it up. That may be your 5% down payment on your first condo, or $5,000 for your first significant investment in a financial instrument of some kind."

"But, Grandpa, having cash just sitting around in a savings account sure won't earn you much money," argued Kevin.

"That's true, Kevin. But as Jenny said earlier, before you can consider how to best invest your savings, you have to have some to invest. Initially, we need an automatic, and relatively painless way to build savings. Once the account hits our target level for a better-value investment, then we can move it – but first, let's save it. Think of it this way. Before you can make that omelette you really enjoy, you need enough eggs."

....

"We've been using as an example, a student like Jenny who with determination, can manage to save 5% of even her small part-time income.

Now let's adjust the example to someone starting a first full-time job, at a salary to be expected after attaining a trade qualification or college graduation.

*Let's call our graduate by her nickname, **Sam**. Her first full-time job pays $3,000 per month. Sam adopts the **Pay Yourself First** principle, arranging for her Credit Union to automatically transfer 5% of her gross earnings to her **Wealth-Creation** account.*

Because her savings go into the highest-interest savings account offered by her Credit Union, this approach saves her almost $2,000 a year.

*As a result of her great work performance, and a bit of overtime, Sam's income at work increases steadily. Within four years it reaches $4,000 per month. By the end of year four, she finds it quite easy to increase her **Pay Yourself First** monthly transfer to 10% of her gross income.*

After just four years Sam has, with her savings and interest earned, accumulated almost $10,000. She has enough saved for the minimum 5% down payment on her first home, a condo priced at $200,000. Her monthly income and lack of debt allow her to easily qualify for the $190,000 mortgage.

If Sam decides to stick for her entire working life, to the 10% level with her *Pay Yourself First* savings habit, she will amass a substantial nest-egg which can regularly be invested in various wealth-building assets.

We'll discuss those various investment options in the next few Saturdays."

TIP #25..... **The *Pay Yourself First* savings formula, begun as early as possible in one's working life, and built up to 10% of gross income, is a relatively painless, but major step, on the path to significant wealth-creation.**

....

"So, Grandpa, if I remember correctly, we said a few Saturdays ago that minimizing *debt drag* was the most important foundation for wealth-creation. Are we now saying that this *Pay Yourself First* approach is the *next* most important stepping stone?" inquired Jenny.

"Absolutely, Jenny. Just imagine the results if the average 25-year-old Canadian couple with a combined annual gross income of $70,000, were to use this approach throughout their working life.

Even if their income were never to increase, but they automatically saved 10% of their salary for 40 years, they would amass $280,000 in savings. If those savings were invested monthly, and earned a reasonable average of 6% annually, their savings would almost quadruple to around $1.1 million.

At age 65, their income from this substantial sum could, if still invested but earning a reduced amount of 5% annually for the next thirty years, pay them an annual sum not much different than their $70,000 earnings before retirement.

Of course, our example has not taken into account the fact that *inflation* will take its toll on the *real* value of the post-retirement earnings. But neither have we at this stage, considered the added retirement benefits we are eligible to receive by age 65, which may well solve the inflation problem for us."

"But, Grandpa, aren't you also forgetting that *taxes* eat into and therefore reduce that $1.1 million as it's growing?" asked Kevin.

"Not necessarily, Kevin. Several tremendously valuable options are available to Canadians to help them grow their net-worth tax-free. Aside from their home ownership, the primary ones are the:

- ***Registered Retirement Savings Plan (RRSP)**, and*

- ***Tax-Free Savings Account (TFSA)**, newly introduced in 2009.*

Since both the RRSP and the TFSA are such important vehicles for the growth of our personal wealth, it's useful to spend a bit of time understanding each of these programs, made available to all Canadians by our federal government.

Again, at this stage we're not going to discuss the many investment options that we have *within* each of these programs. Rather, we simply want to understand *what* they offer as a *vehicle* for investment."

CHAPTER NINE

REGISTERED RETIREMENT SAVINGS PLAN (RRSP)

An RRSP is a retirement savings account, available to all Canadians. Tax-deductible contributions may be made, to specified annual limits. Any earnings within the plan remain totally exempt from tax until withdrawn – usually upon retirement.

"The RRSP vehicle has been, and continues to be, an extremely powerful tool for wealth-creation, and eventual financial independence. While Ottawa parliamentarians are talking more often about the need to expand eligibility and contribution limits, as of 2009 the rules governing RRSPs are:

• Contributions may not exceed 18% of earned income in any calendar year, with an annually increasing maximum ($24,270 in 2014). While the 18% tends to remain unchanged, the dollar contribution limit has risen by $1,000 annually for some years.

   EARNED INCOME as defined by the Canada Revenue Agency is quite complex, and is best reviewed on the CRA website.

• The annual contribution limit is reduced by the value of an employer's contributions on your behalf, to a company-sponsored pension plan. This is designed to level the playing field between those with, and without, company pensions.

• Any unused contribution room is carried forward indefinitely, allowing the annual contribution limit to be exceeded in those 'catch-up' circumstances.

- There is no minimum age for individuals to begin building contribution *credits*. Even a twelve-year old for instance, who files a tax return to record babysitting or lawn-care income, will begin accumulating RRSP contribution room, at the rate of 18% of the reported income. This proves useful for topping up the RRSP in later years.

- Investments within an RRSP can consist of almost any financial instrument available to Canadians. This includes savings accounts, stocks, bonds, mutual funds, index-based funds, and mortgages.

- Subject only to the contribution room of the *contributor*, an individual may contribute to a *Spousal RRSP* rather than his own RRSP. This option is useful for couples wishing to balance their retirement incomes. Although pension-splitting options introduced in 2007 have reduced the need for spousal RRSPs, for many couples, in some circumstances, it remains useful.

  One notable difference between these two tax-reducing vehicles is that with a *spousal RRSP*, the spouse actually *owns* the contents. Income-splitting on the other hand, conveys no ownership interest to the receiving spouse. It is simply a *calculation* made for tax purposes.

- In the year that they are made, all contributions are fully tax-deductible. This usually results in significant tax refunds to the contributor.

- No later than the year in which the holder turns 71, an RRSP *must* be converted to a **Registered Retirement Income Fund (RRIF)**.

- Withdrawals from the RRIF *must* commence in the following calendar year, at a minimum of 5.4% of the account's value. This percentage increases annually, until at age 95, it peaks at 20%. All withdrawals are fully taxable.

- On death, any balance remaining in an RRSP or RRIF passes tax-free to a *designated spouse*. Otherwise, its full value is included in the final tax return of the deceased, and taxes are paid on the full amount remaining at that time.

Are you still with me, Jenny and Kevin?"

"Well, Grandpa," replied Jenny. "I *think* I follow the basic concept and benefits of an RRSP, but it's kind of mind-boggling trying to get my head around talking about retirement when I haven't even started a career yet!"

"I agree with Jenny," commented Kevin. "It's sort of weird even to be talking about retirement. But I do understand that it's useful to know about an RRSP now rather than later, especially since it helps us grow part of our net-worth tax-free, and gives us a tax refund too. Too bad I didn't start filing tax returns in my early teens – I would have had more RRSP contribution room by now."

"That's exactly it, Kevin. The dual benefits of tax-deductibility on annual contributions, and tax-exemption for any income or growth *within* an RRSP, make this an incredible wealth-creating vehicle that no Canadian should ignore.

Add to these benefits, the power of *time* and *compounding* which we will discuss shortly, then it's no wonder that an RRSP becomes such a powerful tool for building our net-worth."

....

"Because of the immense value of this dual benefit, some individuals, with unused contribution room in their RRSP, actually opt to borrow the funds from their bank or credit union. This is especially so, if they are in a high tax-bracket."

"Aha!" exclaimed Kevin. "I do believe that's what you called 'leverage'."

"Good for you, Kevin," added Jenny. "That just occurred to me too."

"You're both on the ball! In general, I would discourage the use of borrowing for the average person. However, for the highest marginal-tax-bracket wage earner with no corporate pension plan, this option *may* make sense."

MARGINAL TAX BRACKET is the rate at which one's next dollar of income will be taxed. The higher the income, the higher the tax percentage on the next dollar earned. Varying somewhat from province to province, this rate peaks at around 45%, when taxable income exceeds $136,000.

"A $20,000 RRSP contribution for example, can result in a $9,000 tax refund just a few months later. Even for this worthy purpose however, I would borrow on only two conditions:

- *If* I had the discipline to *immediately* apply the refund toward the loan's repayment; and

- *If* I knew that I could *repay* the balance of the loan within a very short time-frame, say twelve months.

It is *always* better to make monthly RRSP contributions *ahead* of the annual end-of-February deadline for the previous tax-year, than it is to contribute a single last-minute lump-sum, followed by payments on a loan taken out to finance that contribution."

. . . .

"Let me introduce you to **Buck**, an energetic high-tax wage-earner who had a $20,000 annual contribution allowance in his RRSP.

Buck could borrow the $20,000 and invest it in his RRSP. Upon receiving a $9,000 tax refund, he could immediately apply it to the loan. He would then need to make payments of around $1,000 monthly, including interest, for the next twelve months, to repay the balance of the loan.

Alternatively, and more astutely, Buck could have begun his saving effort in January of the tax-year at issue, struggling hard without a loan to contribute the same $20,000 at a monthly rate of $1,667.

The following Spring, when he received the $9,000 tax refund on his $20,000 total contribution, Buck could have immediately applied the $9,000 as a lump sum to the next year's allowable limit in his RRSP. He would then be able to lower his monthly contribution to only $917. At this more manageable amount he would still reach the same $20,000 level before the following year's deadline.

Other than for minor annual limit increases, or 'catch-up' contributions, Buck could repeat this pattern every year, budgeting to contribute no more than $917 monthly.

With the annual refund, the government in effect was giving Buck 45% of the funds toward his annual $20,000 contribution limit.

Clearly, for those in a lower tax-bracket, this benefit decreases. However, contributing to an RRSP is usually worthwhile for all but the lowest tax-brackets."

TIP #26..... **An RRSP is an incredibly useful, long-term vehicle for tax-deferred wealth accumulation for Canadians. Most individuals with an earned income should over time, try to utilize as much as possible of their RRSP contribution allowance.**

....

"One major caution is in order: An individual carrying outstanding balances on high-interest debt such as credit cards, retail store cards, or car loans, generally should *not* invest in an RRSP, until *after* those debts have been fully retired.

The unused RRSP contribution allowance is carried forward from year to year and is not lost. It makes sense therefore, for an individual to pay off the high-interest debt first, and then work to catch up on his accumulated RRSP contribution allowance."

> **TIP #27..... Even an RRSP, with all its identified benefits, is not as good an investment as is the liquidation of high-interest debt.**

"As beneficial as an RRSP is, it may *not* be the best savings vehicle for those in very low tax-brackets. The *Tax-Free Savings Account*, dealt with in the next chapter, is likely the better option."

....

"If an RRSP is so useful, do most people have one?" asked Kevin.

"Given the plan's huge advantages, Kevin, you would think the answer would be a resounding 'yes'. Unfortunately, that is not the case. About 90% of Canadian wage earners are eligible to make RRSP contributions. Surprisingly though, in any given year only about 30% actually contribute to an RRSP. Those who do contribute, average less than $3,000 annually. This is despite being allowed on average, to contribute more than twice that amount. Why do you think that is?"

"It's probably the same old story of not knowing how to save, spending too much, or owing too much money," suggested Jenny.

"You're right, Jenny. Many of us need to pay off debts first, and learn to apply the **Pay Yourself First** principle we talked about earlier."

"Not to mention the even harder challenge of trying to stay out of debt in the first place," added Jenny.

"It's probably easiest for individuals to set up an RRSP at a financial institution, along with a *Pre-Authorized Contribution Plan*. With this plan, the Bank will automatically transfer a specified portion of pay deposits to the RRSP – and place it in the investment of choice.

You're probably both aware of automatic bill-payments which you can set up with your Bank. Well, this is the same automatic process. In this instance, the transfer is your savings portion going into your RRSP – before you can get your sticky fingers on it."

TIP #28..... **Most Canadian wage-earners should strive to be making regular contributions to an RRSP by *no later* than their 30th birthday.**

....

"You keep teasing, Grandpa, with information on ways to save and stay out of debt, but I'm still waiting. How do I become that millionaire?" exclaimed Kevin.

"Patience, Kevin, the light bulb will come on. You'll very soon understand how continuing to build your RRSP with 5 to 10% of your income for 30 or 40 years, can make you wealthy, probably beyond your wildest dreams.

But first, more teasing. Let me tell you both about the *Tax-Free Savings Account (TFSA)*, newly introduced in January, 2009."

. . . .

CHAPTER TEN

TAX-FREE SAVINGS ACCOUNT (TFSA)

"The Federal Government's TFSA plan, introduced in 2009, is a tremendous financial innovation which will complement RRSP plans, and further assist Canadians in their wealth-creation efforts."

"We Canadians sure like to use acronyms," observed Jenny. "But I guess it's easier than using the whole title every time. So how is the TFSA different from an RRSP?"

"A TFSA can work hand-in-hand with an RRSP, in a sort of partnership.

But first, let's understand what a TFSA is:

- It's an account to which every Canadian who is at least 18 years old may contribute. The original annual contribution limit was set at $5,000. This was raised to $5,500 in 2013, and to $10,000 in 2015.

- Upon turning eighteen, every Canadian begins accumulating TFSA contribution capacity, even if no account is yet set up.

- *Like* an RRSP, investments within a TFSA can be made in virtually any financial instrument.

- *Unlike* an RRSP, contributions are **not** tax-deductible when made.

- However, *like* an RRSP, earnings in the account grow tax-free.

- *Unlike* an RRSP from which after age seventy-one, you are *forced* to withdraw funds, as well as pay tax on them, there is **no** deadline for forced withdrawal or termination of a TFSA.

- *Unlike* an RRSP, funds in the TFSA account **can be withdrawn** at any time, in part or in full, with **no tax** consequences. Although an RRSP can be accessed at any time, doing so would trigger full marginal tax assessment on any amounts withdrawn.

- *Like* an RRSP, an unused contribution allowance in a TFSA can be topped up at any time.

- Any amount withdrawn from a TFSA is immediately added to the individual's *unused* contribution allowance. This permits him to replace the withdrawn funds in any *future* year.

- Should the holder of a TFSA die, the remaining funds pass to his estate, with no tax-liability arising. A TFSA holder can name a beneficiary, in which case the estate can be bypassed."

TIP #29..... **By age eighteen, every Canadian begins accumulating contribution room in a TFSA. Regardless of one's ability to contribute to it in any year, the carry-forward feature may prove in future years to be extremely valuable. A TFSA account need NOT be opened for contribution allowance to start accumulating at age eighteen.**

....

"Wait a minute, Grandpa. I'm confused," declared Jenny. "If both the RRSP and TFSA plans have such great benefits, how do I know which is the better one to contribute to?"

"Good thinking, Jenny. Both plans *are* excellent tools. And, unless you have enough savings to top up both, they can each be best-used in specific circumstances.

Take **Sam** for instance. She could use her TFSA to save for a down payment for her first home, for furnishings, or for a trip. You'll notice that each of these expenditures has a much shorter time-horizon than does an RRSP account, which is meant to build wealth over the *long* term.

However, if you should be lucky enough to one day earn more money than you know what to do with, here's a golden tip."

TIP #30..... **If one has sufficient financial flexibility to do so, he is wise to *regularly* make the maximum-allowable contribution to both an RRSP and a TFSA.**

"By contributing to *both* plans, you get the maximum, tax-sheltered benefit of each program."

"Not any time soon, Grandpa!" exclaimed Kevin. "It makes sense, but it'll be a long time before either of us have those kinds of spare dollars."

"You're probably right, Kevin. But you never know. One day you may receive a huge bonus at work, or make a large profit on an investment, or even inherit a significant sum. Unless you have debts to pay off first, what better use for such windfalls than to *strategically* load them into both plans? You would be maximizing the long-term, tax-free growth of an increasing sum of money – not to mention receiving the benefits of the tax refund flowing from each RRSP contribution.

I intentionally used the term *'strategically'*. There is no downside to loading as much as you can, up to the maximum allowable, into a TFSA.

On the other hand, you may be best advised to spread out, over a number of years, *large* contributions to an RRSP. Remember, you receive your tax deduction *only* in the year you make an RRSP contribution. You want to make sure you receive the greatest *total* refund possible from those contributions. In the case of a large sum, that may take several years."

....

"Jenny, I promise we'll return to your question about contributions – if you don't have enough funds to top up both, and you have to decide where to put the limited dollars at your disposal, how to choose between an RRSP and a TFSA.

But first, I want to better acquaint you with one other tax-protected savings vehicle, with which you are both somewhat familiar. You, Jenny, have already in fact been taking advantage of it, and Kevin will begin to do so very soon."

CHAPTER ELEVEN

REGISTERED EDUCATION SAVINGS PLAN (RESP)

"We know about the superb tax-saving advantages of both a TFSA and an RRSP (or RRIF, after conversion from an RRSP). A third valuable tax-protected savings vehicle is the *Registered Education Savings Plan (RESP)*.

So let's take a closer look at understanding the RESP, which is offered by the federal government.

But first, back to you two. Since your early childhood years, you've each been registered in an RESP. The day will likely come when you yourselves, will have children and family responsibilities. You'll want *your* children to know that they'll be able to afford a higher education."

"You're making me dizzy, Grandpa!" exclaimed Jenny. "First you've got me planning for my retirement. Now you've got me planning to send my unborn children to university or something! What next?"

"Careful, Jenny," responded Kevin. "Next, Grandpa'll have you making a will!"

"You're right! I *am* throwing a lot of information at you. But RESPs fit in logically with TFSAs and RRSPs, so you're stuck with it!"

. . . .

> *A REGISTERED EDUCATION SAVINGS PLAN (RESP) has the sole function of helping to finance a child's post-secondary education. It is registered by the Canada Revenue Agency on behalf of the child enrolled.*

"As of 2014, the specifics of an RESP include:

- No annual limit on contributions; however, each account's total contribution is capped at $50,000 for each child.

- Regardless of family income, the federal government adds to the RESP, an annual grant, called the *Canada Education Savings Grant*. Subject to a $500 annual limit, and a $7,200 lifetime limit for each beneficiary, the government's grant equals 20% of the subscriber's annual contribution. If the beneficiary does not pursue a post-secondary education, these grants are subject to recapture by the government.

- The funds in the RESP may be invested by the plan *subscriber*, usually the parent or grandparent, in any investment vehicle of the subscriber's choosing. Alternately, the RESP may be managed and invested by various organizations specializing in these plans.

- As with a TFSA, annual contributions to an RESP are *not* tax-deductible. However, while in the plan, *increases* in the fund's value are *not taxable*.

- The subscriber's initial contribution is never taxed, even when withdrawn years later.

- RESP payments to the student, *beyond* the amount contributed by the subscriber, are taxed when withdrawn, but only in the student's hands as a scholarship. Generally, because of the student's minimal income, this makes the scholarship payments subject to low tax, or possibly, no tax at all.

Most financial institutions will assist in setting up an RESP for a child beneficiary, and will provide the detailed rules governing the plan.

One caution: Government rules governing RESPs are very complex. Details are available online on government sites, as well as those of most financial institutions. Review those rules *thoroughly*, before setting up an RESP."

TIP #31..... **An RESP is an incredibly useful, tax-protected vehicle for accumulating post-secondary education funds for children. It should be a key element in any financial plan for families with children.**

TIP #32..... **The earlier a child's RESP is established, the higher its likely value at the time of high school graduation, and the greater its potential to fully finance the child's post-secondary education.**

"In your case, Jenny, your RESP was set up when you were about five by your mom, with help from the grandparents and great-grandparents. It is now substantially covering the cost of your post-secondary education. From a total investment of $8,000, your RESP had become worth about $24,000 by the time you graduated from high school.

In *your* case, Kevin, because you're younger than Jenny, the plan has existed longer. As a result it's worth closer to $30,000."

"Sometimes it pays to come second," quipped Kevin.

"Perhaps, Kevin. But keep in mind that the cost of *your* education will also be higher than Jenny's. Inflation must be factored in. Does either of you want to take a stab at defining 'inflation'?"

"The money you have today will buy less in the future?" offered Jenny.

"Not bad, Jenny. More formally it could be defined as:

INFLATION is the increase in the price level of goods and services, over time."

....

"You don't know how much I appreciate my RESP, Grandpa," declared Jenny. "It has essentially allowed me to use my *meager* part-time earnings for miscellaneous expenses, while my tuition and books are pretty well covered by the plan."

"RESPs play a significant role in helping to finance the post-secondary education of our young people.

Only about half of Canada's post-secondary graduates begin permanent employment with a student loan to repay. Those who do graduate with an outstanding loan however, do so with an average debt of $27,000. You're both very fortunate to not have to start your career with such a debt hanging over your heads."

"Yes, don't we know it," added Kevin. "It's a huge relief to know that we aren't likely to need student loans before we finish our formal education. And just so you know we've been listening, Grandpa, we both realize that avoiding this huge debt gives us a great advantage for jump-starting our net-worth fortune."

"And I can tell both of *you*, it gives us all a great deal of satisfaction to know that we've been able to help ensure your education – *and* to know that the government has contributed a good chunk as well!"

....

"OK, Jenny, now let's get back to your question about how to choose between investments in a TFSA or an RRSP."

· ·

CHAPTER TWELVE

TFSA vs. RRSP DECISIONS

"At various stages throughout our working life, we will have many different reasons for choosing one of these plans. Here are a few guidelines which *generally* may assist with selection of the best plan.

In the early stages of a career and family formation, Canadians will usually be better off opting to make the *maximum possible contribution to a TFSA, while delaying contributions to an RRSP.*

TFSA ADVANTAGES – The Early Years: The Twenties

- Earnings, and therefore marginal tax-brackets, tend to be lower at this age. Use the TFSA to accumulate tax-free savings for early family expenses such as furnishings, summer camps, and orthodontists.

- A TFSA is a great vehicle for accumulating a first down payment for a home, or perhaps the purchase of a vehicle.

- A TFSA can serve as an emergency fund to cover a major, unexpected expense, such as a job loss or lay-off.

- Since, in addition to each annual contribution entitlement, withdrawn funds may be replaced in any *future* year, you can rebuild the account as quickly as financial circumstances permit.

- As mentioned previously, on the death of the owner, any balance in a TFSA attracts no tax as it passes to the estate or to a designated beneficiary.

Remember, if you are lucky enough to max out the limits on your TFSA, you can and should, divert any additional savings capacity to your RRSP."

TIP #33..... **A TFSA is a great vehicle for tax-free accumulation of funds that may be required within a few years. It is also a useful savings tool for retirees who do not immediately require all the funds they must withdraw annually from their RRIF.**

....

"On the other hand, if you were to use your RRSP as an accessible fund into which you periodically tap, you will pay a heavy price for withdrawals. You'll pay taxes on the full amount withdrawn, probably at a higher rate than existed at the time of your tax deduction when you first contributed the funds. This is because when you make the withdrawal, you're probably in a higher tax-bracket than when you initially contributed the funds to your RRSP."

"But, Grandpa, I heard from one of my friends that you can use your RRSP for a down payment on a condo or a house. Is that wrong?" asked Jenny.

"Your friend is right, Jenny. The government allows *first-time home buyers* to withdraw without tax consequences, up to $25,000 each from an RRSP, but *only if the funds are used for a down payment.*

This one-time privilege has another very important condition. The full amount is considered as only 'borrowed' from an RRSP. It *must* be repaid over the subsequent fifteen years, or tax penalties are assessed.

This fact leads to another useful tip."

TIP #34..... The first-time home buyer with both an RRSP and a TFSA, should consider withdrawing allowable funds from both plans, in order to maximize his down payment. A down payment of 20% or more eliminates the cost of high-ratio mortgage insurance, and reduces the initial mortgage loan. This helps achieve faster net-worth growth.

....

"Here's something to consider. *In future*, by age 30 each Canadian adult will have had twelve years of TFSA eligibility. This would provide the *opportunity* for at least $101,000 of contribution capacity. This is never lost, even if the eligibility is not fully utilized as it arises.

I emphasize '*in future*' because the TFSA program, begun in 2009, is still in its infancy. This means that a 30-year old in 2015 will have accumulated only $41,000 of contribution room by that date. But an individual aged 18 in 2009, will have $101,000 of accumulated contribution credits by the time *he* reaches 30.

By this age also, many individuals will have formed personal partnerships. This means that a couple will, in future, have accumulated at least $202,000 of TFSA eligibility by age thirty."

TIP #35..... The TFSA is a tremendous vehicle for tax-free wealth accumulation for Canadians. Every adult should strive to take full advantage of his TFSA savings eligibility throughout his lifetime. In the early years of a career, unless one can afford to maximize contributions to both plans, a TFSA is likely the more appropriate savings vehicle over an RRSP.

"But, Grandpa, did you forget what you advised earlier? That contributions to either plan should take place only *after* all credit card and other high-interest debt is paid off?" asked Kevin.

"An excellent reminder, Kevin! *All debts*, other than perhaps a low-interest mortgage or a student loan, are your biggest roadblocks to wealth-creation. It makes no sense to be saving money on the one hand, while at the same time, wasting hard-earned cash on high interest payments.

You've heard me say this often – *Pay off those debts first!*"

....

RRSP ADVANTAGES – The Middle Years: 30's Through to Retirement

- Earnings and marginal tax-brackets, generally now higher, shift the greater advantage for savings from a TFSA, to an RRSP.

- Tax refunds resulting from annual RRSP contributions should ideally be used to:

  - Pay down allowable, penalty-free portions of mortgage principal; *or*

- Contribute to still-available eligibility in one's RRSP; *or*

- Top up accumulated contribution room in one's TFSA.

"Remember, the ideal situation is to contribute to both an RRSP *and* a TFSA, once you have the financial resources to do so. However, by about age thirty, it is *generally* beneficial to fully utilize your RRSP capacity *first*, because of your higher tax bracket.

I can't say it too often – both a TFSA and an RRSP are wonderful wealth-creation programs. While, depending on your circumstances, it may be necessary to opt for one over the other, the important decision is to *contribute to at least one of these plans* as early as possible, and to the maximum of your financial capacity."

"Okay, Grandpa, we hear you. If we can't handle both, we know you'll haunt us if we don't contribute to at least one plan," quipped Jenny.

"As we continue to our next subject of discussion, *the power of compound interest*, you'll come to understand why the earliest-possible loading up of *both* a TFSA and an RRSP, will pay huge dividends in your long-term efforts at wealth-creation."

....

> **TIP #36..... Saving money does not constitute investment.**

"Till now, we've talked only in general about these two key, tax-sheltered *savings* vehicles. We haven't yet made an attempt to identify and examine the many *investment options* that we can utilize within each of these plans. We'll eventually come to that as well."

INVESTMENT is the strategic allocation of savings to produce the best-possible returns over a selected time frame, consistent with the level of risk-tolerance of the investor.

"Before we can indulge Kevin's desire to discuss specific investments, we have to first understand:

- The power of compound interest;
- The types and categories of investments which are available;
- The relationship between *risk* and *return*.

If I haven't worn you out yet, and you're both still keen to carry on, we'll try to deal with all three of these important subjects next Saturday."

"You bet, Grandpa!" enthused Kevin. "Sounds like we're finally getting to the real meat of wealth-creation. I can't wait to learn more."

"It's a date," added Jenny. "Much of this is actually beginning to make sense. See you next Saturday. Lunch first? Please remember, I'm just a starving student on a minimal income, some of which according to the gospel of Grandpa, I'm supposed to be saving!"

. . . .

CHAPTER THIRTEEN

THE MAGIC OF COMPOUNDING

"Well, here we are again! Our fourth Saturday get-together. We're actually making good progress. So far we've discussed how to:

- Manage our cash spending;
- Control our debt, especially credit cards and mortgages;
- Save regularly;
- Utilize three key, tax-efficient savings vehicles – the TFSA, the RRSP, and the RESP.

Today, as I promised you, we'll become familiar with several topics and terminology key to understanding future investment decisions which we'll be called upon to make throughout our lifetime."

. . . .

"The first of these is the **_power of time and compound interest_**.

Kevin, have you any objection to our using _your_ finances as an example? You might enjoy discussing _your_ investments which with my advice, you've been accumulating since your early teens."

"Go for it, Grandpa," enthused Kevin.

"Great! In round numbers, I believe your present _portfolio_ is worth about $5,000. Am I right?"

"_Portfolio_ – I kind of like the sound of that; it makes me feel like a successful businessman. But yes, according to my last _statement_, it was within a hundred dollars of that," replied Kevin.

"Wow! How did you manage to save so much, Kevin?" asked Jenny.

"Kevin's too modest to answer. It's mainly because his wants and needs are few. Up to now, he's been able to save far more of his allowance and part-time earnings than he has spent. He has shown an incredible degree of dedication to savings, which is most unusual not only for someone as young as he is, but for most of us at any age. Of course, we've been careful to invest his savings prudently, and they've grown significantly.

If Kevin is able to maintain this same discipline throughout his working life, he and his family will end up very wealthy indeed – due in great part, to the magic *power of compounding and time.*"

....

"We understand the basic concept of *simple interest*. But now let's understand what is meant by *compounding* interest when we use it in terms of investments.

Usually we are most interested in the *compounded annual rate-of-return* achieved on our investments over a set period of time. In simplest terms:

> *COMPOUNDING is a process by which the original value of an investment increases exponentially over time. As periodic dividends or interest are automatically reinvested, they escalate the dividends or interest earned in future.*

Let's clarify this with an example. You have a $1,000 investment. It earns 5% interest annually. All interest earnings are *reinvested*. At the end of:

- Year One – the investment has grown to $1,050

- Year Two – the investment has grown to $1,103

- Year Three – the investment has grown to $1,158

- Year Ten – the investment has grown to $1,629

- Year Twenty – the investment has grown to $2,653.

By contrast, had you chosen to *not* reinvest the interest earned each year and instead spent it, you would have been earning only *simple interest* on your $1,000.

By the end of year twenty you would have earned but withdrawn *$1,000* in total interest payments. Compare this to the *$1,623* interest which accumulated when you allowed the annual interest to compound. The magic of compounding earned you an extra $653 over 20 years."

"Maybe rabbits are nature's example of compounding," joked Jenny.

"The annual effect of this *interest-on-interest* growth doesn't at first, seem particularly significant; but as the definition states, it increases *exponentially* over time."

....

"Let's look at Kevin's current investment of $5,000.

Kevin, how much do you think you would end up with if, never touching the interest earned, nor adding to the original investment, you had invested this $5,000 at 5% annual and compounding interest, for a 40-year period?"

"I guess it could be worth over $10,000?" ventured Kevin.

"You'll both be shocked!

Invested today, at 5% compounding interest, for 40 years – about the length of your working life, Kevin, your $5,000 would actually become worth approximately $35,000."

"No way! That's so awesome," exclaimed Kevin.

COMPOUND ANNUAL RATE-OF-RETURN is the percentage by which a given investment would need to increase each year, over a specified period, to reach a desired end value.

"So, if we were asked what the annual compound rate-of-return would be if Kevin's $5,000 increased to $35,000 after 40 years, our answer would be?"

"Five percent," promptly replied Jenny.

"Right you are! These two definitions are crucial to our understanding of the differing results we might achieve with various types of investments. But more on that later."

....

"For now, let me share with you some more compounding magic.

To keep it simple, we'll again use Kevin's $5,000 investment, the same 5% compounding interest yield, and the same 40-year term.

But we'll add another component – an additional $200 monthly contribution to the original investment.

Kevin, would it be reasonable to assume, since you've managed as a teenager to achieve a $5,000 portfolio value, that once you have a full-time job, you should be able to add at least $200 a month to your initial $5,000?"

"Sure!" exclaimed Kevin. "That should be easy."

"Easy for *some* of us," muttered Jenny.

"*If* you were disciplined enough to actually do that, Kevin, and I've no doubt you will be, then your initial $5,000 investment would after 40 years, amount to an impressive **$332,000!**"

"Incredible!" exclaimed a stupefied Kevin.

"The actual cash you invested would have been:

- The initial **$5,000**, *plus*

- $200 monthly for 480 months, for an additional **$96,000**.

Your total *combined* investment would be **$101,000**.

That $101,000 would have mushroomed by another **$231,000** due solely to the 5% annual interest earned on all invested contributions *as well as* all the extra interest earned on the *reinvested* interest. This is the ***magic of compounding***."

"That's truly unbelievable!" declared a shocked Jenny. "It's like buying one Lamborghini, and getting two more for free!"

....

"I'm getting a kick out of throwing surprises at you two. Let's look at another scenario.

Let's assume that instead of investing your $5,000 in a fixed-interest instrument, you invested it in the ***Toronto Stock Exchange (TSX) Index***. We'll also factor in the impact of your continuing to add $200 monthly to your initial investment.

The TSX Index produced an actual average annual rate-of-return over the years 1940 through 2007, of 10.6%. At this rate of return, your initial $5,000 over 40 years would become:"

	Initial Investment	TSX Average Annual Yield (1940 to 2007)	Value After 40 Years
With No Additional Investment	$5,000	10.6 %	$281,000
With an Extra $200 Per Month Invested	$5,000	10.6 %	$1,592,000

"Wow!" exclaimed Kevin. "That is *some* difference! All that extra benefit from only $200 a month of additional investment."

"Kevin, you are the *only* one I know who would say *'only'* when referring to saving $200 every month!" teased Jenny.

....

"If you're impressed by *that* example, here's another which illustrates the startling effect of **early-in-life investments** on ultimate wealth accumulation. Let me start by introducing you to two lifelong friends, **Jake** and **Larry**.

Jake, at age 25, begins investing $400 a month. He's able to keep this up for 10 years, and then, at age 35, stops making further contributions. His investment averages a 7% annual return through those 10 years and continues to do so, until he retires at age 65.

His friend Larry also invests $400 monthly, earning the same 7% return. He however, is a few years older and only begins investing at age 35. He continues to invest the same amount monthly, for thirty years, until he retires at age 65.

Larry started investing at an older age than Jake. However he was diligent in keeping up his monthly contributions for the next 30 years, compared to Jake's relatively brief ten years of contributions.

Who do you think will have the larger portfolio at age 65?"

"Logic tells me that Larry, by investing the same monthly amount over a 30-year period instead of just ten years, should end up with the most money," offered Jenny.

"Well, Jenny, most people would agree with you.

Surprisingly, despite having contributed a total of only $48,000, Jake would end up with **$521,000** at age 65.

Although Larry's monthly contributions would have totaled a much greater $148,800, he would end up at age 65, with only **$468,000**."

"How can that be, Grandpa?" asked Kevin. "Somehow it doesn't seem possible."

"The sole reason, Kevin, that Jake's investment grew so dramatically is that, despite his much shorter contribution period and smaller cash investment, his money not only compounded over the initial 10-year period during which he contributed, but *then*, the accumulated sum had a full 30 more years of compounded growth.

Larry on the other hand, had a total of only thirty years for compounding to work its magic. In other words, the effect was less dramatic than in Jake's case because Larry's accumulated savings and earned interest after ten years, had only 20 years of growth remaining, compared to Jake's 30 years.

Jake was able to contribute only one-third as much as Larry, but by starting ten years sooner, ended up with a larger nest-egg."

"Wow, I still can't believe it!" exclaimed Jenny.

> **TIP #37.....** **The combined magic of compounding, time, and self-discipline, can produce phenomenal results, especially for those whose saving and investing habit begins early in their working life.**

"I'm beginning to understand how we can actually become millionaires by the time we retire," exclaimed Kevin. "But there's a slight problem. What I know about *investing* is basically zero."

"Don't worry about that, Kevin. You're not alone. Many of us lack this knowledge at first. Later in our chats, I'll describe investment products that will eliminate much of the mystery for both of you."

....

"What about *inflation?*" asked Jenny. "Forget the Lamborghini. What if forty years from now, Kevin can't even buy a basic clunker for the $1.6 million he might have accumulated in the example you just used?"

"That's stretching it a bit, but still a great question, Jenny! This is a really good time to understand the eroding power of inflation.

In terms of inflation's *effect* on all of us, it means that our dollar generally, will buy less in future than it does today.

If we say that inflation is running at 4% annually, we mean that the average cost of goods and services is expected to be about 4% higher than it was a year ago."

"So what do you think my almost **$1.6 million** in today's purchasing power, would be worth after forty years, Grandpa?" asked Kevin.

"To begin, I used 4% as an example because that was the *actual* average inflation rate that existed over the period 1940 to 2007 – the same period that averaged 10.6% in stock market returns. If we were to apply the same **4%** inflation rate to *your* 40-year investment horizon, we would find this sum of money to be *worth* about **$330,000** in today's dollars."

"All those years of saving, investing, and planning, and that's all my efforts would be really worth?" exclaimed Kevin.

....

"Now you're beginning to see, Kevin. Because of the very real effect of inflation, targeting a one million-dollar retirement fund by the time you reach sixty, may be way too low a number, *unless* at that time you have other sources of income, like pensions.

Fortunately, in the last twenty years inflation in Canada has moderated greatly, averaging about 2% annually. Nevertheless, to be on the safe side in our calculations when trying to set your long-term investment goals, we may be smart to use a higher inflation figure of 3%.

Using this **3%** rate of inflation over a 40-year period would make the **$1.6 million** worth about **$485,000** in today's purchasing power."

> TIP #38..... Because of the eroding effect of inflation on purchasing power, savers and investors must adjust their long-term objectives to compensate for inflation's drag on future values.

"So what you're saying, Grandpa, is that having $1.6 million today is a lot of money, but forty years from now, because of inflation, that amount may buy only the equivalent of what $485,000 will buy today?" queried Jenny.

"Assuming a 3% inflation rate, yes, that's correct, Jenny. It will still buy a lot, but not nearly as much as we might have wished for, or expected.

And we *must* take into account that eroding purchasing power, when we do a *Financial Plan*, later in our discussions."

....

"Does it now make sense why *sheltering* your growing investments as much as possible from income taxes becomes extremely important? Imagine if, in addition to the *inflation drag* we've just discussed, your investments were further eroded by *taxes* on increases in value!"

"I've heard people complain about the high taxes they pay, but this is the first time it's really hit home for me," observed Kevin.

TIP #39..... **Protecting investment gains from income taxes is an extremely important element of every individual's wealth-creation strategy.**

"The *TFSA* and *RRSP* savings and investment vehicles we discussed earlier are the primary tax-minimization tools available to every Canadian investor."

"I definitely get the importance of putting my money in a long-term savings plan, like an RRSP," agreed Jenny. "But the thought of *investing* in the stock market or something like that, makes me very, very nervous. It strikes me a bit like gambling. I've heard a lot of horror stories about people who've lost tons of money in the market."

"It's good that you're nervous about it, rather than flippant, Jenny. There's nothing wrong with wanting to invest more conservatively. But I think that a good part of your concern is based more on a lack of understanding. One *can* invest reasonably safely in the stock market, in a manner that greatly reduces risk, especially over the long term. I think our next discussion will help you with that.

It's also important to realize that any long-term investment plan needs to be *balanced*. The stock market is only one investment possibility. Our discussion on various investment options will I think, make you feel more comfortable."

UNDERSTANDING
INVESTMENTS

CHAPTER FOURTEEN

FIXED-INCOME INVESTMENTS

"Before contemplating actual investments, we need to become familiar with the various investment *options* available, and their associated risks.

We'll go slowly. This subject can be overwhelming for the novice investor. There are literally thousands of investment options in existence. By grouping them into main categories, they become easier to understand.

Given your concerns, Jenny, you'll probably be at your most comfortable with our first category – the various **Fixed-Income Investments**.

As the name implies, these investments will produce a yield or *fixed-income* which is largely predictable. Let's look at the main ones:

- **Bank or Credit Union Savings Accounts**

    These usually pay a very low rate of interest, often less than 1%. Useful for very short-term saving purposes, they should be avoided for larger savings, or for longer-term investments.

    These accounts are 100% secure in that your *principal* (the cash deposited) is government-protected, at least to $100,000 per account, by the ***Canadian Deposit Insurance Corporation (CDIC)***.

- **High-Interest Savings Accounts**

  Many financial institutions offer the option of higher interest rates on larger minimum-balance savings deposits. For example, because they are expected to grow to a significant amount of money over time, TFSA savings accounts are generally able to attract higher rates.

  The CDIC protection applies to TFSA accounts *if the investment is in a savings account*. This makes the high-interest savings account a risk-free, modest-return savings vehicle. At best however, it is unlikely to keep up with inflation.

- **Treasury Bills (T-Bills)**

  Treasury Bills are short-term investments issued by both the federal government and some provinces; as such, they are risk-free. They can be purchased for various terms, generally ranging from 30 days to one year. A minimum investment of at least $1,000 is required. Yields may be better than in a typical savings account, but at best, still barely on pace with inflation.

- **Money Market Funds**

  This is the most conservative type of *fund*. Most such funds are *not* CDIC-insured. The fees charged by the mutual fund service-provider are generally low, but so are the returns earned.

  Most money market funds are invested in government or government-guaranteed securities. Some may include *somewhat* riskier investments such as mortgages. Investment returns are neither guaranteed, nor are they specified. Over time however, the returns tend to be better than savings accounts or T-Bills.

- ## Guaranteed Investment Certificates (GICs)

  Also CDIC-insured, these certificates are issued by the lending institution, such as a Bank, for specific terms, usually ranging in length from one year through five years. Generally, the longer the term, the higher the rate paid. Yields will be better than savings accounts, T-Bills, or most money-market funds. Your investment however, is usually locked-in for the duration of the term selected.

- ## Government and Corporate Bonds

  These are *debt* instruments issued by governments or corporations. In buying them, you are lending the government or corporation a sum of money. In return, they offer a specified interest rate, and a return of your capital at a set maturity date. Since North America's government bonds are considered to be risk-free, they pay a much lower rate of interest than do corporate bonds.

  Bonds are such an important category for most investment portfolios, we'll delve into them in greater detail shortly.

- ## Mortgage-Backed Securities (MBS)

  These are fixed-income securities that are invested in a *pool* of residential first mortgages. These mortgages are insured under the National Housing Act. As such, they are unconditionally guaranteed by **Canada Mortgage and Housing Corporation (CMHC)**. Though these investments are very safe, their returns will not be very attractive when interest rates are low."

"So, Grandpa, you're saying that all these types of investments are really safe, and if we invest in them, we're not likely to lose our money. Is that right?" asked Jenny.

"That's right, Jenny, but keep in mind that because they *are* safe investments, they don't earn you very much. In fact, remember what we discussed about the impact of *inflation* on your investments? If all your money were for example, in only government bonds, you would be very lucky over the years to even keep up with inflation.

So yes, all of these investments are safe, slow and steady earners. On the other hand, they don't contribute substantially to growing your wealth much beyond covering the effect of inflation.

If we're to achieve financial independence, we'll need to at least *balance* these safe investments by also investing in products that can earn us more."

"Sounds like you're still suggesting we risk a good part of our hard-earned money, Grandpa. Why not just go to Vegas and take our chances there?" asked Jenny.

"By the time I finish explaining in detail the other investment options, Jenny, I think you'll agree that investing in a *prudent* manner is nothing like the gamble you'd take in Vegas.

Look at it in terms you're both familiar with.

When you play cards with the family, you're holding a hand with cards of various values. You try to build up a solid winning hand (a portfolio). To do this, you want some high-value aces and face cards (high-risk) which will net you higher points, but if caught with them in your hand at game end (market downturn), it could result in a loss. The boring lower-value cards (low-risk) won't add up to a lot of points (interest), but they also won't lead to huge losses. To win the game (a comfortable retirement), you need, and try to achieve, a balanced hand."

"Cards, I understand," commented Jenny. "But with cards I'm only playing with points, not my retirement funds."

TIP #40..... The prudent investor will always consider, and almost always include in his portfolio, some very conservative, cash-preserving investments. To prudently balance risk, the closer an investor is to retirement, the greater should be his proportion of fixed-income investments.

....

"Grandpa, how do you know when you *have* achieved financial independence?" asked Kevin.

"I'll give you *my* definition, Kevin. It should work pretty well for most of us."

FINANCIAL INDEPENDENCE exists when, without having to be employed, one earns sufficient income from investments, pensions, or other sources, to maintain a desired lifestyle.

....

"I mentioned earlier that *bonds* are such an important investment option for any portfolio, that they're worth a more detailed examination. Let's talk more about them right now."

CHAPTER FIFTEEN

BOND INVESTMENTS

A BOND is a debt instrument. It is used by governments, municipalities, and corporations to raise capital. It represents both a promise to pay periodic interest at a set rate (coupon), as well as a promise to repay the principal on a specified date (maturity).

"An investor who buys a bond becomes a **creditor** of the issuer; he is **not** a shareholder.

A *bondholder* has a priority claim over that of a shareholder, on an issuer's income. This means that a bondholder must receive his interest payments in full, *before* any dividends can be paid to a shareholder.

Every bond has a **par value**, set by the issuer.

PAR VALUE of a bond is the predetermined amount to be paid out on its maturity date.

When an investor buys a bond, the price he *pays* may be above or below par value. This is because the prevailing interest rates in the market may have changed up or down since the bond was first issued.

If comparable-term interest rates have *decreased* since the bond was issued, then the bond will be more valuable and priced higher than when first issued. This is because the interest rate paid on the bond is now more attractive than that of the general market. In this situation, a bondholder who bought at issue date, could sell his bonds for a capital gain."

"Whoa, Grandpa!" exclaimed Jenny. "What exactly is a capital gain?"

A CAPITAL GAIN is the increase in value of an asset, from its purchase price to its selling price – not taking into account either interest or dividend payments.

....

"Let's look at the other side of the coin. If interest rates have *increased* since the bond was issued, it will now be worth less. If this occurred prior to its maturity, and the bond were sold, the selling price would be below its purchase price, to make up for its below-market interest rate."

"I guess in that case you would have a *capital loss?*" asked Jenny.

"Exactly, Jenny. But keep in mind that you can avoid the loss by holding on to the bond until its maturity date."

....

"To put all this another way, the interest rate (*coupon*) attached to a newly-issued bond does not change throughout the bond's life. The original purchaser, and any subsequent buyers on the resale market, will always receive the same pre-determined interest payment. However, the *effective* interest rate of the bond *will change* as, until maturity, its market value slides up or down relative to its par value.

As you might expect, a bond's *market value* will approach *par value* as the maturity date nears. That is because, regardless of prevailing market interest rates, par is the value payable to the bondholder at maturity."

"Grandpa, this is a tough one. If we were on a golf course, I'd definitely understand '*par*'. I *think* I understand, but could you please clarify in *simple* terms, the value movement of bonds, just to be sure?" asked Kevin.

"I'll be glad to, Kevin. The key principle to remember, is that individual bond values will fluctuate up or down over time, generally in the *opposite direction* to changes in market interest rates. These fluctuations matter little to the bondholder if he holds the bond to maturity – *as long as the issuer remains financially sound*."

....

"Financially sound? Does this mean that when I invest in a bond, I *could* actually lose not only my interest earnings, but even my capital investment too?" asked Jenny.

"Unfortunately, Jenny, the answer is yes. There are *some* circumstances under which a bondholder *can* lose. But with a little care, the risk is minimal:

- Government bonds, considered risk-free, will pay the lowest interest.

- Investment-grade corporate bonds will pay a higher rate because the issuer has *some* risk of encountering financial difficulties.

- Below-investment-grade bonds, sometimes called *junk* bonds, pay a much higher interest rate to compensate for their increased risk."

....

"When buying an individual bond, it's very important to carefully consider the *credit rating* of the bond issuer.

Bond ratings range from AAA (highest quality) to D (highest risk). If an investor seeks a very low risk to his bond-generated income and invested capital, he should probably avoid individual bonds with a rating below AA."

"Sounds a lot like school," observed Jenny. "Aim for an *A*, avoid a *D!*"

117

"And I," added Kevin, "cannot believe anyone could be tempted by something called a 'junk' bond!"

"You're right, Kevin. Investing in an individual *junk bond* would be sheer folly. But what some investors do is buy a *fund* holding a large number of such bonds. This reduces the risk of individual bonds failing. Because of their high risk individually, such bonds pay very high interest rates. The much higher average yield of the corresponding bond funds makes them attractive to some investors.

I personally, would never put more than 10% of my total bond holdings into such funds."

....

"There is a category of bonds that *can* protect the long-term investor against the risk of *inflation*. In Canada, these are called ***Real Return Bonds (RRBs)***.

RRBs are similar to regular bonds in all respects but one. The interest rate they pay floats at a fixed percentage **above** the official rate of inflation. Hence the protection from inflation.

RRBs are not great investments when inflation is low. But because their interest rate is pegged at a constant percentage *above* the rate of inflation, they will outperform regular bonds when inflation is high.

Several notes of caution with RRBs:

- RRBs are long-term investments, maturing some 15 to 20 years in the future. Your capital investment is protected *if held to maturity*. Like all bonds however, they are subject to market fluctuations if sold before maturity.

- Unless held in a TFSA or RRSP account, all interest earned by RRBs is, as with all bond products, fully-taxable at the same rate as other earned income."

....

"Another bond category with which it is useful to be familiar is known as the **Strip Bond**.

Also known as *zero-coupon* bonds, they differ from regular bonds in that they pay no periodic interest. The interest coupons have been *stripped* from the purchase price of the bond.

An investor buys strip bonds at a discount to the bond's face value, which he will receive at the bond's maturity date. The difference between the purchase price and maturity value is the investor's return.

Federal, provincial, municipal, and some corporate bonds are available as *strip bonds*. Terms may range from less than a year to several decades.

Some investors like strip bonds because, not needing an ongoing interest income, they are happy to defer it. They prefer to have the foregone interest reflected in the cash value of the bond at its maturity.

An investor can buy this bond and forget it, knowing precisely how much he will receive at a future date.

Even though payment of interest is deferred to maturity, these bonds should not be held in taxable accounts. The investment will be taxed as if interest were received annually.

These bonds can be a useful investment component of a tax-sheltered account such as an RRSP or RESP.

As an example, a family celebrates the birth of a child. An RESP account is immediately established. A deeply-discounted strip bond with a 17-year maturity date is purchased for the newborn's RESP account. This provides a safe and fully-predictable value when the child is ready to begin post-secondary studies."

> TIP #41..... Bonds are an extremely valuable, low-risk element of any portfolio. If carefully selected from enterprises with very high investment-grade ratings, individual bonds represent little risk to capital, when *held to maturity*. Corporate bonds generally produce a higher annual return than do savings accounts and GIC alternatives. They also offer the *potential* for capital gains if sold prior to maturity.

....

"Grandpa, instead of buying just one bond, can't you hold a *bunch* of them so that you don't have all your eggs in one basket?" asked Kevin. "I'm thinking that if you spread your investment among several bonds, it would reduce your risk, and reduce the pain of any one bond failing."

"That's a very good observation, Kevin. Just like my reference to *junk bonds*, there are easy ways of diversifying your bond investments:

- Buy a selection of individual high-quality corporate and government bonds.

- Buy *bond funds*, each of which will hold a wide variety of individual bonds.

The upside of owning *bond funds* is that you achieve broad diversification and reduce risk.

The downside however cannot be ignored, and must be carefully evaluated:

- As you will come to understand when we talk about any kind of mutual fund, investment in *any* fund comes with a management fee – *sometimes* a very significant one. A fee can seriously erode your interest yield.

- With a bond fund you lose an important protective feature of individual bonds. With a single bond, the issuer guarantees a specific interest rate, *as well as* the payment of par-value at maturity. A bond fund can guarantee neither. Bond funds never *mature*. They are invested in a large number of bonds, each with a different interest payment and maturity date.

The consequence of this difference between individual bonds and a bond fund is twofold:

- Because a *fund* often sells bonds, or redeems maturing ones and replaces them with other bonds, the interest rate paid by a bond fund will fluctuate, though not significantly. More importantly, the fund's redemption value will change up or down, depending on the direction of interest rates in the marketplace.

- When you sell a *bond fund* you *may* achieve a capital gain if interest rates have decreased since you bought. However, you are also exposed to the possibility of a capital loss, if rates have risen since you bought into the fund.

   Because a bond fund does *not* have a specific maturity date, you *cannot*, as with individual bonds, eliminate this risk of capital loss by holding the fund to maturity.

   If your bond fund is valued below your purchase price, you can hold on until prevailing interest rates again decline, and the value of your Bond Fund increases. This means you have *some* control over an eventual gain or loss. However you do not have a specific date at which the risk will disappear, as you do with individual bonds.

If prevailing interest rates are very low when buying into a bond fund, your risk of future capital loss is magnified, because a high probability exists that market interest rates will increase at some future time.

For example, with interest rates at historically-low levels during most of 2009, I was very hesitant about purchasing bond funds. For the bond portion of my portfolio in 2009, I chose instead to invest in high-quality corporate bonds. Their guaranteed par value at a fixed maturity date was for me, the better investment."

TIP #42..... **Bond funds are useful for diversification among various bonds. This benefit however, must be balanced against the reality of some fluctuation in interest paid, as well as capital-value changes if market interest rates change after the date of your fund purchase.**

....

"Whether you buy individual bonds or bond funds, they serve not only as a solid fixed-income investment, but also, as a great hedge against major downturns in the stock component of your portfolio.

When stock markets trend downward, it's generally the result of a sluggish economy, and poor corporate performance. In such circumstances the ***Bank of Canada*** tends to lower interest rates. As we've discussed, when market interest rates go down, bond values tend to go up – because the interest rate at which they were purchased has become more valuable to the new investor.

In addition to their other benefits, this stock-market-balancing feature of bonds and bond funds makes them a key component of a well-balanced investment portfolio."

....

"Thanks, Grandpa, for explaining this so thoroughly," acknowledged Jenny. "I know this is kindergarten stuff for you, but for Kevin and me, it's all brand new. We appreciate your patience."

"No problem, Jenny. I enjoy sharing this information with both of you. If you really *do* grasp the basic principles, then every minute we spend on this is worthwhile. You'll find it much easier to manage your lifelong wealth-building efforts.

Shall we continue? Since I've just mentioned *stocks* as an investment option, we may as well discuss them next."

"It just may bring me to my knees, Grandpa," moaned Jenny. "But if you take it slowly, maybe it'll get easier."

"I've just three words for you, Grandpa," added Kevin. "Simplify, simplify, simplify!"

"I'll do my best, Kevin, without overlooking anything important."

CHAPTER SIXTEEN

STOCKS (*also referred to as* EQUITIES)

A COMMON STOCK or SHARE, denotes an ownership position (called equity) in a corporation.

"A *common shareholder* has a claim on the profits and assets of that corporation. He in fact, is one of the owners of the company. His ownership interest is in proportion to the number of shares he owns relative to the total number of shares issued. For example, if he owns 1% of the shares, he will have a 1% claim. Common stocks also provide voting rights to shareholders on certain, major corporate decisions."

. . . .

"The *risk vs. benefit* spectrum of equity investments (stocks) has the widest range of any investment we have yet discussed, except perhaps for 'junk bonds'.

Generally, the higher the risk-profile of a stock, the more volatile its trading value. It's therefore worth some extra elaboration to help you understand this trade-off for various types of stocks."

"Grandpa, I actually heard of something called a '*Large-Cap*' bunch of stocks. What are they?" asked Kevin.

"Interesting that you've heard of them, Kevin. They aren't exactly everyday vocabulary. There are actually *three broad categories* of common stocks. 'Large-Cap' is one of them. By the way, 'Cap' is an abbreviation for *Market Capitalization*."

MARKET CAPITALIZATION is a company's share value, multiplied by the number of shares it has issued.

COMMON STOCKS – THREE BROAD CATEGORIES

"Because fund companies tend to use these definitions, it is important that the prudent investor at least be familiar with these three categories of common shares. In order to select the investment category that is right for *his* level of risk-tolerance, an investor must understand the differences.

1. Large-Cap Shares ($$$$$)

A LARGE CAP corporation is a long-established business, among the largest of publicly-traded companies. Although definitions vary widely, it will usually have a market capitalization of over $10 billion. Many corporations in this category pay regular dividends to their shareholders.

Often, large-cap shares will be referred to as *Blue Chip stocks*. In Canada, approximately thirty companies fall into this large-cap definition.

While there are no guarantees of positive performance with *any* common stock, large-cap stocks tend to be the least risky of the three categories, particularly if held over an extended number of years. This is especially so for those that pay dividends.

Dividends provide shareholders with regular cash payments which, when added to market-value increases of the stock itself, serve to enhance the overall return to the shareholder. Dividends also serve to moderate the effect of periodic market-value declines in the stock.

2. Mid-Cap Shares ($$$)

A MID-CAP corporation's capitalization will generally fall between $2 billion and $10 billion.

Mid-cap shares are those of generally solid companies, with the potential to become large-cap corporations. Some may show phenomenal growth and hence great market returns. Others are susceptible to major negative value swings.

Some mid-cap shares may also pay dividends.

If an investor selects carefully, or is lucky, or perhaps both, he *may* receive great returns from mid-cap stocks, even in a short-to-medium investment period. However, value volatility risk will tend to be greater than that of large-cap companies.

To reduce the downside risk of individual mid-cap stocks, an investor is wise to moderate his risk by using either *actively or passively-managed funds*. Such funds provide broad diversification across many such companies, and hence reduce the volatility and risk of individual investments.

As I said earlier, we'll deal separately with the important subject of *funds*, and key differences between them, when we discuss the broad category of *mutual funds*.

3. Small-Cap Shares ($$)

SMALL-CAP companies typically have a market capitalization of between $300 million and $2 billion.

Small-cap share values will tend to be the most volatile. They are therefore riskier than investments in both large-cap and mid-cap companies. Small-cap companies are very unlikely to pay dividends.

The prudent investor with a somewhat conservative risk-tolerance, would be wise to place only a relatively minor portion of his portfolio in this category. Again, broad diversification through various funds is advisable."

> TIP #43..... As a general rule, the higher the capitalization (cap) of your equity (stock) investments, the less risky the profile of your investment.

> TIP #44..... The lower the capitalization (cap) value of your equity (stock) investments, the more important it is to achieve a high degree of diversification by using carefully-selected funds.

....

PENNY STOCKS

"This is a fourth common stock component of Canadian equities. This category is highly volatile and extremely risky, relative to the three I've just outlined.

Although the conservative investor is not likely to invest in *penny stocks*, it's useful to understand what they are, along with their risk and potential reward.

PENNY STOCKS, as the name implies, are those with an individual share value of less than one dollar.

As you might expect, penny stocks represent the riskiest end of the spectrum among common stocks. In Canada, they trade primarily on the **TSX Venture Exchange**.

Sometimes you get lucky. For instance, you happen to buy a stock in a fledgling mining company, at 80 cents a share. Suddenly, because the corporation has just announced a major new find, the value zooms to over $8 a share. Very excited by your savvy investing, you're tempted to buy more penny stocks to add to your net-worth.

Unfortunately, this winning example is little different than the one-in-a-thousand luck of the individual who hits a jackpot in Vegas. It can happen, but it's very unlikely.

Far more penny-stock corporations fail financially, with major losses to their shareholders, than succeed dramatically.

Unless you are particularly knowledgeable about a specific company, its business, its market, and most crucial, its management, it is generally wise to refrain from investments in penny stocks. Buying penny stocks is often closer to gambling than to investing."

"That's what's so scary," observed Jenny. "Even though they call it investing, I've heard of some people who practically throw away their futures on a hodge-podge of what they call 'investments', when what they're really doing is gambling."

"You and Kevin won't be among those 'gamblers', Jenny. You're already asking the right questions.

Despite the high risk, the lure of even a slight potential for an astronomical return causes a significant number of investors to buy penny stocks.

Understandably, this tendency is welcomed by fledgling and start-up companies. Such investments are an important financing vehicle for them. With little to no established track record, issuing bonds is next to impossible. The equity market therefore becomes their main source of both initial funding and expansion capital."

TIP #45..... **Due to the extraordinarily high-risk profile of penny stocks, the prudent investor is wise to limit his investment in this sector to *no more than 5%* of his portfolio.**

DIVIDEND-PAYING STOCKS

A DIVIDEND-PAYING STOCK is one which pays a regular cash distribution to shareholders.

"As we saw, penny stocks are at the highest end of the risk spectrum. At the opposite end of that scale are dividend-paying stocks which over time, tend to have the lowest portfolio-risk of any common stock investment.

Historically, *dividends* have accounted for more than 40% of the overall returns of the Canadian **S&P/TSX Index**.

Dividend-paying equities are much better long-term risks because:

- Dividend-paying corporations are usually among the largest, well-established businesses, with proven long-term track records. They typically represent a *minority* of the companies listed on an exchange.

- Dividend-paying companies tend to have the most secure financial outlook. As the cream-of-the-crop listed on any stock exchange, they can afford to pay regular dividends to their shareholders, while continuing to invest capital for future growth.

- If invested in dividend-paying equities, an individual's portfolio will benefit from the regular dividend payments, in addition to any gains in capital value. In a market downturn, these dividend payments moderate the negative impact on the portfolio."

....

"An investor *must* realize however, that despite these advantages, dividend payments of individual corporations are *not* guaranteed. A company can reduce or eliminate dividends at any time, particularly if it encounters difficult economic circumstances."

"How do these companies decide when to pay a dividend to

shareholders, and how much to pay?" wondered Jenny.

"It's a major decision, Jenny. The Board of Directors of a corporation must first decide whether it's financially strong enough to pay a dividend. In determining its magnitude, the Board must take into account capital requirements for future growth, and the company's ability to withstand economic downturns.

Perhaps most important, the Board must weigh the corporation's continuing ability to sustain or increase the dividend in future years. It knows the market will react very positively to a new dividend announcement. On the other hand, it will react extremely negatively, to future decreases or worse, elimination of a dividend."

> TIP #46..... Dividend-paying stocks, or funds which contain them, represent a *significant* percentage of the equity investments in a well-designed portfolio.

....

"An added advantage of owning *individual* dividend-paying stocks, is that many such stocks offer the investor a **Dividend Reinvestment Plan (DRIP)** option.

A DIVIDEND REINVESTMENT PLAN (DRIP) offers an investor the option to automatically reinvest all dividend payments toward the purchase of additional shares.

No commission is charged for these additional share purchases. Effectively, your current dividends will generate more dividends in the future, through the extra shares bought in this manner."

"Is this another example of compounding at work, Grandpa?" inquired Kevin.

"Absolutely, Kevin! The extra shares acquired in this manner pay dividends, which in turn buy more shares which pay more dividends, and so on until you sell that particular investment. It's a great example of compounding at work.

And here are a few other features of *Dividend Reinvestment Plans (DRIPS)* which are worth noting:

- Some DRIPS further enhance their value by offering a reduction of up to 5% on the cost of additional shares purchased through dividends;

- Many DRIPS require the ownership of a minimum number of shares. That number however, tends to be quite low;

- Toronto Stock Exchange lists more than one hundred companies offering this advantageous DRIP feature."

"This is more like it, Grandpa," enthused Kevin. "I invest enough to meet the minimum share requirement, then just like watching dandelions re-seed themselves, my number of shares keeps increasing. Cool."

"It is cool, Kevin. Now you'll understand that I wasn't being insulting when I told you that all of your present portfolio investments are DRIPS."

PREFERRED SHARES

PREFERRED SHARES issued by a corporation yield a specific dividend which must be paid to its preferred shareholders, before any dividends may be paid to its common shareholders.

"Unlike dividends on common shares, dividends on preferred shares *must* be paid. They are a contractual obligation. If their payment is suspended due to economic difficulties, the company will be considered to have defaulted on its obligation. It will be prevented from paying any dividends to its common shareholders until after the default is first remedied to the preferred shareholders.

- *Like* common stock, preferred shares represent an ownership interest in a corporation;

- *Unlike* common stock, preferred shares confer no voting rights on their holders."

"You're kidding! The owner of preferred shares owns part of the company, receives a more or less guaranteed dividend payment, but has no say?" questioned Jenny.

"And the common-shares holder also owns part of the company, receives a slightly less secure dividend payment, but gets some say," continued Kevin. "Weird!"

"Because of their *preferred-dividend* feature, the market prices of these shares tend to be less volatile than those of common shares. On a risk scale, preferred shares would fall between the somewhat riskier dividend-paying common stock of the company, and its more secure corporate bond.

Due to their slightly-higher risk profile compared to bonds, the yield (dividends) on preferred shares will tend to be somewhat higher than the yield (interest) on the same company's bonds."

> **TIP #47.....** For an investor striving to achieve a good return at a very modest risk, preferred shares can play a useful role in his portfolio.

....

"Grandpa, you've mentioned *funds* as an effective way to diversify investments," commented Kevin. "Can I presume that this includes all these different stock investments too?"

"Yes, Kevin. A huge variety of funds exist for pretty well all the products we've talked about since our discussions first began."

....

"This might be a good time to stop today. But when we return next Saturday, it makes sense to spend some time better understanding these funds. Usually they're called *Mutual Funds*."

"We're in *mutual* agreement about calling it quits for today, Grandpa," agreed Jenny. "My brain is just about overflowing! It's been interesting. But I'm curious. What about real-estate related investments? Way back when we started these discussions we talked about Great-Grandma and Great-Grandpa investing in real estate. How does that fit in with all these financial options?"

"You're right, Jenny. We should cover that subject too. Real estate investments are an important way of adding to our net-worth. We've talked about it, but only as it related to ownership of our *personal* home.

Since you've raised the subject, let's delay our discussion on mutual funds, and instead begin with a discussion of real estate investment options when we meet next Saturday. Then we'll return to understanding mutual funds as an investment vehicle.

How about lunch first, as usual? See you around noon?"

"No argument there, Grandpa. Thanks. See you then," echoed Kevin and Jenny.

....

CHAPTER SEVENTEEN

REAL ESTATE INVESTMENTS

"Here it is, our fifth Saturday already. I don't know about you, but I'm impressed by the number of topics we've discussed."

"Just don't expect us to pass a test," retorted Jenny.

"It's so beautiful outside, what do you say we have our chat in the fresh air, on our balcony?"

"Great idea, Grandpa," replied Kevin as Jenny nodded her head in agreement and led the way to the outdoor deck.

....

"For starters, remember we agreed that generally, we buy our own home primarily as a comfortable and secure place to live? Only secondarily do we view it as a proven, excellent long-term investment.

There are however, a number of other options for investing in the real estate sector, in which our *primary* purpose may well be the potential *investment value*.

In some cases it may be a fortunate combination of both personal enjoyment and the expectation of long-term appreciation."

1. THE SECOND HOME

"Long a favourite of many Canadian families is the *second home* – in most cases, a cottage. About 9% of Canadian families own a second home.

As with a family home, most second homes are bought primarily for family lifestyle. However the investment value may play a greater role in the purchase decision, than it does with a primary residence.

Canadians are well aware that cottages, particularly those on a waterfront, have over the past decades, increased dramatically in appeal, and therefore, value. Many have in fact, shown a capital appreciation often greater than that of the owner's principle residence.

Once a homeowner's main residence is substantially mortgage-free, purchasing a cottage property can bring great satisfaction to the family, as well as superb long-term growth in the homeowner's net-worth."

"I'd love to be able to afford a getaway cabin one day," mused Jenny. "I remember how much fun we had when we rented them for family vacations."

"Well, I'd rather have a little ski shack," reflected Kevin. "Hey, Jenny, you get the summer place and I'll get the winter one. That way we'll have one of each in the family!"

"It costs nothing to dream. Not only is a second home both a getaway haven, and a great investment, but it can also *work* for you, by earning income. It could be rented out when not in use by family. You could even be fortunate enough to not only cover your ongoing operating and maintenance costs, but also put a few extra dollars in the bank."

....

"Because your country cottage, ski chalet, city condo or farm getaway is a *second* residential property, tax issues will force you to make a key decision when selling."

> TIP #48..... Canadian tax laws permit an owner to designate *either* his second residence *or* his personal home, as his *primary residence* for income tax purposes. This choice must be made by the filing date of the first tax return, *after* the sale of either property.

"When you sell the property you have designated as your tax-exempt primary home, you are not required to report a capital gain on the sale. However, if you subsequently sell your other home, you *must* report, after all costs and improvements are factored in, any profit on the sale. You will then be assessed the *capital gains tax* on that profit."

CAPITAL GAINS taxes in Canada are currently assessed at your marginal tax rate, on 50% of the increase in capital value of your investment.

"Grandpa, it'll be a long time before either of us have *one* home, let alone two! But just in case, how would we decide which home to select as tax-exempt?" asked Kevin.

"Most likely, Kevin, you would exempt the one that had gained the most in value. But the best idea is to consult with an accountant just before you make the first sale. That way he can point out the tax consequences of choosing one home over the other, and guide you in the correct procedure to follow."

> TIP #49..... A secondary home or cottage, if clearly affordable, can be a great asset both for family enjoyment, and as an investment for long-term capital appreciation.

"By the way, interest or dividends earned on investments are taxed differently. They are *not* included in the calculation of capital gains. Of course as we have discussed, if your eligible capital asset is held in an RRSP or a TFSA, any capital growth, interest, or dividends, are *not* taxed within either plan."

"By 'capital asset', Grandpa, do you mean only financial investments, or can Kevin's ski shack or my cottage also be held in an RRSP or a TFSA?" asked Jenny.

"I should have been more clear, Jenny. No, a real estate asset cannot be held in either a TFSA or an RRSP. However, under some circumstances, a first mortgage in a real estate property *may* be included as an RRSP investment. Before considering that however, it would be wise to consult an accountant to make sure that your mortgage qualifies, and that you follow the complex rules imposed by the *Canada Revenue Agency* on such a registered investment."

2. RENTAL-INCOME PROPERTY

"Think back to our early get-togethers, when we chatted about your great-grandparents' investments in rental properties. Because of their underlying property value and rising income stream, they were an excellent long-term investment.

Over the long term, a rental property's value should increase in roughly the same proportion as personal residences in the same area.

As always, several cautions are appropriate:

- Owning a rental property is *not* a hassle-free exercise. Don't underestimate the amount of work and expense required of you, the owner. Unless your budget includes paying a property manager 10 to 15% of your revenues to oversee the property on your behalf, you will be the one responding to all tenant issues, and arranging for ongoing maintenance.

- Before proceeding with the purchase of a rental property, do your homework. Check out the rental market in your target community. Satisfy yourself that a sufficient long-term rental demand exists, to minimize vacancy risk.

- Calculate carefully, *all* the costs of ownership. Include mortgage payments, property taxes, maintenance, and an allowance for vacancies. Match those total figures *realistically*, against your projected rental revenue. Satisfy yourself that the economics make sense for you.

- As with any real estate investment, remember the three key rules for selecting any property – *location, location, location.*"

TIP #50..... **With at least a 20% down payment on the purchase price, the addition of a rental property to a family's asset mix can provide an impressive boost to its net-worth. With the combination of tenants paying down the mortgage, and capital appreciation over time, the positive net-worth impact can become substantial.**

---

3. MORTGAGES

"Mortgages as an investment can be made available on a direct basis, to both individuals and developers.

More common however, is the purchase of a *share* in a pool of mortgages managed by a third party such as a *mortgage fund*.

Many companies, large and small, exist for the sole purpose of lending funds as mortgages. These firms may choose to invest in first mortgages, second mortgages, or a combination of both. By creating a *pool* of funds, raised from individual investors, the mortgage fund managers acquire the necessary financial resources.

An ownership share in a *pool* of mortgages reduces investor risk through diversification.

These mortgage-based investments can produce impressive returns for the investor, at times in the 9 to 12% annual range.

Again, a few cautions:

- Careful *due diligence* is in order, in researching the caliber and reputation of the company with which you plan to invest. We've all read or heard of more than a few unfortunate examples in which investors, at times due to outright fraud, lost most or all of their capital.

- Be sure you recognize and accept that, with higher potential returns, comes higher risk. This is particularly so with investments in *second* mortgages.

  First mortgages are considered to be of much higher quality and therefore less risky than second mortgages. Should foreclosure become necessary due to default by a borrower, *second mortgages* rank behind first mortgages."

TIP #51..... **Mortgage funds *can* be a useful, modest component of an investment portfolio. If carefully chosen, they can add significantly to the income stream within the portfolio.**

"Kevin, are you thinking the same as I am?" asked Jenny. "We'll probably be old and retired before we can handle more than our *own* mortgage, let alone invest in someone else's."

4. REAL ESTATE INVESTMENT TRUST (REIT)

A REIT is a corporation or trust that uses the pooled capital of many investors to purchase and manage income-property (an equity REIT) and/or mortgage loans (mortgage REIT).

REITs can be bought as individual stocks in either a corporation, or an individual trust.

Again, maximum diversification will be achieved if these products are bought as a **REIT Index Fund**, such as the **iShares CND REIT Sector Index Fund (XRE)**.

REIT investments offer an investor a number of advantages:

- By definition, a REIT will provide an investor with far more diversification of risk, than could any single property or mortgage investment.

- Contrary to the purchase of an actual property, no minimum investment amount is required.

- Contrary also to property ownership, a REIT investment, no matter in what form, is extremely liquid. REITs can be bought or sold on any business day.

Investors *must* accept however, that despite the promise of attractive yields at time of purchase, the returns will fluctuate over time, as will the value of the investment itself. REITs therefore are *not* a fixed-income product.

For some investors, their potential for much higher yields *may* compensate for the higher risk level.

One cautionary note. Despite the distribution to shareholders of REIT income in the form of dividends, REIT dividends paid into a non-registered account – unlike other dividends paid on Canadian common shares – are taxed as if they were interest payments. REITS therefore, are best held in a Registered account."

"Jenny, maybe investing in a REIT is the closest we'll ever get to being landlords," mused Kevin.

> **TIP #52.....** A REIT may be an excellent addition to one's portfolio as a modest-risk investment in the real estate sector. The broad, low-cost diversification achieved through investment in an index-based REIT product will serve to reduce risk.

....

"It's important to understand, Jenny and Kevin, that in no way have our discussions exhausted all of the many and varied investments available to investors.

In addition to those we've touched upon, there are many other, often very complex investment options, such as:

- Hedge funds,
- Foreign-exchange products,
- Limited partnerships,
- Commodity futures,
- Options,
- Flow-through shares,
- and other, even more exotic-sounding investments."

"Grandpa, my eyes are crossing!" exploded Jenny.

Don't let it worry you, Jenny. Actually, my advice is to always stick to the *KISS* principle of investing:

KISS ... KEEP IT SIMPLE, STUPID!"

"That doesn't sound very politically-correct, Grandpa," retorted Jenny.

> TIP #53..... Unless you are an experienced investor, avoid investment products that are complex and difficult to understand. The less one understands an investment, the riskier it usually is.

....

"Wow, Grandpa, there's a lot more to this investment game than I thought!" exclaimed Kevin.

"Now I'm beginning to understand why so many people get confused, and why so few of us do really well with our investments," added Jenny.

"You are both so right. It *can* be very complicated. What is important right now however, is that you gain a sufficient understanding of the investment *categories* we've discussed. This will equip you in future, to more intelligently decide the best fit for both *your* own *investment plan* and your *risk profile*.

I promise that when we finally begin to discuss your personal investment decisions, I'll share with you some simple techniques that should serve well over the long term, to help you make smart and uncomplicated investment decisions."

"Grandpa, the word 'simple' is music to my ears. But I really hope you're keeping good notes for your book," interjected Kevin. "It's for sure we'll need it!"

....

"Grandpa," added Jenny. "You *really* have talked a lot about *investment risk*. I'm not sure though I really understand how anyone can actually *manage* that risk. Can you tell us how a person can deal with risk and still be able to sleep at night?"

"That's an excellent point, Jenny. It's almost impossible to separate investment and risk. And since you raise it, I think it would be appropriate to discuss that topic now, before we turn to my long-promised mutual fund discussion."

. . . .

CHAPTER EIGHTEEN

INVESTMENT RISK

"Jenny, hopefully I'll now answer your concerns on risk, and help you see how an investor *can* understand and manage the role it plays in making investment decisions.

Remember, we agreed that if we're to grow our net-worth by much more than the level of inflation, *prudent* measures of risk are *necessary* in our investments.

But to be ready to assume that risk, we *must* understand it. We must know both how to balance it against its potential benefits, and when to vary our level of risk-tolerance.

First you need to understand the **risk-versus-benefit tradeoff**, over the long term. These figures show the actual, *compounded annual rates-of-return* for different Canadian investment categories, over the 67-year period between 1940 and 2007:

- Stocks (Equities)   10.6%
- Bonds   6.5%
- Treasury Bills (T-Bills)   5.2%

By comparison, during this same period annual inflation in Canada averaged 4.0%.

The next set of figures shows the growth of *a single Canadian dollar* invested in 1940, in each of these three categories. It assumes that *all* income from each investment was reinvested annually, through to the end of 2007.

This example is for illustrative purposes only since realistically, one would be unable today to invest only one dollar.

- Equities: $1 in 1940 - Value in 2007: $854
- Bonds: $1 in 1940 - Value in 2007: $ 68
- T-Bills: $1 in 1940 - Value in 2007: $ 30

These results show the huge incremental returns achieved by stocks over an extended time-frame, as compared to those of the much lower-risk bonds and T-Bills."

"By the way, Grandpa, this looks like another example of the power of time and compounding. It sure works miracles," observed Kevin.

"You're so right, Kevin. It's the power of compounding that makes all three of these growth figures so dramatic.

Despite the benefits of compounding, did you notice the compelling differences in value growth between the three asset classes?

As you both made abundantly clear throughout our discussions, you acknowledge the importance of *controlling risk* in any investments you make. Given that none of us is too likely to be dealing with a 67-year investment time-frame, we need to strike the right balance for us, between *risk* and potential *return*."

"You'd better believe it, Grandpa," exclaimed Kevin. "I'll be lucky 67 years from now, if I can remember the *name* of my bank, let alone what I have in it!"

"History shows us that equities, while providing a dramatically higher return over the very long term, have much greater volatility over shorter time frames. We need therefore, depending on our stage of life and investment horizon, to balance our investment portfolio to produce what is for us, an ***acceptable level of risk***."

....

"Grandpa, you've convinced me that we have to take *some* risk when we're investing," said Jenny. "But I still don't have the faintest clue how I'll get a good night's sleep. I'll be a nervous wreck!"

"I think this next part of the discussion should help chase away those nightmares, Jenny.

Controlling risk effectively may at first seem a daunting task. You'll be relieved though, to learn that *investment risk* can be broken down into simple, ***individual risk elements***:

- Expense
- Advisor
- Tax-erosion
- Investment term
- Lack-of-diversification
- Political and currency issues
- Trading frequency
- The 'sure-thing'
- Timing
- Inflation
- Age
- Lack-of-a-plan

Each of these individual elements is easy to understand; most are easy to manage.

Let's examine these risks one at a time, and see what we can do about reducing their negative impact on both your portfolio, *and* your peace-of-mind."

1. EXPENSE RISK

"We've all heard that '*location, location, location*' is the single-most important criterion when buying a home or an investment property.

By the same token, when making *financial investment* decisions, perhaps the three most important considerations over the long-term are '*expense, expense, and expense*'.

Let's elaborate, using a real-life example:

*Remember our young friend, **Sam**? Let's say she inherits **$100,000**. She wishes to invest it for the long-term, in a well-diversified, Large-Cap fund.*

*Sam has narrowed her choices down to either an actively-managed mutual fund, or an exchange-traded fund (**ETF**).*

*The management expense ratio (**MER**) on the actively-managed fund is **2.5%**. On the exchange-traded fund it is **0.5%**. We'll define all these terms in our pending discussion of mutual funds. For now, it simply indicates the difference in fees that Sam will have to pay for the management of her potential investment.*

*We'll make the assumption that over the **40 years** before Sam retires, both funds will be able to achieve an average annual return of **7.5%, before** expenses. This is a reasonable expectation in view of the very long-term time frame.*

At the end of 10 years, a comparison of the two options shows Sam the difference in end-values:

	Original Investment	*MER Expense (Annual)*	*Net Value to the Investor (40 Years)*
Actively-Managed Mutual Fund	*$100,000*	*2.5%*	*$704,000*
Exchange-Traded Fund	*$100,000*	*0.5%*	*$1,497,000*

Earlier we learned about the positive power of compounding. However, compounding can either work *for* you, or *against* you. In this example, the *adverse* compounding effect of an extra 2% annual MER cost ends up eroding more than half the potential return on Sam's investment.

The *extra* annual 2% management fee in this example, would cost Sam $793,000 over a 40-year investment time frame. Another way of looking at this, is to conclude that by reducing her investment expense by 2%, Sam could more than *double* her total investment gains over a 40-year period.

The message in Sam's case is a simple one, and leads to the next tip."

> **TIP #54.....** **Minimizing the costs associated with an investment will over time, have a huge, positive impact on investment returns. If paying a higher fee, an investor must ensure that the long-term return of that particular investment is proportionately higher, to at least compensate for the higher fee.**

"When we talk about *investment costs*, MER costs may not be the only expense. We have to include all other costs such as:

- front or back-end loads on funds;
- commissions charged when purchasing stocks;
- monthly or annual fees charged on accounts.

To minimize the potential high costs of investing in stocks and in many funds, *online* discount brokerages are available. Using a discount service can result in the cost of your purchase or sale being as little as one-tenth that charged by a full-service broker."

2. ADVISOR RISK

"Given the relative complexity of the investment world, it's understandable that many of us prefer or require financial planners or investment advisors to assist us."

"Ha!" interjected Jenny. "Here I am having a nervous breakdown about all of this, and you call it 'relatively complex'?"

"Financial advisors or planners can be very helpful. Unfortunately however, we often end up consulting an advisor who also sells financial investment products. He is both an advisor, *and* a vendor of specific products from which he earns fees. Even though, by law, any potential conflict of interest must be revealed to the investor, it is often glossed over by investors themselves as being not terribly important.

The conflict however, does become an issue if the advisor guides the client toward an actively-managed mutual fund for example, when a comparable product, such as an exchange-traded fund also exists, but at a much lower cost.

The advisor can't be blamed for encouraging clients to invest in one of his mutual funds. That fund gives him an initial purchase fee, as well as an annual *trailer fee* of perhaps 0.5% of the entire value of the investment, for as long as the client holds it."

"That's probably why," quipped Jenny, "I've heard the comment that even as your mutual fund is crashing in value, your financial advisor may be buying a new set of luxury wheels!"

"Grandpa, would *'Buyer Beware'* be another of your famous tips?" asked Kevin.

"To be fair, Kevin and Jenny, advisors are generally very honest individuals, trying to earn a living. Simply put, unless they are truly *independent*, they have no incentive for pointing out comparable investment options with much lower fees. Many advisors probably believe that their recommended fund will, through better performance, more than make up for its higher fee. If they were correct, then this would be a win-win scenario for both the advisor and his client.

We'll examine *actual* performance differences when we finally get to our mutual fund discussion.

Truly **independent** financial advisors do exist. They do **not** offer for sale, specific products. Usually you will be charged either an hourly, or a flat fee for their advice. The cost in this case is well worth it. The independent advisor, having nothing more to gain, will provide totally objective input and advice."

"Grandpa, you're an anomaly," chuckled Jenny. "You're our advisor, you have nothing to sell, and you're free to boot! What a deal!"

> TIP #55..... For objective financial advice, consider consulting a truly *independent* professional who has no vested interest in the advice provided.

3. TAX-EROSION RISK

"To refresh your memory, Jenny and Kevin, investments *within* TFSA or RRSP accounts are tax-protected."

"*That* fact is pretty well etched into our brain now – but I guess it doesn't hurt to keep reminding ourselves," agreed Kevin.

"If however, your portfolio is invested *outside* these accounts, its value, no matter how well-invested, will be severely eroded by income taxes."

> TIP #56..... Only if the maximum allowable investment in both a TFSA and an RRSP account has been utilized, should funds be invested outside these two tax-efficient investment vehicles.

"Let's look at a few facts about *income taxes* on investments *outside* TFSA or RRSP accounts:

- All interest earned by your savings account, GICs, treasury bills, bonds or bond funds, is taxed as *ordinary income* in the year it is earned. This means that the tax you pay on earned interest will be no different than the tax you pay on earnings from your job.

- Dividends from common or preferred stocks receive *preferential* tax treatment. This means that you pay much less tax on dividend income than on interest income.

- Capital gains, whether on the *sale* of real estate, stocks, bonds, ETFs, mutual funds, or any other investment, are taxed at the investor's normal tax rate. Fortunately however, the tax calculation is applied to only *one half* the increase in value."

"So what exactly does this mean for us when we're investing, Grandpa?" asked Jenny.

"The simple rule, Jenny, is twofold:

- Invest everything possible in either a TFSA or an RRSP;

- If you have additional investments (other than an RESP), beyond the maximum capacity of these tax-sheltered vehicles, be sure that at least your *interest-generating* investments are in either your TFSA, or your RRSP."

> **TIP #57.....** **Different tax treatments on investments, and their impact on returns, should always be considered when deciding *where* to hold investments.**

....

"*Before* you ask, I'll clarify. Because it is taxed the most severely, an interest-generating investment should be in either a TFSA or RRSP account. It doesn't matter which account, *if* you are not drawing down the earnings.

If however, you are planning to draw income in the shorter term, try to favour your TFSA, because you will pay no tax on your withdrawals. Withdrawals from RRSPs on the other hand, attract full taxes as if they were earned income.

That tax penalty is usually mitigated by the **retiree** withdrawing funds from an RRSP, because he has likely dropped to a lower tax-bracket than when he was contributing."

"So in withdrawing funds from an RRSP or RRIF, the retiree will usually pay less tax on the withdrawal than the amount of the tax refund he received when he originally made the contribution? Is that correct, Grandpa?" asked Kevin.

"Generally, that's true, Kevin. But remember the original contributions are likely to have grown dramatically over time. More *actual* tax will eventually be paid on withdrawals, but only because the amount withdrawn will be far greater than originally contributed."

"So originally, you might have received a tax refund of 40% on the $10,000 you contributed to your RRSP. Once you retired, your marginal tax rate may have dropped to 28%, but it will be applied to say, the $30,000 that the investment had become?" asked Jenny.

"That's exactly the point I was trying to make, Jenny."

4. INVESTMENT-TERM RISK

a) Fixed-Income Investment

"Generally, your *missed-opportunity risk* is greater, the longer the term of your *fixed-rate* investment.

Consider for example, a 5-year GIC. Because the return of your principal is guaranteed, your *capital risk* is zero. However, your interest rate is locked in for the full five years. This means you lose any *opportunity* to take advantage of higher rates which may become available before your GIC term ends.

To partially compensate for this risk, longer-term fixed-income investments usually pay a higher return than those offered for shorter terms."

"Fixed-income investments certainly are attractive to those of us who like to feel safe," commented Jenny. "Maybe we just have to live with their being locked in for some years."

"There is a way, Jenny, to reduce this risk of locking in for the longer term. You can *ladder* your fixed-income investments."

LADDERING is the staggering of investment maturities over various terms.

"The intent of laddering is to help smooth out the impact of interest rate fluctuations, and to allow a gradual reinvestment at current rates. This strategy also prevents drastic changes to the earnings generated by your fixed-income portfolio.

For example, you decide to place $25,000 of your investment portfolio in GICs or bonds. You split it into five individual investments of $5,000 each, with 1,2,3,4,and 5-year maturities. The first matures after one year, the second in two years, and so on, until the fifth reaches maturity in five years.

At the end of year one, you will reinvest the now-matured one-year investment (with or without the interest earned) in a new 5-year term. Repeat the procedure each year, with every subsequent maturity."

TIP #58..... Laddering of fixed-income investments is an effective tool for gradual adjustment to rising or falling interest rates, thereby avoiding drastic rate changes and earnings fluctuations.

"As an added benefit, this 5-year laddering strategy also provides for the investor, annual access to one-fifth of his invested capital."

"So, Grandpa, if I eventually decided to go back to school for a PhD or something," asked Kevin, "I could crater one-fifth of my GIC investment each year, and still leave the other GICs earning me interest till I need more money the following year?"

"That's exactly how it could be done, Kevin."

b) Equity Investments

"For equity investments, the risk is different. *The shorter the time frame, the higher the risk*, whether invested in stocks, or in equity mutual funds.

We do know that over many decades, a *well-diversified* portfolio of high-quality equity investments has consistently outperformed all other categories of investments, by a wide margin.

Equity investments, unlike fixed-income investments, have neither an underlying guarantee of value, nor of regular dividend payments. They are subject to the ups and downs of the economy, and to the changing fortunes of individual corporations. Equity market returns in the shorter-term do *not* gravitate around the high, average long-term gains. Instead, they tend to *spike* above or below the average.

This extreme example will illustrate:

In 2008, the TSX Index plummeted by approximately 35%. However, over the preceding 67-year period, from 1940 to 2007, it produced on average, an annual rate-of-return of 10.6%."

....

"This is frustrating, Grandpa," complained Jenny. "If I invest in stocks for a short time, I might lose money. If I invest for a really long time, like my *whole* working life, I'm likely to make a great deal. But then, because of inflation, it will be worth less anyway. Yikes!"

"It isn't as bad as it seems, Jenny. Although *time* is only one investment risk factor, this TIP may help simplify your decision."

TIP #59..... To reduce the risk of negative, short-term market fluctuations, equity investments should always be made with a longer time-horizon than fixed-income investments.

5. LACK-OF-DIVERSIFICATION RISK

"Putting all your eggs in one investment basket, or even in a limited number of products, is clearly a higher risk than investing across a wide range of options. Let's consider a few examples:

• *Owning one stock only, no matter how highly recommended, is at the extreme high-end of the risk spectrum for equity investments.*

*The safest place on the equity-risk spectrum, would be to own shares in the **total equity index**, whether through an actively-managed mutual fund, an index fund, or an ETF.*

• *Owning equities only is riskier than having a portfolio with a **mix** of GICs, bonds, and equity investments.*

• *Owning fixed-income investments with a single maturity date is riskier than laddering the investment to staggered maturity dates."*

TIP #60..... Diversification *within* an investment class, *across* investment classes, and over varying time-frames, are all key to achieving a well-balanced portfolio, with a prudent level of risk.

6. POLITICAL and CURRENCY RISK

"If you, as a Canadian investor, were to invest in only one nation's financial products, it should be Canada. That's where you live. That's where you'll spend the benefits of your investments. By sticking to Canadian investments only, you won't encounter exchange-rate risks. You'll be earning returns in the same currency that you spend.

Also, if your investment is held in taxable vehicles outside an RRSP or a TFSA, it's important to keep in mind that advantageous dividend tax-credit rules are applicable to Canadian investment products only.

Canada, however, represents barely 3% of the world's investment opportunities. By limiting yourself to Canadian-based investments only, you *may* be missing out on some great growth opportunities.

On the other hand, if your investments were to include those of other countries, such as for instance, Brazil, Japan or Germany, you'll add a major new dimension to your risk exposure, namely political and currency risk.

Global diversification is worth considering for every long-term portfolio, but *only* with the appropriate level of *currency protection*, and with due regard to *political* risk.

Currency risk can be substantially eliminated through Canadian *currency-hedged ETFs* or other funds. You will pay a slightly higher annual fee for the hedge cost, *but* you will have eliminated the currency risk.

There is no real hedge available, other than wide multi-national diversification, against the risk of, for example, a third-world country defaulting on its government's bond obligations.

The prudent investor is wise to ensure that any international fund in which he invests holds only a small proportion of its total investments in the products of less politically-stable countries."

"I'm sorry, Grandpa," interrupted Jenny, "you just lost me again. The only hedge I know about is the one in our back yard, and I know that's not what you're talking about. So what is a *'hedge'*?"

"Sorry about that, Jenny!"

*A **HEDGE** is an action taken to protect against an unfavorable price move of an investment product.*

"Now I understand – I think," replied Jenny.

"And now you'll understand the next TIP."

TIP #61..... **A modest diversification into international investment products should be considered as an element of a prudent investment portfolio, but ONLY if it can be purchased on a fully-hedged basis, to eliminate currency risk.**

"Failure to hedge foreign financial products greatly magnifies the investment risk. If an international investment were to decline due to cyclical economic or political upheaval for instance, *and* at the same time, the currency-value of the investment falls, the double-whammy could be catastrophic for your portfolio.

On the other hand, the opposite can also be true. If the international investment value were to increase dramatically, and its currency-value relative to the Canadian dollar were to rise at the same time, you could stand to make a huge return.

Relying however, on *two* key factors moving in the right direction at the same time, is more akin to *speculating* than to prudent investing.

> TIP #62..... In considering international financial products, the prudent investor always balances currency and political risk against potential benefits, and errs on the side of caution.

7. HIGH-FREQUENCY TRADING RISK

In today's world of easy, accessible, and inexpensive *online* trading, the temptation for frequent trading – buying or selling of almost any financial instrument – arises all too often.

Many of us, believing in our abilities as independent investors, trade too often, at times making several online trades weekly, or even daily. For the most part, these individuals are not investors. At best they're *traders*; at worst, *gamblers*."

"This reminds me of another question, Grandpa," interjected Kevin. "Remember on our last trip to Mexico, you were talking with a woman who said she pays for all her vacations with her earnings as a *day-trader*? Exactly what is a '*day-trader*'?"

A DAY-TRADER is an individual who buys and sells a financial instrument in the same trading day, and often, multiple times in the same week.

"That sure sounds like gambling to me," exclaimed Jenny. "Why would anyone want to take that kind of risk?"

"It definitely is not an activity for the faint-of-heart, nor for those who cannot afford to comfortably absorb losses. I'm certain that a *very small* percentage of day-traders do quite well, but in the greatest majority of cases, trying to outguess the market's movement in such short time spans is not a winning strategy."

> **TIP #63.....** Day-trading is one of the riskiest strategies for most individuals. In fact for many, it is not an investing strategy, but at best, speculation.

"We already know how very difficult it is to time the market properly. The odds of making *frequent*, successful, buy-and-sell decisions over extremely short time-frames, are very slim to none.

This point is important enough to merit another TIP, a corollary to the previous one."

> **TIP #64.....** If you do plan to *try* to predict market moves on a frequent, short-term basis, do so with no more than 5% of your total portfolio. Be aware that frequent trading rarely leads to long-term success.

"Etch the following in your brain. It won't let you down:

> *PRUDENT INVESTING* combines the elements of:
> - *QUALITY*
> - *DIVERSIFICATION*
> - *MAGIC OF COMPOUNDING*
> - *PATIENCE, and*
> - *TIME.*

Prudent investing is *not* the impatient flipping of investments in a perpetual search for the get-rich-quick fortune.

Trying for a quick return is best left to buying the odd lottery ticket or heading to Vegas for a fun holiday. It is not for the prudent investor."

"After all this, I doubt I'll have the nerve to buy even a raffle ticket," quipped Jenny.

8. THE 'SURE-THING' INVESTMENT RISK

"Unless it's a GIC, or other *guaranteed* investment, there is no such thing as a *sure-thing* investment. If someone tells you there is, run the other way fast!

By the time the average person learns about a truly exceptional investment opportunity, you can be sure many others are also aware of it. Chances are that by the time you buy in, the price will already have reflected the higher value."

TIP #65..... Leave *tips* for servers in restaurants. Never use them as a basis for investment decisions.

---

9. MARKET-TIMING INVESTMENT RISK

"Regardless of *when* you make a major investment in the equities market, you are always at risk of making it just before a major downward market correction. This could in the short term, see your initial investment plummeting.

No matter how we reassure ourselves that the investment will serve us well over the long haul, such a quick drop in the value of our investment can be traumatic. It may even lead us to doubt the very wisdom of investing in equities.

But a simple technique, available to all of us, virtually eliminates that risk.

Remember our *Pay Yourself First* strategy? We talked about combining it with an automatic investment program that regularly diverts 5 to 10% of our gross income to specified investments. This same approach can benefit our portfolio, even during periods of equity downturn.

During downswings, our *regular* contribution to our portfolio will buy a greater number of *units* of our chosen investment product, at the lower price. This tends to average-down the per-unit cost of our earlier purchases. Once the market recovers and turns up again, our portfolio will recover more quickly than had we not averaged-down."

TIP #66..... **Regular, periodic investments in the equity portion of a portfolio will serve to smooth out the impact of major market corrections.**

---

10. INFLATION RISK

"As Jenny continues to remind us, the effect of inflation is a key factor in the *actual* future value of our investments. We saw how the purchasing power of our investments can be eroded, even by modest 3% annual inflation rates. This impact becomes even more dramatic when continued over several decades.

Inflation is a fact of life. For your investment portfolio, it presents such a huge potential risk, that it warrants more emphasis. Investing exclusively in fixed-income instruments presents the real risk that over time, our returns may barely keep pace with inflation.

On the other hand, **equity indexes**, pretty well world-wide, but most certainly in Canada and the U.S., have over the decades, dramatically outpaced inflation. So why not invest everything in either an index-based equity product, or in individual, high-quality equities?"

"Trick question, right? I think we answered it earlier, Grandpa," retorted Jenny. "We know there's an added risk from having too many eggs in one asset class, or any other *single* basket."

"You really have been listening! Good for you, Jenny."

"And, Grandpa," added Kevin, "we know the three magic words this time…. *'balance, balance, balance'* – a little bit of this, a little bit of that."

"Well put, Kevin!'"

11. AGE-RELATED RISK

"In your 20's – your early investing years – your investment strategy is not unduly risky, even if 70 or 80% of your entire TFSA and RRSP portfolio is in equity-based products. This is especially so if the majority of these investments is in dividend-paying equities.

At this age, you have the advantage of the magic power of *compounding* and *time*. As we have seen, these two factors dramatically reduce risk while at the same time, enhancing your ultimate returns.

On the other hand, a 55-year old investor who plans to retire at 60, and who plans to draw on his investments as soon as he retires, will need a much different mix. By this age, his portfolio should have gravitated toward a more conservative investment mix – perhaps 60 or 70% in fixed-income investments, with only 30 to 40% remaining in riskier equity-based products."

> **TIP #67.....** **Every investor must strive to balance the assets in his portfolio between equities and fixed-income instruments, in a proportion appropriate to his circumstances at each particular stage of his life.**

"Over shorter periods of for instance five years, stocks can be highly volatile. The near-retirement individual cannot afford during his last few working years, to risk a significant portion of his portfolio on the possibility of an equities downturn. On the other hand, he must still protect against inflation. Knowing that he may live into his 90's, he still needs to keep a *portion* of his portfolio in equities, or he risks outliving his funds."

....

"Grandpa, is there some easy *formula* that we can use to determine the best mix at various ages?" inquired Kevin.

"Unfortunately there isn't one that fits everyone, Kevin.

We each have different circumstances and personal levels of risk-tolerance. These differences will influence how we build, balance, and manage our individual portfolio.

Let's look again at a real example:

*Meet **Mike**, an electrician with 35 years of government service. He enjoys a defined-benefit pension plan which, when he retires, will pay him 70% of his pre-retirement income. Knowing this, Mike can comfortably maintain a higher proportion of his portfolio in equities, even after retiring. With such substantial pension income, he will not have a major need to regularly draw on his investments.*

For those *without* a significant pension plan or other safety-net, the reverse will be true."

"A public-sector career looks better and better," quipped Jenny. "What do you say, Kevin, should we go for municipal, provincial or federal?"

> TIP #68..... As one ages, the age-driven risk to an investment portfolio can be moderated by a gradual shift in emphasis from equities to fixed-income investments. The degree of the shift should be governed not only by the timing of planned withdrawals, but also by the magnitude of such withdrawals.

12. THE LACK-OF-A-PLAN RISK

"It's important that each of us, as potential investors, educate ourselves on:

- The various investment classes;
- The products within them;
- The various risk factors we've just talked about; and
- How to manage them.

All of this knowledge however, will prove to be of little value if we don't have an individualized *plan*.

Take the vehicle owner who gets into his car. He knows how to drive, but has no idea of where he wants to go, how best to get there, or how long it will take. The driver needs a destination, and a travel plan to reach it.

So too, does the investor need both a goal and a plan. He needs to determine his:

- Periodic shorter-term objectives as he moves through various stages in life;
- Long-term objective for his retirement years;
- Strategies for achieving these goals, including prudent risk-decisions.

These various elements are all part of what is commonly referred to as a *FINANCIAL PLAN*.

A Financial Plan is so critical to an investor's success that we'll make time on a future Saturday to dig in and really understand what we mean by such a plan."

TIP #69..... A periodically-updated financial plan is one of the most crucial stepping stones to successful wealth-creation.

....

"Grandpa, that's quite an eye-opening insight into investment risk," observed Jenny. "What amazes me, is that when you break risk down into its individual elements, it's so much easier to understand – and not so scary."

"I'm glad you now see that, Jenny. Not only is risk easy to understand, but also, relatively easy to reduce to acceptable levels.

As a result of today's rather lengthy discussion, I hope we've laid the foundation for your becoming wise *and* prudent risk-takers. If you succeed in blending this with the other information you've acquired, you should both become very successful wealth-builders."

....

"Grandpa, you keep teasing us with this 'wealth-building', but we still have to get to the good part – the actual investing," prompted Kevin.

"Patience, we'll get there, Kevin."

"Actually, I'm beginning to see how, if I plan it right, I can actually become a millionaire," added Kevin. "But I'm still worried about inflation chewing up the value of my million bucks."

"And that's why, Kevin, I said that one million dollars may *not* be the right objective for you. This will become more clear when we eventually put together a customized *financial plan* for each of you."

"I'll probably be as grey as Grandpa by the time we get around to it," muttered Kevin to Jenny.

"I heard that, Kevin! But first, I've been promising we would delve deeper into mutual funds, particularly the pros and cons of actively and passively-managed funds.

I think though, you've had enough information for today."

"You can say that again, Grandpa!" two voices echoed in stereo.

"Let's meet again for lunch before we head back to our place next Saturday. Is that still OK with both of you?"

"You've got a deal, Grandpa," replied Jenny. "But if we can talk about something other than wealth-building during lunch, *we'll* buy *you* the dessert!"

MUTUAL FUNDS

CHAPTER NINETEEN

MUTUAL FUNDS – An Investment Vehicle

"Our sixth Saturday – we're moving along nicely, Kevin and Jenny. I'm impressed! If you stick with me for a few more Saturdays, I think you'll have a really good foundation for managing and investing that money you'll eventually be earning – not to mention building your long-term financial independence."

"We do appreciate your spending this time with us, Grandpa," replied Kevin. "But we'll remember these Saturdays even more fondly once we become millionaires!"

"You certainly don't lose sight of your objective, Kevin! And by the end of today's discussion, your understanding of mutual funds is almost certain to become a very important part of your future success in wealth-creation.

As we mentioned near the end of last Saturday's session, most of the investment options we've discussed so far can be purchased individually, or through some form of *Mutual Fund*."

A MUTUAL FUND is offered by a company that attracts many individual investors who wish to own stocks, bonds, or other securities, on a pooled basis. Each investor buys into the fund, purchasing shares or units, which represent his proportional investment.

BENEFITS OF MUTUAL FUNDS

- "Mutual funds are an investment *vehicle*. An investor can buy units (shares) of the fund on a one-time, or regular-contribution basis. The latter allows over time, for automatic averaging of unit-costs, thereby smoothing out the bumpy effect of major market changes.

- They are instruments of easy diversification, allowing individuals to own a share in a basket of investments in any category of their choice. This averages the investor's risk across many products.

- They are easy to invest in, providing opportunity for achieving easy balance between equities, bonds and other fixed-income investments.

- They are easily convertible on short notice, into cash.

- Over the long-term, consistent investment in solid mutual funds should produce a significant, cumulative return. This helps the investor achieve his wealth-creation objectives."

TYPES OF MUTUAL FUNDS

"Mutual funds fall into two basic categories:

- Actively-Managed Funds
- Passively-Managed Funds

It's extremely important, *before* choosing a mutual fund for his portfolio, that an investor understand the differences between these two types of funds."

1. Actively-Managed Mutual Funds

An ACTIVELY-MANAGED MUTUAL FUND is one in which its managers make many individual decisions to buy or sell specific investment products, in an effort to outperform a particular benchmark index.

"These funds are operated by an investment firm or bank. It raises money from individuals and invests the proceeds in a particular group of assets, in accordance with a stated set of objectives, which it shares with its investors.

Each fund will purchase various investment products such as stocks, bonds and money-market instruments, depending on the fund's objectives. They can focus on various sectors such as mining or financials, or on individual countries or regions.

Many actively-managed mutual funds require a minimum initial investment.

Because of its *active* portfolio management, each fund charges an annual fee, called the ***Management Expense Ratio (MER)***.

Many funds also charge:

- An entry fee (*Front-End Load Funds*) or,
- An early-exit fee (*Back-End Load Funds*).

The **disadvantages** of *actively-managed* mutual funds are their **high fees**, and very *spotty* performance relative to index benchmarks, such as the overall S&P TSX Index, or many of its sub-indexes, such as the Resources or Financial Index."

2. Passively-Managed Mutual Funds

PASSIVELY-MANAGED MUTUAL FUNDS simply strive to track, rather than exceed, the performance of a particular index or sub-index.

"There are two main avenues for acquiring passively-managed mutual funds. They can be bought either as:

- Index funds, or
- Exchange-traded funds (ETFs)."

a) Index Funds

An INDEX FUND is a passively-managed mutual fund that strives to mirror the performance of a specific index such as the S&P 500 (broad-based U.S. Stock market index) or TSX 60 (top 60 companies on the Toronto Stock Exchange).

"As of 2014, Index funds in Canada are offered primarily by Banks.

Index funds enjoy exactly the same advantages as actively-managed mutual funds, but with much lower management fees.

Since portfolio decisions are relatively automatic, and transactions infrequent, costs incurred by the fund are lower. As a result, the fees charged to investors are dramatically less than those of actively-managed mutual funds."

b) Exchange-Traded Funds

An EXCHANGE-TRADED FUND is very similar to an Index Fund. It also tracks a specific index. It is however, bought and sold like a stock.

"Even fewer decisions are required of the fund manager, since the index is tracked relatively automatically. Fees as a result, are even lower than those levied for Index Funds."

....

"So, Grandpa," clarified Jenny, "do I hear you saying the main difference between an Index fund and an Exchange-traded fund is basically the way you buy and sell them?"

"That's generally correct, Jenny. But as I'll explain in a minute, there *are* nevertheless good reasons for choosing one over the other."

....

"Grandpa, in comparison to the *individual* investments we discussed, how *risky* are all these different types of mutual funds?" asked Kevin.

"Well, Kevin, it depends on the *specific* products in which a particular fund invests:

- Clearly, if a mutual fund is invested in a diverse basket of *fixed-income* products, it will be very safe.

- If the investment is in *equity-based* products, then due to the inherent volatility of stock markets, the risk will be greater, especially over the short term.

  On the other hand, particularly over a longer period of time, equity-based mutual funds will have a much greater upside.

Because mutual funds by their very definition contain a broad basket of individual investments, the **diversification** factor makes *any* type of mutual fund less risky and less volatile, than if you were to invest in specific stocks or bonds.

The real challenge for the investor is to invest in funds:

- With a low cost-base; *and*

- Which strike the right balance between fixed-income and equity-based products.

With this careful balance, such a portfolio will often be referred to as a ***balanced portfolio***."

. . . .

"It seems to me," suggested Jenny, "that what's important is whether the actively-managed mutual funds do well enough to make up for their higher fees, compared to how Index and Exchange-Traded Funds do, with their much lower fees. Right?"

"Absolutely correct, Jenny.

Remember our reference to the TSX Index performance over the years 1940 to 2007? Over that period, we saw that the Index increased by an average, compounded annual rate of 10.6%.

Many of today's financial products such as Index Funds and Exchange-Traded Funds did *not* exist decades ago.

But if, using products available *today*, and over that *same* time span, you had been invested in the TSX Index through either of these *passively-managed* funds, you would have netted an annual return of at least 10.1%, because the average management fees would have been no more than about 0.5%.

Now, let's assume the same 10.6% rate-of-return over the same 67 years. But this time the investment is in an *actively-managed* mutual fund. The actual yield to the investor would have had to be reduced by management fees of some 2.5%. This would have resulted in a much lower net annual return to the investor of only 8.1%.

The 2.5% figure represents *approximately*, the average annual Canadian ***Management Expense Ratio (MER)*** of actively-managed mutual funds. If the fund had also had a *front-end* load cost, the yield to the investor would have been even less than 8.1%.

In this example, with both types of funds performing equally, the net return to the investor of the actively-managed fund would have been at least 2% less on an annual basis, than if he were invested in the low-cost, passively-managed fund."

"I remember in our earlier discussion, when you showed us the incredibly negative effect of a 2% greater annual cost on our friend *Sam's* investment returns," recalled Kevin.

....

"This is so important, Kevin and Jenny. Because of these much higher fees, actively-managed mutual funds represent a *higher* level of *risk* to your investment returns than does either a passively-managed index fund or an exchange-traded fund."

"Charging the same high fee, whether the actively-managed mutual fund goes up or down in value, doesn't seem fair," offered Jenny. "Why would the cost be the same to the investor if the fund has a bad year?"

"Well, Jenny, the fund management's argument is that their costs continue at the same level, whether a fund is up, down, or unchanged in value. To be fair, the same also holds true for index funds and exchange-traded funds. At about 2.5% however, the average MER of an actively-managed mutual fund is about five times the approximate average of 0.5% charged by index funds and ETFs."

....

"I'm glad we don't need to write a test on all this," commented Kevin. "It's a pretty convoluted subject, even for someone like me who *enjoys* math problems."

"This subject *can* take some time to digest. I've been at it for decades and there's always something new to learn.

It may become more clear as we look at the specific performance of actively-managed funds, compared to that of passively-managed funds.

It makes sense that an investor would *not* mind paying higher fees for an actively-managed fund, *if* its long-term performance were to more than compensate for the higher fees.

Let's consider that next, as we compare the relative performance of these two categories of funds.

But first, a short break?"

"Yes, yes, yes!"

TIP #70..... **A successful investment portfolio will often include in its investment mix, well-managed mutual funds with good track records. However, great care must be exercised to properly consider each fund's performance *for* the investor, after the impact of all costs: Front-End Load (entry) and Back-End Load (early-exit) charges, as well as annual Management Expense Ratio (MER) fees.**

CHAPTER TWENTY

. . . .

ACTIVELY-MANAGED MUTUAL FUNDS

"Earlier we referred to the choice faced by our young friend **Sam**, as she deliberated how to realize the best potential long-term return on the investment of her $100,000 inheritance. She mulled over whether to opt for a broadly-diversified, actively-managed mutual fund, or a passively-managed fund, such as an ETF. She had *assumed* that before fees, both funds could achieve the same average annual return of 7.5%.

Sam was shocked to discover that, with *no* difference in fund performance, the 2% extra cost in annual fees of the actively-managed fund would, after 40 years, produce about 43% less total return than would the low-cost ETF."

. . . .

"I remember discussing Sam's situation," commented Jenny. "I also remember wondering if the 2% higher fee could have been justified by the possibility of better performance of the actively-managed mutuals."

"You're right, Jenny. We did wonder if her *assumption* of an equal rate-of-return from both types of funds was a valid one.

If in fact, the actively-managed fund *did* produce a higher return than for example, an ETF, Sam's underlying assumption that they would both achieve the same average annual return would have been false.

But why speculate? Let's look at some real data, extracted from various reliable publications which regularly track actively-managed fund performance compared to the key benchmark Indexes."

EQUITY FUND PERFORMANCE

"Fund performance statistics show:

- Over the three years, 2005-2007, only 13.3% of actively-managed Canadian equity funds outperformed the TSX Index.

- Over the five years ending June 30, 2009, only 7.6% of actively-managed Canadian equity funds beat the TSX Index.

- In the 15-year period from 1993 to the end of 2008, the TSX Index returned an average of 7.1% per year. Canadian actively-managed funds averaged a return to the investor of 5.4%.

- In the 25 years from 1980 through 2005, the average U.S. actively-managed equity fund provided its investors with an average annual return of 10.0%. The average annual rate-of-return for the S&P 500 Index (U.S. benchmark index) during the same period, was 12.3%.

- A 2009 study by *MyPrivateBanking.com* found that over the previous five years, the *equity funds* of about 80% of the world's largest wealth-managers lagged behind benchmark index returns."

"With the odds of beating the index so low, it's a wonder that anyone invests in an actively-managed mutual fund," offered Kevin.

"I'm with you, Kevin. There are *some* select situations, especially for higher-net-worth individuals, where an actively-managed mutual satisfies a unique niche that the investor wants. But I for one, would not look too far for such exceptions for my portfolio."

....

Investors can remain current on the latest fund performance comparisons by going online and googling: Index Versus Active Funds Scorecard for Canadian Funds.

"The poor long-term performance of the *actively-managed* mutual fund sector, compared to index performance, as reported in detail by **SPIVA (S&P Indices Versus Active Funds)**, will astound you."

"I bet Sam's actively-managed mutual fund provider wouldn't be too likely to refer her to this site!" quipped Jenny.

"This site also provides an up-to-date statistic on the 5-year survivorship rate of actively-managed equity funds. Early in 2009 for instance, it indicated that survivorship of the average Canadian equity fund was 44.9%. This **does not** mean to imply that more than half the investments were lost. Funds may either have merged, or been discontinued. Regardless of the reason, this indicates a huge turnover of actively-managed funds.

Market indexes by contrast, tend to survive for the long term. New ones may be added, but few disappear."

....

"Is this difference in performance the same for actively-managed funds that invest in other products – like bonds?" inquired Kevin.

"Good question, Kevin. Let's take a look at the performance of Bond Funds."

BOND FUND PERFORMANCE

"Actively-managed Canadian *equity* funds have average MERs of about 2.5%. Actively-managed *bond* funds tend to have MERs on average, about 1% lower, mainly because there are many fewer investment options for bond funds to evaluate.

In its October 3, 2009 issue, the *Globe & Mail* newspaper listed Canada's largest funds, as measured by asset values. The list included 18 *actively-managed* bond funds.

As a useful reference point, the list also included these two *exchange-traded funds (ETFs)*:

- The *iShares CDN Bond Index Fund* (listed as XBB on the TSX). This fund seeks to track the Scotia Capital Universe Bond Index. This in turn tracks the performance of a large collection of short-, mid-, and long-term bonds, with an average duration of 6.49 years.

  The 5-year performance of this ETF showed an average annual yield to the investor of 5.35%. The MER was a low 0.3%.

- *The iShares CDN Short Bond Index Fund* (listed as XSB on the TSX). This fund seeks to track the performance of an Index of short-term bonds only, with an average duration of 2.56 years.

  The 5-year performance of this ETF showed an average annual yield to the investor of 4.86%. The MER was an even lower 0.25%.

And now, the results of a comparison between these two ETFs and the 18 actively-managed funds:

- *Not one* of the 18 actively-managed bond funds showed a return to the investor over the previous 5 years, that exceeded or even matched the returns of either of these two ETFs.

- Of these 18 funds, the *average annual yield to the investor was **3.99%***.

- The average ***MER*** of the 18 actively-managed funds was ***1.53%***.

Clearly, an investor would have been much better off investing in either of the low-fee *passively-managed* bond ETFs during these five years, than in any of the eighteen actively-managed bond funds.

For the investor, most of the shortfall in performance of the actively-managed funds, was attributable on average, to the ***1.2%*** higher fees these funds charged through their MERs."

Had the MERs for the two fund categories been competitive, the yield to the investor would have been fairly similar."

"This pretty well hammers home your previous comment that '***expense, expense, expense***' is an investor's number-one risk-factor," commented Jenny.

"You're right about that, Jenny. Particularly when considering the impact over a long-term investment, keeping the management expenses low can be the greatest enhancer to overall returns."

MANAGEMENT EXPENSE RATIO (MER) – COST COMPARISON

"A recent international academic study found that world-wide, more than 50,000 actively-managed mutual funds are available to investors. Of this total, over 4,000 are available in Canada."

"No way!" exclaimed Kevin. "No wonder we see so much glossy advertising by mutual fund companies. The competition must be fierce."

"It is, Kevin, and that high advertising cost is one of the key reasons why the investor pays such high MERs with actively-managed funds.

The *MER* for the average actively-managed ***Canadian*** *equity fund* was reported to be ***2.68%*** – the highest of all 18 countries surveyed.

By comparison, the average ***U.S.*** *equity fund MER* was found to be much lower, at ***1.42%***."

TIP #71..... *In any given year* the average actively-managed Canadian mutual fund manages to outperform its comparable Index only 20 to 30% of the time. When making an investment decision, an investor must be cognizant of this industry-wide, much-below-average performance.

ADDITIONAL FUND COSTS

"When an individual chooses to invest in an actively-managed mutual fund, MERs may not be the only expenses he faces.

Many actively-managed funds also have either a ***Front-End Load*** or a ***Back-End Load*** charge. Often the investor is given a choice between the two:

- The ***front-end*** option – effectively an entry fee, can lead to a one-time charge of 2%, or even more, of the initial investment.

- The ***back-end*** option – the early-exit fee, replaces an up-front fee. The fund *may* charge up to 5% of total value, if an investor terminates his fund ownership during the first seven years after purchase. After seven years, this fee obligation generally disappears."

....

"Are you saying that *in addition* to the MER it's almost impossible to buy into actively-managed mutuals without being nailed by a bunch of additional fees?" asked Kevin.

"In fairness, Kevin, actively-managed funds offered by Canadian Banks do not have either a front-end or back-end load. They do however, charge a substantial MER. So if you purchase one of these Bank funds, you can generally limit your costs to their MER charge."

TIP #72..... **It is not unusual for investors whose portfolio largely consists of *actively-managed* Canadian mutual funds, to incur total annual expense charges approaching 3%. Such high costs make it very unlikely that the portfolio will over the long-term, exceed or even match the overall yield of a well-chosen, passively-managed fund.**

....

"But, Grandpa, surely *all* these under-performing funds aren't run by incompetents," exclaimed Jenny. "How come so many of them can't beat the Index averages?"

"Good point, Jenny. You're absolutely correct. Many of these actively-managed funds are run by extremely smart professionals.

The problem however, is that with such a high fee-structure for actively-managed funds, the fund manager must on average, beat the comparable Index by close to 3%, simply to achieve a break-even performance for the investor.

Remember we just finished talking about the 18 actively-managed Bond Funds where the performance shortfall on average, was essentially due to their higher MERs? The funds themselves may have produced comparable results to ETFs, but their much higher fees resulted in a much lower *net* return to the investor."

TIP #73..... It is virtually impossible for an individual investor, *or* fund manager, to consistently outperform a comparable Index by 3%.

This reality is why *actively-managed* mutual funds often produce a lower return for the investor than a *passively-managed* fund such as an index fund or exchange-traded fund."

"So, Grandpa, what this means is that if **Sam** had chosen to invest her $100,000 inheritance in actively-managed funds, she likely wouldn't have done nearly as well, as opting for *passive funds*, such as index funds or ETFs. Is that right?" asked Kevin.

"That's generally correct, Kevin. But we must recognize that in any given year there *will* be exceptions to the general reality of underperformance by actively-managed funds. Those exceptions however, are very difficult to identify in advance.

We can look back on which fund did very well last year or over a number of years. But there is absolutely *no* assurance that its extraordinary performance will continue into the future, or over the long term. Often, it does not."

TIP #74..... Strong past performance of an investment, particularly actively-managed mutual funds, provides absolutely no assurance that it will continue to excel, relative to index-benchmarked funds.

....

"*Here's another compelling statistic that may surprise you. Studies have shown that more than one-half the managers of actively-managed funds have **none** of their own money invested in the funds they manage. This pretty clearly suggests that even they themselves feel there are better investment options.*"

PERFORMANCE-REPORTING DEFICIENCIES

"For an investor to remain current, and to know exactly how his actively-managed fund is performing, he must receive accurate comparative performance data. He needs to see the cumulative year-to-date and year-over-year performance data for his fund, with comparisons, not only to other funds in that class, but particularly to relevant *benchmark market Indexes*.

Very few rules specifically govern required reporting. Although investors do receive reports from their fund managers, these reports can be of minimal value for making meaningful performance comparisons.

Some funds may do well in a given year. Managers are happy to report the fund's position in the top quartile of their category. Unfortunately, the investor cares little even if the fund is number one among its peers. What really matters to an investor is how well the fund's *net* growth (after all fees) compares to benchmark index funds with their much lower fees."

"This sounds like my prof giving out test results – Zack gets the best mark, but no one gets higher than a C," commented Kevin.

"Only if the *net* performance of the fund matches, or exceeds index fund benchmarks *over the long term*, can the much higher fees of the actively-managed fund be justified.

Fund managers are reluctant to provide detailed comparative performance reports. They will contend that *their* fund is unique and cannot be compared to a simple index fund. That's nonsense.

Regardless of the fund's holdings, it surely is the investor's *right*, in return for the high fee he is charged, to *expect* that his investment will perform at least as well as an equity or Bond Index – especially over a longer period like five years. The key reason fund managers do not provide this comparison is, as we have seen, that very few actively-managed funds can *consistently* outperform an index over the long term.

You can bet that if actively-managed funds were consistently outperforming Indexes, fund managers would very quickly find a way to report that data!"

....

> TIP #75..... Primarily because they charge much lower management fees, and do not try to second-guess the market, passively-managed funds have a record of consistently achieving better net returns for the investor.

*"Equity and bond **markets** are the result of many thousands of individual investor decisions on what values should be. As such, these aggregate markets (indexes) are smarter over time than any single investment manager can be. The weak long-term performance of most actively-managed funds has proven this conclusion to be correct."*

> TIP #76..... The wise investor will always be mindful of the fact that the entire financial services business is an industry unto itself. It is designed for maximum profitability. The hefty fees charged on investors' portfolios feed it handsomely, regardless of actual performance.

....

"But, Grandpa, if we invest only in passively-managed funds like ETFs or Index Funds, we have to make our *own* fund selections," worried Jenny. "Doesn't that seriously increase the risk of an investor doing something stupid?"

"Good question, Jenny. But if you think about it, you would have to take similar risks in selecting a specific, actively-managed fund.

The key is to stick to the *basic* ETFs and Index Funds. Stay away from the more exotic varieties, particularly those that leverage their investments.

This issue of selection isn't as difficult as you might think. In fact, once an investor, regardless of education level, has the same modest level of knowledge that you now have, he can select appropriate passively-managed funds without losing too much sleep.

Remember too, that for extra peace-of-mind, an investor can consult a truly *independent financial advisor* to help make the best choices. As we said before, a few hours of such advice can be well worth the cost.

Jenny, once we've finished our discussions, you *will* have the basic knowledge you need to make good investment decisions. Really, all you lack now, is the confidence to trust yourself."

"And the small matter of a dollar or two," added Kevin.

"If we spend a little time looking at a typical *passively-managed portfolio*, I think you'll gain some of that confidence."

"I'm willing to be convinced, Grandpa," replied Jenny. "I need a good share of your confidence. But once I'm investing on my own, don't be surprised if I call you in the middle of the night because I can't sleep."

· ·

CHAPTER TWENTY-ONE

PASSIVELY-MANAGED PORTFOLIO

"The lowest-risk passively-managed portfolio is one that invests exclusively in a mix of the broadest-possible *Indexes* in both the equity and fixed-income markets.

ETFs and *Index Funds* are the simplest vehicles for such investments.

If you, the investor, plan to build your investment portfolio through regular monthly contributions, it is best to utilize *index funds*, such as those available from most Banks. While the management fee will be slightly higher than that of an ETF, you will, by using an index fund, avoid the brokerage fee on each monthly purchase.

On the other hand, you may opt to make larger but infrequent contributions, perhaps only once a year. Your lowest cost in this case, would be to invest in ETF products *online*, through one of the many discount brokerage services available in Canada."

· ·

"Excuse me, Grandpa," interrupted Jenny. "I think this is the first time you've mentioned a brokerage fee. What exactly is it?"

A BROKERAGE FEE is the cost you pay whenever you buy a stock or an ETF that's listed on any stock exchange. The brokerage firm, and its broker who is licensed to buy or sell securities, earn the commission.

The commission can be extremely low, as little as $4.95 per trade, *if* you are using your *online discount brokerage* service. Using a full-service broker may cost several hundred dollars for the same trade.

For the cost advantage, I tend now to almost always use the online discount broker.

....

As of 2014, the major Canadian *exchange-traded fund (ETF)* providers are:

- Blackrock (i-Shares)
- BMO Financial
- Horizons
- Power Shares
- Vanguard
- First Asset
- RBC Global Asset Management
- Purpose Investments
- First Trust.

As of 2014, these Canadian ETF providers offer about 300 individual ETF products – many with a ***Dividend Reinvestment Plan (DRIP)*** feature.

In addition, more than 1,000 ETFs are offered on both the New York Stock Exchange and the Nasdaq Exchange."

"Grandpa, ...," began Jenny.

"I'm way ahead of you this time, Jenny."

The NASDAQ Composite Index is a U.S. Index of primarily technology stocks. It is value-weighted for all the stocks listed on this exchange – it thus takes into account not only share prices, but also the market capitalization of the companies it tracks.

TIP #77..... To minimize the ongoing costs of managing your portfolio, choose ETFs for large, infrequent contributions. For regular, perhaps monthly investments, consider using Index funds.

"By constructing a portfolio using these two index-driven products, several key advantages are achieved:

- Lowest-possible acquisition and management cost, leading to higher net returns;

- Broadest-possible, and therefore least-risky, diversification of products within the chosen investment class;

- Ease of broad geographic diversification, with optional hedging of currency-risk."

TIP #78..... Whenever considering international investments, the most prudent course may be to choose *only* those products which are fully-hedged against the Canadian dollar. Hedging eliminates foreign-currency risk, usually at minimal cost.

....

"You both know that learning about new financial products, and applying new investment strategies have always been among my favourite interests."

peter dolezal

"I bet you even read the financial pages *before* the sports pages!" teased Jenny.

"After many years of experimentation with variations on the passive-investor strategy, the best one I have yet come across, is the **Couch Potato Investment Strategy**, proposed by our excellent all-Canadian, **Money Sense** magazine."

"With a name like 'Couch Potato', I'm already in favour of it!" declared Kevin.

"The **Couch Potato Strategy**, brilliant in its simplicity, is outlined on the magazine's website: **www.moneysense.ca**.

It provides all the detail an investor might require. The site also provides historical data, demonstrating how their uncomplicated strategy has consistently *outperformed* the average actively-managed mutual fund.

To follow this investment strategy, the only decisions required of the investor, are to determine:

- What proportion of his total investment should be in *equity vs. fixed-income products*?

- Should the equity component represent an *entire Index*, or a more focused sub-index, such as the *financial index*?

- Should the *bond index* be in shorter-term bonds, longer-term, or a combination of both?

- Should the investments be wholly Canadian, or a mix of Canadian, U.S., and/or other international products?"

"This sounds too simple, even for me," commented Jenny. "What's the catch?"

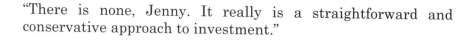

"There is none, Jenny. It really is a straightforward and conservative approach to investment."

....

"Let's think back to our earlier discussions, when we determined that the answers to these questions are very *personal* individual judgment decisions, very much dependent on our age and risk-profile.

We also agreed that for *your* age group, the 20's and 30's, having 70 to 80% of your portfolio invested in equities, and only 20 to 30% in bonds or other fixed-income products is reasonable, given the long-term investment horizon.

At the same time, we also concluded that as we approach our retirement years, it may be wise to gravitate toward a much less aggressive split, to reduce the risk of shorter-term market volatility.

On the question of geographic diversification however, the decision was a little trickier. We considered that on the one hand, we're living and spending our investment proceeds in Canada. We initially concluded that the majority of the portfolio should be in Canadian investments.

But then we also realized that since Canadian equity investments account for less than 3% of those available world-wide, we really should not ignore the potential of that other 97% of investments, available internationally.

We also concluded that if we do decide to invest in indexed products outside Canada, we are wise to do so in a manner that substantially eliminates the currency-risk. Fortunately, both partially and fully-hedged Index products are available, for both U.S., and many other international investments."

....

"With these broad guidelines in mind, here's *one* scenario demonstrating how, as we age, we might achieve an increasing *comfort level* with our portfolio:

	Ages 20 to 40	Ages 40 to 60	Retirement (60 +)
Canadian Equity Funds	50%	40%	30%
U.S. Equity Funds (Hedged)	15%	15%	10%
International Equity Funds (Hedged)	15%	15%	10%
Canadian Bond & Other Fixed-Income Funds	20%	30%	50%

As I said, this is only *one* potential plan. ***Money Sense magazine's 'Couch Potato Strategy'*** provides other options for investors to consider."

....

"At the very least, an *annual* review and rebalancing of your portfolio is a simple but necessary process during which you:

- Sell a portion of the category that has increased beyond your target allocation;

- Use the proceeds of the sale to buy more of the categories that have declined;

- Confirm that you have re-established your targeted percentages between asset classes.

Not only are you rebalancing, but you're *selling high and buying low* – a rather sound approach to investing!"

TIP #79..... The wise investor will review and rebalance his portfolio at least annually, to re-establish his targeted allocations between investment categories.

....

"Grandpa, I really do like the sound of this *'Couch Potato'* strategy! I know I already said the name alone appeals to me," enthused Kevin. "But if such a simple strategy can be the path to our millionaire's club, with less risk and least cost, why on earth would anyone do anything else?"

"I can't argue with that, Kevin. I've used this approach for some time, and it certainly works for me.

However – that's not to say that no actively-managed funds will beat our passive investment strategy. That would be misleading and unfair. In any given year, *a minority* of actively-managed funds may perform exceptionally well for their investors.

Our problem as investors however, is how to consistently pick that minority of winners, in advance of their successful years. No one has yet found a crystal ball that does that."

"And we know, Grandpa," teased Jenny, "the only magic *you* believe in is the power of compounding and time!"

"You're right, Jenny. I for one, have no intention of playing Russian roulette with my investments. Nor does it make sense to incur much higher investment costs, while *trying* to pick one of the few funds that end up producing a superior return in a particular year."

TIP #80..... The power of time and compounding is proven. So is the fact that indexes increase in value over time. Combining these realities into a passive, index-based investment strategy should, with least risk to the investor, produce substantial long-term benefits.

....

"I'm bushed. I think *explaining* everything is as exhausting for me, as trying to understand it, is for you. We've covered a lot of ground in just six sessions.

Next Saturday, I'd like to discuss with you the important subject of *Financial Planning*, and one of its key components, *Investment Planning*."

"Great, Grandpa! Thanks for today. Speaking of planning, should we *plan* to meet for lunch again next Saturday?" begged Jenny.

"Thanks, Grandpa," exclaimed Kevin. "It gets better and better. I can't wait to see how soon I can take up residence on millionaire's row."

FINANCIAL PLANNING

. . . .

CHAPTER TWENTY-TWO

THE FINANCIAL PLAN

"I can't believe we're on our seventh Saturday," exclaimed Jenny. "Did you ever think we'd stick it out this long, Kevin?"

"Nope," replied Kevin. "I thought that within two or three Saturdays we would have covered everything. But obviously there's a lot more to this wealth-building than meets the eye."

"Jenny and Kevin, I'm as surprised as both of you, at how extensive and interesting our discussions have become, and how long they've taken. Your questions have caused me to dust the cobwebs off my brain and elaborate quite a bit, but that's great. It shows that you're interested and absorbing the subject.

Now here's my little pep talk. Don't get discouraged if you can't recall a lot that we've discussed. I'm speaking from a lifetime of hard-won experience. For you, this is a beginning.

When you consider how significantly an understanding of these concepts can help you eventually become financially comfortable, and perhaps even very well off, I think you'll agree that spending ten or so afternoons on this subject is time well-*invested*."

"Well, I'll tell you one thing," observed Kevin. "It sure beats sitting in a stuffy classroom."

"Kevin, I can't believe you didn't mention the bonus of fine lunches every week," scoffed Jenny.

. . . .

"So let's start today by trying to define a *financial plan*. Any ideas?"

"I think it would have to answer that same old question of mine. How much money do I really need to become financially independent?" offered Kevin.

"You're partly right, Kevin. We certainly need to know our ultimate objective, but just as important, we need to have a plan of how to get there. Would you agree?"

"That makes sense, Grandpa," replied Jenny. "You once said that we need both a destination and a road map. But I thought we *have* been talking all along, about the right strategies to follow for saving, managing debt, and investing."

"We have, Jenny. However, what a financial plan does, is pull all those pieces together in a logical manner. It's customized to fit *your* specific circumstances, and *your* specific objectives."

A FINANCIAL PLAN is a personal road map toward one's financial objectives.

"Studies have shown that those who have a financial plan, whether drawn up by themselves or by a professional, tend to realize about twice the long-term financial results of those with no plan."

TIP #81..... **Every individual or family unit, seeking to build long-term wealth and financial independence, should strive to follow a financial plan, updated regularly as personal circumstances change.**

"To be worthwhile, a financial plan must be a dynamic document. Your initial plan, hopefully established in your early 20's when you are just starting a career and perhaps your family, will need to be refined and adjusted often, as you move through the various stages of job-growth and family-creation.

If, like our electrician friend **Mike** for example, you and/or your eventual partner are employed in the public sector, with a defined-benefit pension plan, your ultimate investment objective can be significantly different than if neither of you were to have an employer-sponsored pension plan.

A large family will require more of your earnings than will a small one. The cost of higher education for each child will require extra planning. Even the size, cost, and operating expense of your home will be influenced by your family size.

To ensure that it remains relevant and realistic, a regularly-updated financial plan must reflect *all* of these, and other relevant-to-you emerging realities."

....

"So how do we go about making a proper financial plan?" asked Jenny. "I wouldn't know where to start."

"It's not at all unusual, Jenny, for most of us to need the help of a professional *financial planner*, in constructing at least the first financial plan."

"Is a financial planner the same as a financial advisor?" asked Jenny.

"The terms are often used interchangeably, Jenny. Usually the *planning* function goes together with the *advising* role."

"We've got you, Grandpa, right? And it's for sure, the price can't be beat!" added Kevin.

"Absolutely, Kevin. I'm glad to help for as long as I'm able. But most people will need to find professional advice outside the family."

FINANCIAL PLANNING ASSISTANCE

TIP #82..... **To construct an initial financial plan, and for assistance with its periodic refinement, retaining the services of a professional financial planner is a wise investment.**

"Do you remember in our earlier discussions, we identified the *type of financial advice* as one of the key risks of investing?"

"I sure do," responded Jenny. "You said that if we're going to obtain *objective* advice, it's best to select an advisor who is totally independent, and who preferably does NOT sell *any* financial or insurance products."

"That's right, Jenny. Only by retaining a truly independent advisor can you be certain that the advice you receive will focus solely on meeting *your* needs."

....

"*Independent financial planners* generally, will offer services in one of two ways:

- **Fee-Only Charge**

   Charges usually range between $150 to $250 per hour. Once you provide sufficient insight into your situation and your needs, the advisor should be willing to provide a maximum-cost quotation.

- **Asset-Based Charge**

   This fee is usually set as a percentage of your portfolio value. A fixed annual fee might also be negotiated. For significant portfolios approaching or exceeding one million dollars, it's reasonable to cap this fee at no more than 1%.

In the early stages of an individual's financial planning, the simple fee-only advice is all that should be necessary. A $1,000 to $2,000 cost to set up a financial plan, including its investment-plan component, should be all that one initially requires.

As your portfolio grows, more frequent reviews become advisable. The fixed-annual-fee alternative may then make more sense."

TIP #83..... **Anyone can call himself a financial advisor or planner. Insist on checking credentials and references. If the references leave you feeling less than comfortable, find another advisor.**

"Unless you personally are very knowledgeable in the field of financial planning and investing, the money you spend on *reliable*, independent financial advice, should yield you a huge benefit. Retaining a professional advisor should be considered a reasonable cost toward the achievement of your ultimate objective."

FINANCIAL PLAN ELEMENTS

"A *comprehensive* financial plan will include a review and analysis of at least:

- Your net worth
- Your cash flow
- Your fixed and discretionary spending
- Your savings plan
- Your budget, aligning spending with disposable income
- Your debt profile
- Your risk profile
- Your insurance requirements
- Your current investments and their appropriateness
- Your updated investment plan
- Your tax situation and strategies
- Your shorter-term goals, retirement goals, and estate planning
- Your will."

"I don't have *this* much information in my resume," joked Jenny.

"Did you notice, Jenny and Kevin, the ***investment plan***, although essential, is only *one* key element of a financial plan?

Many of us inaccurately use these terms interchangeably. A ***financial plan*** is a much broader document, only part of which is the investment plan.

Your financial plan will assist you in formulating and improving strategies in each of its component areas. It will help you establish short-, medium-, and long-term investment and wealth-creation objectives.

It is frankly, very difficult for most of us to organize all of these details for ourselves, in a totally *objective* manner. Furthermore, as non-professionals in the field of wealth-management, we seldom have the expertise, or the time, to bring the best-possible solution to bear on each of these issues."

TIP #84..... **A financial plan is *YOUR* plan – not your financial advisor's. His task is solely to *help you* develop the best possible plan, and if necessary, to advise you on its specific implementation. *You* are the final decision-maker for each element that requires a decision.**

"It's a no-brainer to have the advice of a financial planner," commented Kevin. "But I'm sure glad we have you to help us, and not only because you won't charge us a fee!"

"As I've said, I'm more than happy to do that for the family, Kevin. But depend on it -there *will* come a time when you'll need a fresh pair of eyes looking over both your financial plan and its investment portfolio."

....

"So even if we hire a financial advisor, we still need to understand all of this financial stuff," observed Jenny. "We have to know enough to ask questions, make suggestions, and then make the right decisions."

"Exactly, Jenny. What I'm trying to give you through these discussions, is sufficient insight into the key elements. Later, when the options are presented to you by an advisor, *YOU* can make the right decisions.

Maybe now you can understand why we've taken the long route, covering so many complex subjects before attempting to construct a financial plan.

We need to understand and use *all* of that information in formulating a meaningful plan.

It isn't too different from understanding how to use each of the carpentry tools before attempting to build that garden shed.

That's also why in our earlier chats, I emphasized that you need to understand how certain elements of your plan must change at various stages of your life, up to and including retirement."

....

"Grandpa, now that you're semi-retired," inquired Jenny, "do you still have a financial plan?"

"Absolutely. However, the emphasis of Grandma's and my financial plan has changed somewhat, as you'll come to understand later when we talk about *retirement strategies*.

In your retirement years, the focus shifts from wealth-accumulation to *wealth-preservation*, as well as the most tax-effective means of *drawing income* from investments.

For now, the point to remember is that *a financial plan never loses relevance*. It remains just as important as one approaches, and enters retirement."

....

"So, Grandpa," commented Kevin, "We must be getting close to looking at Jenny's and my first financial plan. I'm still curious to figure out what my dollar objective *needs to be*, or what it *could be*."

"You make an excellent distinction, Kevin! The most important thing we must plan for, is to be able to meet our *need* for eventual independence and comfortable retirement. This certainly doesn't mean, if it's realistic to do so, that we can't aim beyond that objective. Knowing you two, that will be the case."

CHAPTER TWENTY-THREE

· ·

YOUR PERSONAL FINANCIAL PLAN

"So, Kevin and Jenny, here we are – finally ready to begin work on constructing your long-promised *initial* Financial Plan."

"You make it sound like a major construction project," commented Jenny. "But I guess it's not so different. Both need a solid foundation."

"We'll look at how the plan, and the strategies supporting it might change, probably every five years or so, leading up to your eventual retirement.

Then we'll consider the changes that retirees must make with *their* continuing financial plans and investment strategies.

As Kevin insists, let's *simplify* our building project into six easy-to-grasp steps:

- The Guiding Principles
- Our Assumptions
- Short-Term Investments
- Long-Haul Investments
- Your Risk Tolerance
- Utilizing TFSAs and RRSPs."

STEP 1 – THE GUIDING PRINCIPLES – The Basics for All Ages

- Spend wisely – Shop around – Negotiate where possible.

- Minimize *debt drag* on net-worth growth:

  - Pay zero interest on credit or department store cards;

  - Pay off mortgages as quickly as possible;

  - Except for emergencies, borrow only for mortgage or education loans.

- Save automatically from each pay cheque, using the **Pay Yourself First** strategy. Strive to save 10% of earnings.

- Minimize income taxes through maximum use of TFSA and RRSP accounts.

- Invest outside TFSA or RRSP accounts only if these are fully-utilized.

- Minimize investment costs – use primarily ETFs and Index Funds.

- Minimize risk. Diversify your investments – by asset class, within the class, and internationally.

- Moderate investment risk as you approach and enter your retirement years.

- Be a prudent *investor*, not a *trader*.

TIP #85..... After meeting one's fixed costs, and saving a pre-determined percentage of each pay cheque, the wise individual will, except for true emergencies, *force-fit* all other expenditures to the remainder of his disposable income.

STEP 2 – OUR ASSUMPTIONS

"I know you've both given some thought, fleeting though it was, to when you *think* you might want to retire. If I heard you right, you've both said that you would want to be in a financial position to be *able* to retire by age 60."

"Hey, Jenny. Neither of us has even started a career, and we're already about a third of the way to retirement. How's that for scary?" asked Kevin.

"In terms of actual dollar figures however, have either of you given any real thought to how much money you think you'll need to have saved in order to comfortably retire at that age?"

"I actually have thought about it, Grandpa," offered Jenny. "I definitely know that I don't want to *have to* work past age 60. But then I thought about inflation, *and* what my final income might be, *and* what percent of that I might need. In the end, I found it just gave me a headache trying to come up with an actual number. All I can guess is that it will be big – probably well over the $1 million that Kevin's always jabbering about."

"Age 60 is my target too, Grandpa," added Kevin. "And I can't believe I'm saying this because I've always thought of a million dollars as a big goal, but now I'm having the same trouble as Jenny on the actual dollar objective."

"I'm not at all surprised by your answers. Remember early in our discussions, Kevin, when I said that pulling a number like a million dollars out of the air, isn't the best way to plan?"

....

"Let's roll up our sleeves and see if instead, we can work up a *realistic* target based on some *reasonable* assumptions. Then we can test its adequacy in meeting your retirement *needs*.

Jenny and Kevin, tell me if I'm on track with these *assumptions*, or where we need to change them. Once agreed, they will become the foundation of *your financial plan*:

- *Your RESP accounts will be sufficient to cover the full cost of your post-secondary education, whether a trade, technical program, or university degree.*

- *By age 25, you will have completed your formal schooling, and will have settled into your first full-time job.*

- *With your education, you are likely to begin your career at an annual salary of at least $40,000.*

- *You want to own your first home by age 30.*

- *You wish to **be able** to retire at age 60.*

- *You should average at least a 6% annual salary increase over the course of your career. This takes into account cost-of-living increases, merit increases, and promotions. The actual number may well be much higher, but for planning purposes, we'll be conservative.*

- *The cost-of-living will rise annually, by an average of 2.5%, over the 35 years of your working life.*

- *By age 25, you are prepared to start your **Pay Yourself First** saving and investing strategy. You plan to begin with 7.5% of your **gross** salary, increasing by half a percent annually, until at age 30, you are regularly saving 10% of your salary. You continue to save and invest at that same level annually, until you consider retirement at age 60.*

- *You will **force-fit** all other expenditures to match your remaining disposable income.*

- *By age 25, you expect your TFSA account to have reached a total value, from your part-time jobs, of at least $10,000.*

- *Until age 30, you will invest primarily through your TFSA in order to save enough, with minimal risk, for at least a 5% down payment on your first home. You'll invest in shorter-term, fixed-income instruments. Your average return on these investments will be 4%.*

- *Just before age 30, you will use all your TFSA savings for the down payment and closing costs on the purchase of your first home, whether a condo, or small house.*

- *As your family needs change, you will upgrade your home, using the increasing equity in your previous home, to fund the larger down payments required on subsequent, more expensive properties.*

- *By age 50, you plan to have paid off your final mortgage, and will be able to boost your saving from 10% to 15% of gross income.*

- *After about age 30, your primary investment vehicle will shift from a TFSA to your RRSP. Resulting tax refunds can be used to:*
  - *invest in your TFSA;*
  - *get a head-start on the following year's RRSP contribution;*
  - *or probably best of all options, accelerate mortgage loan repayment.*

- *Using our **passive-investment strategy**, your long-term RRSP investments should average 7% annual return, for the 30 years to age 60. After retirement the average annual rate-of-return will drop to 5%, due to your more conservative investment strategy.*

....

"Wow, that's a lot of assumptions," observed Jenny, "but they sound reasonable to me. They're pretty much in line with what we've been discussing these past several months. It's *me* I'm worried about though – will I have enough willpower and self-discipline?"

"I agree with all of them, Grandpa! I can't see anything that I'd like to change. Let's crunch the numbers!" enthused Kevin. "Let's see where those assumptions lead us."

"Not to belittle your mathematical genius, Kevin, but there's a simple mechanism we can use to, as you say, crunch the numbers.

Thanks to the internet, we can access a large selection of return-on-investment and other relevant *calculators*. They're offered *online* by most Banks and Credit Unions."

"You mean all we have to do is load in our assumptions, and within seconds, we have our answer?" asked an incredulous Jenny.

"Sounds good, doesn't it? Let's do it right now."

STEP 3 – SHORTER-TERM INVESTMENTS
Down Payment Savings Goal (*Age 25 to 30*)

"With the figures in your early-year assumptions, our magic calculator confirms that before you turn 30, you should be able to accumulate over $25,000 in your TFSA fixed-income investment account.

This is more than enough for a minimum down payment on your first home. You can realistically plan to purchase your home between age 29 and 30.

Notice at this stage, we are talking *generalities* only. We're *not yet* identifying specific investments you might make. That, we'll do when we begin to detail your actual *Investment Plan*. For now, we're simply testing whether your assumptions can achieve your objectives.

In any event, the trusty calculator does confirm that your objective of owning your first home by age 30, is realistic."

STEP 4 – THE LONG-HAUL INVESTMENTS – For Retirement (*Age 30 to 60*)

"Here we go! The end number, please!

Believe it or not, *if* you were to follow through exactly as laid out, on the assumptions in your financial plan, you would from age 30 through to age 60, have automatically saved a total of *$295,000* of your own money.

At the assumed 7% *compounded* growth-rate, your savings would have grown by another *$460,000* – to a grand total of *$755,000*.

"Yes!" exclaimed Kevin. "That's the better part of my million bucks!"

"Good going," congratulated Jenny. "What am I saying? This is my plan *too*! *But* don't forget that even a million dollars will be worth a lot less by the time we actually get to 60. Remember the small matter of inflation?"

"Good! You're keeping us on our toes, Jenny. Let's go online to another calculator, and ignoring inflation *for now*, first see without running out of funds, how much of this amount you could draw out annually for about 30 years of retirement, until you reach age 90.

We'll assume that your post-retirement rate-of-return will drop from 7% to a more conservative 5%. By then more of your investments will need to be in safe, but lower-yielding, fixed-income investments."

....

"Interesting! The calculator shows that over 30 years, you could withdraw about *$40,000* annually – about the same amount as your starting salary at age 25!

But – as Jenny was quick to point out, inflation skews the picture.

Assuming 2.5% average annual inflation, the actual value or purchasing power of your $40,000, in today's dollars, would be only about *$17,000*.

"But, Grandpa, at age 65, won't we get to add something like another $17,000 annually, for all those inflation-adjusted pension payments from CPP and OAS?" asked Kevin.

"Absolutely, Kevin. Actually, as we briefly discussed, you can start receiving CPP as early as age 60, *if* you choose to accept a 33.6% lower (36% by 2016) monthly payment. It's strictly the pensioner's choice.

Nor have we factored in whether any of your future employers will have a pension plan. You may well be receiving additional pension from that source."

....

"In any event, given that this is your very first plan, having these initial objectives seems quite adequate. We know you'll need to refine it many times, to adjust for actual incomes, capital invested, investment returns, and the possibility of workplace pensions. You may even, once you have a partner who is also in the workforce, be able to double up on your targeted savings.

Remember also – by age 60, your *net-worth* will have grown by more than just your accumulated financial investments. Your home should be paid off. You then have the option to downsize to a less expensive home. This would generate additional funds for further investment, growth, and income, after retirement."

> TIP #86..... The earlier one sets a *dollar* retirement objective, the less precise it will be because it is driven by many unproven assumptions. As one moves toward retirement, assumptions will become more accurate, and the need for adjustments in savings and investment strategies more clearly identified.

....

"Given that we're still in school, I'd say we've made a good start on our financial plans. Wouldn't you agree, Jenny?" asked Kevin.

"Besides we've got Grandpa who'll keep us on our toes for regular revisions of our plans," teased Jenny.

"*I* know with our initial assumptions, that by the time you reach age **60**, it's reasonable to assume that you will have accumulated an investment nest-egg of around **$750,000**. A significant objective, even if it is before accounting for inflation.

And who knows, if you really love your job, you may decide that age 60 is too early to retire. Working longer will increase the value of your portfolio even more.

For now, this preliminary financial plan becomes your grand vision, to be revisited regularly, as your life actually unfolds.

As I've already mentioned, at this stage we're only *testing* our original assumptions, to see if they *appear* adequate for producing a portfolio value that ought to give you a comfortable retirement.

An initial portfolio target of $750,000, would *seem* at this early stage of your planning cycle, to be adequate."

"*Adequate* and *three-quarters of a million dollars* in the same sentence?" quipped Kevin. "If you had said this when we first started our sessions, Grandpa, I would have thought you were trying to be funny!"

STEP 5 – YOUR RISK -TOLERANCE

"With few exceptions, investing is *not* risk-free. We've already discussed this in some detail. But we need now to review what level of risk is suitable for *your* financial plan.

- We know that TFSA investments made for the shorter-term, such as saving for a down payment on a home, or the purchase of an automobile, need to be invested primarily in fixed-income instruments such as bonds and GICs. This will greatly reduce, and perhaps even eliminate, any risk to your capital. You've agreed that you're happy with this initial strategy.

- Longer-term investments on the other hand, particularly if made early in your career, perhaps between ages 30 and 40, should generally consist *mainly* of a well-diversified, high-quality group of equity investments. While these have a higher degree of short-term volatility, history shows us that they produce superior long-term returns.

- The exact mix between equity and fixed-rate products varies with each individual's comfort zone. However, in these early years, an 80 to 90% mix in favour of equities would seem reasonable, as long as a large proportion of this equity component is invested in a broad selection of high-quality, dividend-paying stocks. This, you've also agreed, makes sense for these early planning purposes.

- You also agree that after age 40, you would be well-advised to consider a gradual shift in the equity/fixed-income balance, perhaps approaching 50/50 around the time of retirement.

- If, as no doubt will be the case when you retire, you are reliant on investments having to last 25 or 30 years, you *may* be wise to not exceed 50% of your investments in equities. This will help preserve your capital. Because of inflation however, you will need to retain a significant equity component to moderate its effects over a significant number of years.

Always keep in mind that your investment time-horizon is *not* the day you retire – it's the day you die."

STEP 6 – UTILIZING TFSAs and RRSPs

"In low marginal-tax earning years, top up your TFSA *before* making RRSP contributions. This builds up an accessible balance for your early needs such as emergencies, or a down payment for a home.

Once marginal tax rates are higher, shift your contribution priority to your RRSP first, TFSA second.

Try to apply tax refunds arising from RRSP contributions first, to accelerate mortgage repayments, and second, to further build up RRSP and TFSA investment accounts."

TIP #87..... **By age 40, do everything possible to top up both RRSP and TFSA accounts to their maximum-allowable limits. Continue this practice through to retirement.**

"Jenny and Kevin, not only you, but all average Canadians who choose to follow strategies similar to these, have an equal opportunity to become financially independent.

When government pension payments are factored in, along with for some of us, workplace pensions, anyone subscribing to these principles can be assured of a very comfortable retirement –

despite inflation. This becomes even more so, if a second income from a partner or spouse enters the equation."

....

"So, Jenny and Kevin, what's the most important key that unlocks the door to your golden retirement?"

"Is this another trick question? Manage your spending and debt, and start saving and investing early," promptly responded Jenny. "*That* answer, I know by heart now."

"Exactly so, Jenny. From what you've both said, I've no doubt that you understand the need to spend wisely and minimize debts. And the next real key is *definitely* to start saving early – the sooner the better, as both of you have already done.

Saving 10% of your income is more than adequate if you start by age 30. The longer you delay, the more challenging making an adequate commitment to savings will become. The larger contributions required, although perhaps not impossible, become progressively more demanding. If you start saving early, you can avoid these later stresses.

Imagine yourself in this scenario:

You buy your first home by age 30. Even with one or two subsequent purchases to upgrade your home, you manage to pay off your final mortgage by age 50. You can then begin to add the monthly mortgage savings to your long-established ten-percent-of-salary savings.

The end result? You give your retirement portfolio a mighty boost. Reaching your dollar-target *sooner* allows it to grow even more by the time you choose to retire."

> TIP #88..... Regardless of age, it's never too late to evaluate your finances, prepare a financial plan, and apply the best-possible strategies to enhance your retirement lifestyle.

....

"Remember, when doing your regular review and revision of your financial plan, to also include an update of your **Net-Worth Statement** – calculate the difference between your *assets* and your *liabilities*, to track the growth of your net-worth.

For *your* initial plan which we've just worked on, this is a very simple process.

Right now, you are both students with few assets and liabilities. You have projected however, that by age 25 you will each have a $10,000 TFSA investment account, perhaps a $3,000 car, and zero liabilities.

This would make your individual net-worth, at that time, about $13,000."

"So, Grandpa," joked Kevin, "would my friend's $200 gas-guzzler be considered an asset or a liability on his net-worth statement?"

....

"You've probably heard the saying – *There is often too much month at the end of the money!* It can be all too true.

But *you* now have a *basic financial plan*.

As an integral part of that plan, you'll need to regularly monitor *all* your income sources *and* deductions, in order to keep track of your net or *disposable income*.

Once you know how much you actually have available each month, subtract *all* your *committed* or *fixed* expenses, including your **Pay Yourself First** deduction – hopefully 10% of your gross pay.

The remaining balance is the **actual disposable income** that remains for everything else including groceries, car expenses, clothing, and entertainment.

This analysis of your income and expenditures is absolutely crucial for understanding any bottom-line shortfalls. This will allow you to make the necessary spending adjustments to **force-fit** your spending to your actual disposable income."

....

"Here's a little anecdote that might interest you:

*For about the first decade of our marriage, Grandma kept track of every expenditure we made as a family. Every day she asked me what I had bought and how much it had cost. Monthly and at year-end, she would tally up all our spending, by category. This gave us a great insight into our spending, right down to how much postage had cost us. This discipline allowed us to set and adjust our spending budget and to always **force-fit** our spending to our disposable income.*

We haven't done a similar budget analysis as part of *your* initial plan because you're still starving students and don't yet have that first full-time job. But you've both learned the rule – ***if you don't have it, don't spend it!***

As students, you live off your Registered Education Savings Plan (RESP), your part-time earnings, and are still at home.

As a result, you *should* emerge at age 25, virtually debt-free. If a student loan does become necessary before you complete your studies, its value will be reflected as a *liability* on the first update of your financial plan."

"Hey, Jenny," teased Kevin, "do you think you'll make it through school like me, with just two pairs of jeans?"

"Believe me, Kevin," retorted Jenny, "You'll be paying your fair share of my gas from now on. No more free rides for you!"

"Time for a break? Then we'll finally begin the drafting of *your* initial ***Investment Plan***.

As outlined in your Financial Plan, we'll need to consider the two separate issues of both your shorter-term objectives to age 30, *and* your long-term goals to age 60."

CHAPTER TWENTY-FOUR

YOUR PERSONAL INVESTMENT PLAN

"We've reviewed the major components of your Financial Plan. You're now clear on your goals, for both the shorter-term and the long-term.

We're finally ready now to focus on the *implementation strategy* for the *Investment* component of your Financial Plan.

By now you may have come to realize that the investment *process* we follow may well be more important than the specific investment products we choose."

. . . .

"Let's begin paving your investment path – hopefully with gold – all the way to your eventual retirement."

"Lead on, Grandpa! We're right on your heels," enthused Kevin.

THE FIRST FIVE YEARS (Age 25 to 30)

"As we identified in your Financial Plan:

- Your expected savings at age 25 are $10,000;

- For you to meet your goal of home ownership by age 30, we've figured that you'll need to accumulate as much as $25,000;

- You have a 5-year time frame after you expect to begin full-time employment at age 25;

- This means that you'll need secure, shorter-term investments with predictable returns, during the 5-year growth period;

- Clearly, your risk-tolerance during these five years will be low, because you absolutely *need* the funds by age 30.

This dictates that, until you successfully buy your home, all investments must be in either high-interest savings accounts, money-market ETFs, Treasury Bills, GICs, or short-term, high-quality government or corporate bonds.

....

By faithfully adhering to your *savings plan*, and following your outlined *investment plan*, you expect by age 30, to have accumulated at least $25,000 for a down payment, and to have bought your first home."

Shorter-Term Investment Plan

"Remember....even if you don't yet have available cash, set up your TFSA account at the earliest possible opportunity after you turn 18. You want to shelter any future investments as much as possible from the eroding impact of taxation.

If you wait till age 25 to set up this plan, you will between now and then, be taxed on *all* investment gains. With your current low income bracket, it won't be much, but you'd rather your earnings be working for *you*, tax-free, *within* your TFSA."

"As you said, Grandpa," agreed Jenny, "it's smart to set up our TFSA immediately after turning 18, even if we're still students. We can begin growing even modest investments like ours without losing any of the gains to taxes. I'm glad I already have my TFSA."

"By age 25, when you begin full-time employment, your anticipated $10,000 TFSA investments could be deployed as follows:

- If you've already invested in *laddered* GICs maturing over the next four years, stay the course.

- If you've invested in lower-yielding instruments such as a savings account, reorganize your $10,000 savings into four $2,500 GICs, laddering them to mature in 1, 2, 3, and 4 years.

- Your objective after year-four, is to have access to all the capital, for your down payment:

    - When year-one matures, reinvest the total proceeds in a 3-year GIC;
    - At year-two maturity, reinvest the proceeds in a 2-year GIC;
    - At year-three maturity, reinvest the proceeds in a 1-year GIC.

- In addition to these GIC investments, initiate your *Pay Yourself First* savings commitment with your first pay cheque after you begin full-time employment at age 25. Deposit your regular monthly 7.5% contribution in a high-interest savings account *within* your TFSA, until it reaches $2,500. Then buy another GIC with a term expiring no later than the end of year-four."

....

"By the end of year-four, your accumulated savings will, according to our online investment calculator, be over $25,000."

THE NEXT 30 YEARS (Age 30 to 60)

"Your *long-term* investment horizon makes it reasonable for you to accept the greater risk of owning higher-yielding investments which may be subject to short-term volatility. Until at least age 40, you can afford to invest a *high proportion* of your portfolio in high-quality equity investments.

In our earlier discussions, we settled on the following allocation strategies:

- 20% in *well-diversified*, fixed-income investments, such as bonds, bond funds, and money-market funds.

- 80% in a *well-diversified* mix of equity-based investments:
  - 50% of *total* investments in Canadian equity funds;
  - 15% of *total* investments in U.S. equity funds – fully hedged;
  - 15% of *total* investments in international equity funds – fully hedged."

Long-Term Investment Plan

"By no later than age 30, you should have established an RRSP account, with online, discount e-trade capability for both index and exchange-traded funds.

Every major bank offers easy-to-use online access to its index-based funds."

> TIP #89..... An individual's RRSP contribution eligibility begins to grow from the date of *first* tax-reporting of earned income. Everyone, including youth with babysitting or lawn-cutting earnings, should take advantage of this opportunity by filing tax returns from an early age, even when no taxes are payable.

"Hey, Grandpa," teased Kevin, "that's a sneaky way to get kids interested in personal finance."

....

"Let's assume you've reached age 30. You're ready to commit on an ongoing basis, to investing 10% of your salary.

To ensure that you choose your best investment option when you are ready to invest, you are well-advised to investigate carefully, or huddle with your independent *Financial Advisor*.

Remember we decided that because our continuing regular investments incur zero acquisition costs while also maintaining low Management Expense Ratios (MERs), Index funds rather than ETFs are the most suitable investment option.

You can arrange with your Bank to auto-deposit your monthly 10% **Pay Yourself First** savings, directly into the Index fund you've chosen."

....

"To recap, here's how, for at least the first ten years after age 30, you had previously agreed to diversify your long-term investments, between asset classes and geographic options:

- Canadian Equity Funds   50%

- U.S. Equity Funds – Hedged   15%

- International Equity Funds – Hedged   15%

- Canadian Bonds and Fixed-Income Funds   20%

....

Since I happen to be familiar with the **TD e-Series** of Index funds, we'll use it for demonstration purposes as our online source of fund options.

As *one* example, fund solutions which match your requirements are:

- **TD Canadian Index: (Equities)**
  - This index tracks the performance of the entire S&P/ TSX Composite Index;
  - MER is **0.33**.

  Allocate 50% to this fund.

- **TD U.S. Index – Currency Neutral: (Equities)**
  - Tracks the performance of the S&P 500 Index (U.S.);
  - Fully hedged against currency fluctuations;
  - MER is **0.35**.

  Allocate 15% to this fund.

- **TD International Index: (Equities)**
  - Tracks the performance of a selection of international equity-markets;
  - Hedged against currency fluctuations;
  - MER is **0.50**.

  Allocate 15% to this fund.

- **TD Canadian Bond Index: (Bonds)**
  - Tracks the performance, in both interest income and capital appreciation, of the DEX Universe Bond Index;
  - Comprised of Canadian investment-grade bonds – maturities exceeding one year;
  - MER is **0.51**.

  Allocate 20% to this fund.

....

By regularly and automatically investing your monthly savings in these products, in these proportions, you will have achieved the following:

- Diversification *between* asset classes;
- Broad diversification *within* each class;
- International diversification, with full currency protection;
- Averaging, over time, of your purchase prices."

....

"Pat yourself on the back, Jenny and Kevin – with this strategy you're well on the road to achieving long-term financial independence.

You are now the proud owners of excellent long-term 'Save-It-And-Forget-It' investment portfolios.

Over time, your portfolios should grow dramatically."

"But, Grandpa, you can't *really* forget it, because you have to review and rebalance your holdings at least once a year, right?" argued Kevin.

"You're right, Kevin. Over time, your actual allocation between investment classes will change from those you originally selected. This occurs because market values will fluctuate differently for each class. To return to your pre-determined allocations, you will have to rebalance your portfolio, at least annually."

TIP #90..... *At least* once a year, the wise investor will rebalance his current investment mix, to return it to his original targets for each investment category.

"Normally, the rebalancing is achieved by selling a portion of those funds which have increased, and buying more of those that have lagged behind."

"We're with you, Grandpa. 'Sell high – Buy low'," quipped Jenny.

"In your case however, because you're contributing monthly, all you need do, rather than having to first sell some funds, is simply acquire more of the laggards, until the desired balance is re-established."

....

"Whichever way you choose to do it, it's a simple exercise that costs very little to implement."

"Amazing, Grandpa! Hard to believe that investing for the long-haul can be such a simple process," exclaimed Jenny. "And if all I have to do after my initial investment decisions, is a once-a-year rebalancing act, then *maybe* even *I* will be able to do it on my own."

"Me too!" added Kevin. "But it's still a good idea to have Grandpa around as our cheap financial advisor. Now I finally understand, Grandpa, why you said *Money Sense* magazine's **Couch Potato** strategy is simple, and makes so much sense."

"It really is an incredibly simple investment strategy. Even if you have help with your initial allocation and investment decisions, you'll be able to do the annual rebalancing yourself."

....

"So, Grandpa, are you saying this strategy is a sure thing?" inquired Kevin.

"Remember, Kevin, what I said earlier. Unless you are in GICs or some other guaranteed fixed-income investment, *there is no such thing as a sure thing*. What we do know however, is that historically, this strategy has proven itself. It minimizes risk while still producing superior *long-term* returns. I have every expectation that this trend will continue for decades to come.

From personal experience, I also know you'll get a big kick out of going online from time-to-time, to check your investment portfolio.

But always remember my earlier cautions:

- Do *not* be tempted to try to outguess the market.

- Do *not* try to sell or buy at what you guess to be the highs and lows.

- Do your buying methodically, only through your regular monthly installment, or when you need to rebalance your portfolio, perhaps once a year."

TIP #91..... Once an investor has made a careful decision on long-term fund investments, he must *not* be tempted to tamper with his portfolio unless periodic updating of the financial plan or annual rebalancing clearly calls for it. The prudent individual will always remember that he is an INVESTOR, not a TRADER.

....

"I'm bushed, Grandpa!" groaned Kevin. "Any chance we can break off here 'til next Saturday?"

"This is a good time to stop. Next week we'll spend most of the afternoon getting to really understand Canadian pensions – where they come from, and how they impact how much we actually *need* to have saved by the time we retire. We'll finish off the day by looking at some smart strategies to use once we're retired."

"There you go again, Grandpa, sending us off into our golden retirement before we've even started a full-time job," joked Kevin.

"Ignore him, it'll be great, Grandpa! I can't wait for another free lunch. See you at our usual time," replied Jenny.

UNDERSTANDING PENSIONS

CHAPTER TWENTY-FIVE

· ·

CANADIAN PENSION-INCOME SOURCES

"Jenny and Kevin, I've another example of the power of 'time and compounding' – my waistline is increasing dramatically with all our lunches."

"Hey, I'll go you one better – my basic financial knowledge has really 'compounded' over the 'time' we've put into these sessions," bantered Kevin.

"We've sure covered a lot of ground," acknowledged Jenny. "But it's been really interesting, and less stressful knowing we'll have your book to refer to. Without it, I'd be really worried about how much I'll be able to retain."

· ·

"Today we're going to add another layer to your knowledge and comfort level by taking a good look at pensions in Canada.

Remember? I mentioned that we really must factor in the *impact of pensions* to be able to come up with a meaningful long-term, financial plan. Hopefully, today's chat will provide you with the necessary information.

We'll divide the topic of pensions into three logical components:

- Federal Government Pensions and Benefits
- Workplace or Employer-Based Pension Plans
- RRSPs and RRIFs."

1. FEDERAL GOVERNMENT BENEFITS

- ## Canada Pension Plan (CPP)

  All employed Canadians must *earn* their CPP retirement benefit by contributing to it throughout their working lives. Those such as a stay-at-home parent, who never work for an income, do not contribute to CPP, and hence do not, in their retirement years, receive CPP benefits.

  Employees, through their employee deductions, *must* contribute 4.95% of their income, on all annual earnings *between* a minimum of $3,500 and a maximum level of $51,100 (2014). These are referred to as *'pensionable' earnings*. The first $3,500 of annual earnings is exempt from contribution, and no contributions are made on earnings over $51,100 (2014).

  The employer *must* match that contribution. Those who are self-employed have double the cost – they must pay both the employee and employer portions.

  If the retiree elects to commence pension payments at the benchmark age of 65, the potential maximum CPP payment to an individual who has worked his whole life in Canada, is just under $12,460 annually (2014).

  If one elects to start receiving payments as early as age 60, those payments will decrease (in 2014) by up to 33.6% (0.56% per month of early withdrawal). By 2016, this discount factor will increase to 0.65% for each month a draw commences prior to age 65. By delaying payments to as late as age 70, monthly payments will increase (2014) by 0.7% for each month of postponement, to a maximum increase of 42%.

  CPP benefit payments are adjusted each January for inflation. Once the monthly payments commence, they continue for life. They are fully taxable.

- ## Old Age Security (OAS)

  Shortly before a Canadian who has lived all, or most of his

life in Canada, reaches age 65, he becomes *eligible to apply for* OAS payments of $6,618 annually (2014). Payments commence the month after his 65th birthday.

Those who have lived in Canada for shorter periods receive a reduced amount.

OAS is a federal government-funded plan that requires no contributions. It is unrelated to one's employment history.

OAS payments are adjusted quarterly for inflation, and are fully taxable.

Monthly payments continue in full for life, *unless* the taxpayer's annual net income exceeds $71,592 (2014). A *clawback*, or decrease in annual entitlement, begins at this level. OAS payments fully disappear at a total net income of $115,716 (2014).

As a result of the allowable, high net-income threshold, fewer than 5% of Canadians are affected by this clawback provision.

For those age 54 or younger as of March 31, 2012, the OAS benefit will be delayed to as late as age 67, for those born after 1962.

- **Guaranteed Income Supplement (GIS)**

   This extra, government-provided safety-net is for Canadian seniors receiving OAS, whose gross annual income, *excluding OAS payments*, falls below $16,728 for single persons, or $22,080 for couples (2014).

   The maximum combined OAS and GIS payment received by an individual cannot exceed $1,299 per month (2014). This maximum can be reached only if there is *no* income other than the OAS and GIS. All payments are adjusted quarterly for inflation.

   GIS payments are *not* taxable."

....

"Wow, Grandpa!" exclaimed Jenny. "All those CPP and OAS payments can really add up. If they're protected from inflation, does that mean we don't have to save as much for retirement?"

"Exactly so, Jenny. That's why I wanted you to be aware of what your government pensions will amount to. Even though mainly taxable, they're a solid, inflation-protected foundation that we need to incorporate into your financial plan.

Knowing that you'll be able to count on about $17,000 of assured, annual pension income which is indexed for inflation, you can build on that with any other employer-sponsored pensions you may have, as well as with your own investments."

> TIP #92..... **Inflation-protected CPP and OAS payments are a significant component of Canadian retirement incomes. They must be factored into financial planning targets.**

"Together, the CPP, OAS, and GIS pensions and benefits provide a significant safety-net for Canadian seniors. When these benefits are combined with various tax-system advantages for seniors, it becomes easier to understand why only about 7% of Canadian retirees live below the poverty-line. Of course we would prefer that *no one* find himself at or below the poverty line. Canadians however are fortunate to live in a country with one of the lowest seniors' poverty rates in the entire world."

....

2. EMPLOYER-SPONSORED PENSION PLANS

"About one-half of Canadian households have at least one individual who belongs to an employer-sponsored pension plan.

Approximately 6 million Canadians, roughly 38% of our workforce, are enrolled in some form of employer-sponsored pension plan. Of those, about 47% are public-sector plans; 53% are corporate plans.

There are two basic types of plan:

- **Defined Benefit Plan**

> *A DEFINED BENEFIT PLAN provides to a retired employee, a pre-determined monthly benefit based on earnings history, years of service, and age.*

Almost 80% of public-sector employees are members of this type of plan. Of the 25% of private-sector employees who belong to a company pension plan, only 16% enjoy a gold-plated defined benefit plan. These numbers are shrinking annually, as employers strive to economize on this expensive benefit.

The cost of the plan *may* be fully funded by the employer. More commonly, the funding is shared in some proportion between the employer and the employee, during his years of employment."

- **Defined Contribution Plan**

> *A DEFINED CONTRIBUTION PLAN has specified, regular contribution levels by both the employer and the employee. The eventual pension benefit depends entirely on the amounts contributed and on investment earnings.*

....

"So, Grandpa, if we're eventually employed where one of these pension plans exists, we'll definitely need, just like we did with CPP and OAS, to take these pension earnings into account in our financial planning, won't we?" asked Jenny.

"Yes, Jenny, *but* it gets a little trickier. With CPP and OAS payments, we'll know precisely how much they are, *and* we know they're indexed for inflation.

Most *public-sector* plans are also indexed for inflation. They're considered the *cadillacs* of pension plans. Relatively few private-sector plans on the other hand, will have inflation protection. Certainly no defined-benefit plan will."

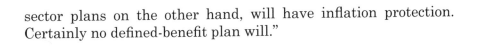

"Here's another question – I've heard people talk about their pensions being 'vested'. What's that?" asked Jenny.

"Good question, Jenny. Many employer-sponsored plans require that an employee remain employed for a minimum number of years, before the *employer's* contribution to the pension plan is *vested*.

Let's say for example, the vesting requirement for a particular plan is 5 years. An employee terminates employment with that employer after only four years. Except for reimbursement of his own contributions, he loses all rights to the retirement benefits provided by the plan."

"A key difficulty for you in projecting *your* future pension values lies in not knowing how many employers you may have over your working life, *or* which ones will have a pension plan of any kind. At this point you can't even accurately predict your income, and hence the level of contributions you may be required to make toward a pension plan."

> TIP #93..... Employer-sponsored pension plans must be factored into the financial plans of employees who participate in them. Because individuals change employers, and because pension plans also change over time, these events are triggers for updating a financial plan to reflect the latest projected retirement benefits.

"Both of you have a reasonable chance of finding employers with good pension plans. It's important that you be aware that having a pension plan represents a very significant, long-term economic benefit to you."

> TIP #94..... If faced with a choice of similar job opportunity, where one employer has a pension plan and the other does not, lean toward the one with the pension, even if the initial salary is somewhat lower.

"An individual who has worked for most of his career for an employer with a defined benefit plan, may find that the overall value of his workplace pension will be worth much more than the equity in his fully paid-off house."

"No way, Grandpa! That's unbelievable! I *never* would have guessed that the value of a pension plan could be more than the value of a house," exclaimed Kevin.

"That is so amazing!" added Jenny.

"To emphasize this remarkable fact, let's look at a typical Canadian public-sector pension plan's retirement benefit:

Remember **Mike**, *the electrician who went to work for the government? He was about 25 at the time. He remained employed in the public sector for his entire* **35-year** *career. He is now about to turn 60, and plans to retire. Over the last five years of his employment, Mike's average annual salary has been* **$60,000**.

As a public-sector employee, Mike belongs to a **defined-benefit plan**. *The plan provides a pension based on a combination of 2% of annual salary averaged over the last five years, and total years of service.*

Using this formula, at age 60, Mike's pension income from this plan will be **(2% of $60,000) times 35 years**. *That works out to* **$42,000 per year** *– fully indexed against inflation!*

Here's another way to look at this incredible value. Had he not had this pension plan, Mike would need to first have accumulated $695,000 and *then* to have achieved a post-retirement annual return of 5%, to be able to draw the same $42,000 annual retirement income until age 95."

"*Now* I understand how a pension like Mike's could be worth way more than the value of his house," commented Jenny. "I *never* would have believed it!"

"Remember too, that once Mike reaches age 65 and adds his annual, indexed CPP and OAS benefits of approximately $17,000, he'll actually end up with a pension close to 100% of his pre-retirement income!

In Mike's case, any *other* investments he has accumulated in his RRSP, TFSA, or other savings plans, are icing on the cake. With those investments, Mike's post-retirement income would actually increase. Not a bad arrangement, don't you agree? We should all be so lucky!"

"Sweet, Grandpa! This sure makes me want to check out a career in the public sector, at least more seriously than I had ever considered," observed Kevin.

"Me too!" added Jenny. "I'm amazed! The value of Mike's pension isn't much different than receiving a huge inheritance!"

"Although it's worth being aware of this impressive pension benefit offered by public-sector employers, many *other* factors will enter into your ultimate choice of employer."

....

"Here's another fact we should note regarding Mike's great pension.

As we just said, once he retired, Mike's pension was clearly equivalent in value to almost $700,000 of accumulated investments. But remember, this did not come entirely free.

Throughout his working years, Mike would have had to contribute perhaps 6% of his gross annual income to his employer-sponsored plan. This means that his contributions, at least partially, funded those retirement benefits. If Mike's contributions averaged $3,000 a year for 35 years, he would have contributed $105,000 in total. Still not much, considering the huge ultimate benefit.

My purpose here is simply to increase your awareness of the value of *any* employer-sponsored pension plans, and to make it clear that such a plan, or the lack of one, will have a huge impact on your retirement-planning strategies."

....

"It's very important to be aware that belonging to an *employer-sponsored pension plan* has consequences for your **RRSP contribution eligibility**."

TIP #95..... An individual with an employer-sponsored pension plan will see his annual RRSP contribution entitlement reduced – often severely. Future pension benefits from the employer-sponsored pension plan should however, more than compensate for this impact.

"This reduction in the allowable contribution limits to an RRSP is the government's effort to level the playing field between those who belong to a pension plan, and those who must rely entirely on their own resources and investments to enhance their CPP and OAS pensions.

RRSP contribution limits aside, participation in a company-sponsored pension plan has no impact on your annual TFSA contribution entitlement, nor on the amount you invest *outside* RRSP or TFSA plans.

If you are a couple, where one belongs to a pension plan, but the other does not, you *will* be able to maximize all the contribution allowance in each of your RRSPs. One RRSP account will simply have less contribution entitlement than the other. Between the two however, the maximum contribution opportunity will still be quite significant."

....

"Do you remember early in our chats, when I mentioned that your *net-worth* at retirement is only *one* indicator of how well you'll manage when you eventually retire? Well, you now have solid evidence of that.

Although your CPP, OAS, and any employer pension plan benefits are *not* shown in your net-worth statement of assets and liabilities, they are in reality, a huge additional asset."

"If pensions are so valuable, why aren't they included in our net-worth statement, Grandpa?" asked Kevin.

"Probably, because at any point in time it's difficult to forecast the actual *dollar* value of the pension. The value is affected by many factors, including your total years of service with that employer, and any future changes in the plan. You can only accurately determine the value of the benefit the day you begin receiving a pension."

....

"Boy, this is incredible information, Grandpa!" exclaimed Jenny. "I had *no* idea that when we retire, we *might* receive such huge pensions, even *before* adding in our personal investment income."

"It certainly is possible, Jenny. But keep in mind that only about 20% of Canada's workforce is employed in the public sector. The other 80% has either much less-generous workplace pension plans, or no plans at all.

Take your mom for instance. She has always been self-employed. Like many others, she must pay into CPP, but has no access to an employer-sponsored pension plan.

If we wish to maintain our standard of living when we retire, most of us, like your mom, must rely *solely* on our own savings and investments to supplement our CPP and OAS benefits."

....

"And now, this brings me to a key, *personal* source of retirement income – your **RRSP**. We've talked about it many times, but usually in terms of putting money *in*, not taking it *out*."

3. RRSP / RRIF (Registered Retirement Income Fund)

"Government rules require that every RRSP holder *must* convert his RRSP to a **Registered Retirement Income Fund (RRIF)**, by the end of the year in which he turns 71.

From then on, beginning the following year, a total of 5.4% of the RRIF's total value *must* be withdrawn from the plan. The minimum withdrawal increases annually, until at age 95, it reaches 20%. Taxes are payable on all withdrawals.

Keep in mind too, an RRSP may be converted to a RRIF earlier than age 71, *if* the owner wishes – for example at age 60, or even earlier. However, and this is an important point – *as soon as* conversion to a RRIF occurs, an *annual* minimum withdrawal requirement arises, although at a lower percentage rate because of the lower age."

....

"I guess at *your* age, Grandpa, this is more important to you than it is to us," teased Jenny. "But I guess I can see where it's useful to have a basic understanding of RRIFs so we can make better planning decisions *long before* we think of retirement."

"You're very perceptive, Jenny. And I don't mean the crack about my advancing age! You *do* need to understand the retirement rules, so they're at least in the back of your mind as you develop your early financial plans."

> **TIP #96.....** **An RRSP / RRIF is a key source of retirement income. Because of the tax consequences on mandatory withdrawals, much thought must go into a decision to convert an RRSP to a RRIF earlier than the compulsory age of 71.**

....

"What about investment income that isn't in an RRSP or RRIF?" inquired Kevin. "One day I might have a large, income-producing TFSA account, or even a rental-income property. Wouldn't that also be considered pension income?"

"Good thought, Kevin. Although additional investment products can add to your income, only payments from your CPP, OAS, RRIF, and employer pension plans are considered to be *pension* income. Any other income is considered *investment* income. For various tax reasons, the distinction is important.

You can set up all your investments so they pay you a steady monthly income, just *like* a pension. *If* that income comes from your TFSA, it will attract no tax. Your other investment income *will*. The level of tax will vary, depending on whether the income is fully taxed as in the case of a RRIF payment, or whether you are receiving interest, dividends or capital gains from investments outside a RRIF. Each category attracts a different level of tax.

Taxation issues are a complicated, multi-faceted topic — this summary is only the tip of the iceberg. But we'll touch on taxes again when we discuss specific retirement strategies.

In most cases, an individual's tax planning for retirement should be finalized only after advice from an accountant."

....

"Now we've arrived at a topic Kevin's been impatiently anticipating for weeks: ***How much income do we actually need, if we are to retire comfortably?***"

"I hope you remind him that inflation plays a starring role, Grandpa," advised Jenny.

"That's definitely one important consideration, Jenny. But first I want to separate some of the *myths* from the *realities* of how much we in fact *need* for a comfortable retirement."

....

"But first, a break. Your sharp observations and questions are *taxing* my brain!"

"You know, Grandpa," offered Jenny, "I'm amazed. All through high school we were exposed to hardly any of this information we've been talking about. Yet, it's obviously so useful. Some of it's even easy to understand!" she chuckled.

"I agree," added Kevin. "Until now, I've always skipped the financial pages in newspapers. I've seen bits and pieces on TV – usually sales pitches for mutual funds or reverse mortgages. But I sure haven't picked up much at school. I'm really enjoying this initiation into the world of personal finance. But as for the details, the sooner you write your book, the better. I'm definitely going to need it!"

"Maybe, Grandpa, your book will one day become part of the curriculum," suggested Jenny. "It is so needed."

CHAPTER TWENTY-SIX

RETIREMENT AFFORDABILITY

"Grab a rocking chair, Jenny and Kevin. It'll set the mood as we examine the important subject of *retirement affordability*.

For the two of you, retirement *is* many years in the future. However, in understanding this key subject, you'll be better equipped to set realistic, *and* necessary, long-term goals in your future financial planning."

HOW MUCH DO WE REALLY NEED IN RETIREMENT?

"A never-ending debate continues among mutual fund organizations and financial advisors, on what percentage of final pre-retirement income is *needed*, to maintain one's lifestyle in retirement.

The suggestions vary dramatically. They range from as low as 50%, to as high as 80%. However, as you will soon see, there really is no one-size-fits-all universal answer.

In reality, for each person planning retirement, the correct answer can only be arrived at individually. This is because each retiree's specific needs will depend on consideration of *at least* the following:

- Upon retirement, will the individual be, and plan to remain, totally debt-free?

- Will the retiree live in a mortgage-free home, or in rental accommodation?

- Will the retiree have health or disability issues?

- Will the retiree be responsible for an aging or disabled dependant?

- Will the retiree live alone, or with a partner, who may also be drawing CPP and OAS benefits?

- How extensive are the pre-retirement, work-related expenses and various payroll deductions, which will cease upon retirement?"

....

"If for example, an individual like *Mike* enters retirement debt-free, lives in a mortgage-free home, and has a partner who will also be eligible for CPP and OAS, it is entirely *possible* to retire from a $60,000 job, yet still maintain his lifestyle on $40,000, or even less."

....

"I see you both frowning. This really *is* possible. Be patient. I'll explain further. Keep in mind the following major changes which accompany retirement:

- Personal CPP and workplace-pension *contributions* cease on retirement. So do union dues and other miscellaneous, work-related deductions.

- Seniors over age 55 qualify for a tax credit equal to the lesser of: pension income, or $2,000.

- Personal tax-deduction allowances increase substantially at age 65.

- Since 2008, retired couples can split eligible pension income between themselves, to further minimize their total tax bill.

  Even before age 65, an individual belonging to a defined-benefit pension plan has the option to split that pension income with a spouse.

Can either of you think of other work-related expenses that disappear or decrease upon retirement?"

"Well," offered Kevin, "I guess your transportation and parking costs would go down."

"You're right, Kevin, and probably your clothing costs too."

"What about lunches and those expensive designer coffees?" piped up Jenny.

"That's looking at the bright-side scenario. Many costs *do* go down."

....

"On the other side of the coin, another employee, also earning $60,000 annually, still has both a significant mortgage, and other debts which make it difficult to make ends meet, even *before* retirement.

Without a major change in lifestyle, he will have difficulty surviving on *any* reduction in income after retiring. He may well have to sell his home and down-size, in order to reduce or eliminate debts."

....

"Recent statistics report that the average Canadian retires on only about 55% of pre-retirement income."

"When you're used to almost twice as much, how can 55% be anywhere near enough to call your retirement comfortable?" demanded Kevin.

"It does seem way too low, doesn't it, Kevin. Remember though, this statistic is reporting only the percentage of income-replacement. It is *not* reporting on post-retirement lifestyle changes.

Let's look at the lowest (less than $20,000) income sector first.

In this income-bracket the retiree's post-retirement income may actually *increase*.

This is a testament to ***Canada's strong social safety-net***. For a retiree with no personal income resources, his CPP, OAS, and GIS entitlements can produce almost $20,000 annually. We saw this in our earlier discussion of these programs."

....

"At the other end of the scale, once he retires, a high-income earner can get by on a much lower income than before retirement. This is possible primarily due to the huge drop in his tax bill and other payroll deductions, as soon as he retires. The higher-income retiree is also more likely, before retirement, to have liquidated all major debts."

> TIP #97..... Generally, the greater the pre-retirement income of a retiree, the lower the percentage of that income that is *needed* to maintain post-retirement lifestyle, particularly if the retiree is debt-free.

....

"Grandpa, I see where you're heading," commented Jenny. "Once again you're emphasizing the importance of trashing all debt as fast as we can. Seeing how debt can be such a drag on our lifestyle even in our far-off retirement, I really get why you've always said there is ***no such thing as good debt***."

> TIP #98..... To effectively address retirement affordability, the most important consideration is to compare the difference in pre-retirement *disposable income* and *living costs* to those in post-retirement.

"Remember this. All the figures I've used represent *averages*.

There *are* retirees whose post-retirement income is at 100% or even more, of their working salary. This does not mean however, that they *need* it to maintain their lifestyle. It simply means they've been prudent managers of their finances, and wise investors, throughout their working lives."

....

"So if I hear you right, Grandpa," observed Kevin, "to have a comfy retirement like yours, we have to do three things in life:

- Climb the salary ladder;
- Manage our spending and investments wisely;
- Have no debts by the time we're over-the-hill seniors like you."

"Such kind words! But yes, you're spot-on, Kevin.

If you start focusing on these objectives early in life, you can easily become extremely well-off in your retirement years. You may even achieve financial independence much earlier than you expect, and be in a position to retire early, if that's your wish."

TIP #99..... The prudent retiree can easily maintain his pre-retirement lifestyle on significantly less than his pre-retirement income.

"At 80% of pre-retirement income, the average Canadian retiree is virtually *assured* of being at least as well-off as he was prior to retirement.

With between 60% to 80% of pre-retirement income, particularly if debt-free and with a partner over age 65, the retiree will *probably* be as well off as before retirement.

This lower 60% threshold will be a relief to those who, aged 40 or more, have few investments and much less time to prudently capitalize on saving and investment strategies."

> TIP #100..... The magic combination of compounding and time, along with prudent debt-management and sound investment strategies, affords every Canadian the opportunity for a very comfortable retirement. The earlier one focuses on his retirement objective, the easier it will be to achieve.

WHEN TO RETIRE?

"There are among us those who have *no* intention of retiring, even at age 65.

Many of us dream however, of being able to retire *before* we reach age 65. Some – with determination, a solid saving and investment ethic, and perhaps a bit of luck – *do* reach that goal.

Often, in the mistaken belief that they cannot afford to do so, other would-be early-retirees often miss out on a golden opportunity to retire early."

....

"Let me introduce you to my somewhat younger friend, **Ann**.

Ann, a nurse, was approaching her 60th birthday. I asked if she planned to retire. She replied that she had no option but to continue working until age 65. Her pension entitlement at age 60 would produce a monthly income of only about $3,600. She was used to her comfortable income of closer to $5,500 per month.

Ann jumped at my offer to work out some numbers for her. I wanted to see if she really could not afford to retire right away. She gave me a recent pay-stub, which showed all her regular deductions, including taxes, pension and employment insurance contributions, union dues and other deductions.

Within a few hours, I was able to demonstrate to Ann that her monthly pension entitlement at age 60, combined with her early CPP eligibility, would produce an after-tax monthly retirement income that would fall short of her present take-home pay, by only about $600.

She could easily make up this deficiency by converting her RRSP to a RRIF, and beginning to draw from it on a monthly basis. I suggested instead however, that Ann might prefer to make herself available on a casual basis, at one of the local hospitals. If she managed to work only four 8-hour shifts each month, she would earn more than the monthly $600 shortfall from her pre-retirement take-home pay.

By working only four shifts monthly as a casual employee, rather than twenty shifts as a full-time employee, Ann could match her pre-retirement disposable income!

Ann was astounded and delighted at this prospect. Within a few months, she had retired.

A year into her retirement, Ann's biggest problem was to not accept every shift offered to her. She was working many fewer hours than before retirement, had more disposable income, and now had both the time and the extra funds to indulge her passion for travel."

"How is it that this seems so simple?" inquired Kevin.

"Well, Kevin, a combination of factors worked in Ann's favour:

- She was one of the 20% of fortunate Canadians who worked for a public sector employer; that meant she had a great defined-benefit pension plan.

- Pension contributions, which had amounted to almost 7% of her gross income, ceased on retirement; so did employment insurance, and other deductions.

- CPP rules allowed Ann to commence drawing reduced benefits as early as age 60.

- Ann worked in a profession where significant casual-employment opportunities exist."

....

"The majority of would-be retirees would not be as fortunate as Ann.

Without the security of the workplace-pension benefit, many individuals opting for early-retirement may need to start drawing on their RRIF, or working more part-time hours than Ann did.

No one however, should rule out the early-retirement option before first examining the possibility in detail. It may in fact, be attainable."

"I'm beginning to understand a bit better how retirees can live on much less than their pre-retirement income," observed Jenny. "The combination of lower taxes, employer pension for some, and CPP and OAS benefits, means the retiree's *disposable income* actually drops by much less than I would have thought."

"Exactly, Jenny! Some of us fail to calculate our post-retirement income accurately. As a result, we often needlessly stay in the workforce till age 65, well past our early-pension entitlement.

Even if we earn $35 an hour during that extra five years, our *incremental* hourly benefit may well be less than $10 an hour, compared to what our post-retirement income would be – hardly worthwhile.

I'm *not* suggesting that everyone plan to retire at 60. For many, work is fun! What I *am* suggesting however, is that many of us may be better off *financially* by accepting an early pension, and then *choosing* to work where, when and as much or as little as we wish."

....

"I've mentioned a number of times, Jenny and Kevin, that you are both at the perfect stage of life to ensure that your wealth-creation and ultimate retirement objectives are not only easily met, but perhaps even exceeded."

"Well," offered Jenny, "I for one, would love to be among those few retirees who *do* manage to replace 100% of their pre-retirement income. And I sure don't expect to *have to* work full-time until age 65! Kevin, can you believe I'm actually talking about retirement?"

"I knew Grandpa would get to you eventually, Jenny. But definitely, I agree," added Kevin. "You're going to help us become well-off dudes, Grandpa!"

"I hope so, Kevin. But as I've said more than once, you need a **balanced lifestyle**. At the same time that you're saving and investing a relatively modest part of your income for the future, you will also want to enjoy life and all that it has to offer. With a little planning and discipline, you can achieve both objectives simultaneously."

TIP #101..... **Saving a modest portion of income, prudently managing and eliminating debt, investing wisely and for the long-haul, should still allow you to enjoy a fulfilling and comfortable lifestyle.**

"Here's a shocking fact, Jenny and Kevin. With today's longer life-spans, you may well live as long in your retirement years, as you spend in your working life. It makes sense therefore, to make a reasonable effort while you're working, to plan for and secure your economic comfort for perhaps 30 or 35 years of retirement."

....

"For even more information on preparation for retirement, you might check out a website sponsored by the Ontario Securities Commission – *Investor Education Fund* at www.investored.ca. It contains much excellent information."

....

"Let's take a quick break, and then we'll finish with a discussion on specific *retirement strategies* to follow, once we actually *are* retired."

"Let's do that," agreed Jenny. "I really need to stretch my legs, *and* wrap my brain around the fact that at my age I'm actually talking about *retirement!*"

....

CHAPTER TWENTY-SEVEN

RETIREMENT STRATEGIES

"When we left off before our break, I said I wanted to finish today by giving you a brief insight into retirement strategies, once an individual actually retires. We don't have to talk about *your* retirement, Jenny, if that makes you feel less ancient.

We'll assume for our discussion, that for most Canadians, retirement means age 65. That's when *full* Canada Pension Plan (CPP) and Old Age Security (OAS) benefits generally kick in. A number of very important, and beneficial tax changes also become available to the retiree at this age."

"This must be the good part, when you finally show us how we can enjoy spending all those investment nest-eggs we'll have racked up," commented Jenny.

"You're right in one sense, Jenny. On retirement, our focus will need to shift from saving and investing for growth, to smart strategies for *withdrawal* and *use* of our accumulated funds.

But remember, we're likely to live a good 30 years or more *after* retirement. So the emphasis on withdrawal must be tempered to ensure that we don't outlive our money."

"Can you believe it, Jenny? For about a third of our lives we're likely to be part of the rocking-chair brigade," cracked Kevin.

"Remember, Kevin, with health care advances, most seniors today remain very active for many years after retirement, even if they own and enjoy rocking chairs! And much of that activity, like travel for instance, requires a good continuing income."

"You're right, Grandpa," agreed Kevin. "Jenny and I have recently enjoyed a lot of lunches on *your* retirement dollar."

INVESTMENT WITHDRAWAL PLAN

"By the time you are 65 and retired, you will, in most cases, have begun receiving both CPP and OAS benefits, as well as any other employer-pension plan payments for which you are eligible.

This may also be the time for you to consider converting your **RRSP** to a **Registered Retirement Income Fund (RRIF)**, and to start drawing income from it. However, since you are not *required* to convert until age 71, you would be wise to do so only if you need the extra income, *or* if there were a tax advantage to drawing the funds earlier."

THE RRIF PLAN

"We touched on this subject earlier while discussing various sources of pension income. Now let's build on that introduction.

You can convert an RRSP to a RRIF at any age – before 65, or after, as long as you *do* so by the end of the year you turn 71.

The obvious advantage of waiting until age 71 to convert to a RRIF, is that your portfolio has the maximum number of tax-sheltered years in which to accumulate value, before withdrawals *must* commence. This is particularly helpful if your portfolio is modest, perhaps because you were late in initiating significant saving and investing.

On the other hand, if your portfolio is very substantial – approaching a million dollars or more, it *may* actually be to your long-term advantage to convert earlier to a RRIF, and to start drawing benefits even before you reach age 65.

If you delay conversion of a large portfolio until age 71, you'll be forced in the following year, to make your first withdrawal at 5.4% of your entire portfolio value. The percentage you *must* withdraw increases annually, until at age 95, it reaches 20%."

"Question, Grandpa," inserted Kevin. "Why can't we take out whatever we want? It's our money."

"Good question, Kevin. You can take out as much as you want, *over* the minimum annual percentage specified, but you cannot take out less. The 5.4% is simply the starting point designated by government.

The reason for a specified minimum withdrawal is simple. The government has allowed us to benefit from tax refunds each time we contributed to our RRSP. Furthermore, it has allowed our investments in the RRSP (or RRIF) to grow totally tax-free for many years. The government now wants some of that foregone income tax back. The way they choose to do that, is to force us after age 71, to withdraw at least a minimum amount each year."

....

"One useful fact to tuck into the back of your mind – the government *permits* a retiree with a *younger* spouse to make use of the younger person's lower minimum withdrawal requirement. That may enable the retiree to withdraw less from his RRIF in any given year, than normally required for a person of his age."

....

"Here's one other useful point. Remember when we discussed the OAS program? I explained that it provides a monthly benefit which in 2014 totals $6,618 per year for most Canadians over age 65. I also pointed out that this sum begins to be *clawed-back* by the government once an individual's annual net income reaches $71,592. The OAS benefit disappears entirely when that net income exceeds $115,716.

Now hold that thought as we get back to the RRIF. When you withdraw funds from your RRIF, you add to your income for that year.

Can you see where I'm heading? If your withdrawals *after* age 71 put you in the *claw-back* zone on your OAS, you may be better off to start drawing down your RRIF earlier, if that helps you avoid the problem of too high an annual net income.

It would be a shame to end up losing the annual indexed $6,618 OAS benefit, simply because your diligence in saving and investing all your life resulted in *too high* an income after retirement."

"Seems to me it would be a nice problem to have," mused Jenny.

"You're right, Jenny. It *is* a nice problem to have – one faced by only about 5% of retired Canadians."

....

"Like you said, Grandpa, we're better to start withdrawing from our RRIF before our birthday cake has 72 candles on it, *if* that means we can keep our OAS," observed Kevin. "So how would that work?"

"Well, first you invest in a fire extinguisher...." laughed Jenny. "Sorry, Grandpa, I couldn't resist."

"We'll ignore that, Jenny! Here are a few options, Kevin:

- Convert to a RRIF earlier than mandated. Withdraw sufficient annual income to ensure that by age 65 when OAS entitlement currently begins, you do not, then or in subsequent years, exceed the lower-threshold of net income at which OAS claw-backs commence.

- Delay conversion to a RRIF, until the required age of 71. In the first year, acknowledging that your tax bill will skyrocket for that one year, withdraw one large sum. Calculate carefully the amount to be withdrawn, to ensure that the resulting decrease in total value of your RRIF is sufficient to ensure that your *subsequent* withdrawals do not put you over the OAS claw-back threshold.

With this strategy, you *will* in year one, have a large one-time tax bill. However, after that one year of major withdrawal from your RRIF, you may preserve your full OAS entitlement for life.

- If you're part of a couple, take full advantage of pension income-splitting provisions, to reduce each partner's taxable income to below the OAS claw-back threshold.

- A *combination* of these three strategies may be the optimum solution. Use your lending institution's online retirement-benefit calculator. Investigate various options, to make the best decision, for your situation.

Reviewing your options with an accountant, *before* making a final decision, is advisable and well worthwhile."

....

"Grandpa, if we were to choose the second option you mentioned and withdraw the one large amount at age 72, there must be something particularly smart we can do with it," mused Kevin. "And I don't mean buy a yacht, or something like that."

"Good observation, Kevin. There are many potentially rewarding uses, such as a gift to children to assist with a house purchase, or a grandchild with his education."

....

"If however, you mean smart *investment* options, here's a particularly good one.

From previous years, you may have unused availability in your TFSA. It continues to accumulate contribution capacity for both you and your partner, currently (2015) at a rate of $10,000 annually, for life.

The TFSA becomes the perfect vehicle for *reinvesting* excess withdrawals from your RRIF."

"And," piped up Jenny, "once *in* a TFSA, any earnings or withdrawals from it are non-taxable, so you don't lose out on your future OAS payments."

> TIP #102..... **A prudent retiree will carefully determine both the year he converts to a RRIF, and the timing and amount of annual withdrawals, in order to minimize the impact of claw-back rules on OAS payments.**

THE TAX PLAN

"Since 2008, retired couples have enjoyed the benefit of a *pension income-splitting* provision. For tax purposes, this feature allows a portion of one partner's pension income to be allocated to the other."

"How does this reduce the taxes the couple pays?" asked Jenny.

"Remember our earlier discussion on pensions? One of the couple may have had a golden employer-pension plan, while the other had none. After retirement, the partner with the pension is likely to have a much higher income. If taxed without the benefit of income-splitting, it would attract a much higher tax-rate than that of the lower-income partner.

By apportioning the income differently, *for tax purposes only*, the couple's combined tax bill will be less, because each will be taxed at a lower marginal tax rate."

....

"Most of us prepare our own *tax returns*. Thanks to the advent of easy-to-use software for this specific purpose, it is no longer the arduous chore of the past. We are guided step-by-step through the process, part of which will lead us to the optimal pension-income split.

If you're not comfortable doing this yourself, by all means consult an accountant. Your tax savings are likely to far exceed the cost of consultation."

....

"Every pensioner, *regardless of age*, will also be eligible for a tax credit on the first $2,000 of *qualified* annual *pension* income. By splitting eligible pension income with the lower-income partner, *both* partners can receive this credit, for a total potential tax credit of $4,000.

As a retiree over age 65, the pensioner will automatically qualify for additional age-related tax breaks previously not available to him."

TIP #103..... Effective tax planning by retirees, particularly couples, can substantially affect disposable income. The advice of an accountant may result in significant financial benefits.

INVESTMENT STRATEGIES

"Although we discussed this earlier, it does *not* hurt to repeat it. On retirement, your priority will have shifted from long-term capital growth, to imminent income withdrawal and *capital preservation*.

Well before retirement, it's *usually* prudent to have shifted our investment mix toward a split of 50% (or less) in equities and 50% (or more) in fixed-income investments.

This reduces the risk to our portfolio of value fluctuations, particularly in the critical years immediately before, and just after, retirement commences.

For those with very large portfolios, or a good employer-based pension income, this short-term fluctuation risk is not as crucial. These fortunate individuals may prefer to continue with their objective of increasing long-term estate value by retaining a more aggressive portfolio allocation than most retirees.

Strange as it may seem to both of you, some retirees do *not* require *all* their retirement income in a given year. As we've just discussed, excess funds are best invested through their or their partner's TFSA. This strategy will optimize tax-free growth, and provide future tax-free income."

....

"A consultation with an ***independent financial advisor*** is advisable to investigate the potential value of investing segments of your retirement portfolio, whether in a RRIF, TFSA, or other savings vehicle, in any of the following, more complicated investment structures:

- **Segregated Funds**

    These *managed* funds generally charge an even higher fee than the previously-discussed actively-managed funds. They do guarantee however, that at the end of a specific time period, usually ten years, the value of the investor's capital will not have declined, regardless of market performance.

    Tracking of equity markets over the past 60 years indicates that an overall decline in equity values, over *any* 10-year period, is highly unlikely. Given that assurance, it is questionable, especially in view of the higher fees, how valuable the guarantee offer really is. However, some retirees, and near-retirees, may find this peace-of-mind worth the higher fees.

- **Guaranteed Minimum-Withdrawal Benefit Products**

These come in many forms. Critical to investment in any of these products is an understanding of the benefits versus the costs in each case.

Basically, these funds guarantee a regular income stream.

For example, plans exist which will make monthly payments for life. Income is guaranteed annually at 5% of the invested sum, as long as withdrawals commence after age 65. The 5% minimum income remains protected, even if the underlying investment value decreases. But if the original investment increases in value, the 5% payment will rise. All of these benefits of course, come with a price which is reflected in the fees charged.

- **Annuities**

An ANNUITY is a contract which one purchases in exchange for a lump sum of money. It provides regular payments, usually on a monthly basis, for either a fixed number of years, or life.

If a substantial portion of a retiree's portfolio is *outside* an RRSP, RRIF, or TFSA, any income from that segment of his portfolio is taxed at the retiree's marginal rate. In this circumstance, annuities *may* play a useful, tax-effective role in generating some of the retiree's income.

Because annuity payments are a blend of earned income and return of capital, they are very tax-efficient. Because they are a *combination* of these two elements, they tend to generate much larger sums than the income earned on most fixed-income investments.

As with any seemingly good deal however, annuities also have their downside. Most significantly, once purchased, these products provide zero access to the capital, and *no residual value* to the estate.

The retiree must therefore balance the benefits provided by an annuity against the income and capital preservation to be achieved from a well-balanced, relatively low-risk investment portfolio.

....

For a healthy retiree, there is a compromise solution to the issue of estate preservation. He can for example, purchase both an annuity *and* a parallel *term-to-100 life insurance policy*. On the retiree's death, the insurance policy would return to the estate, the capital which would otherwise be lost with an annuity.

Obviously, at age 70 or 75, the high purchase cost of such a life-insurance policy would significantly erode the annual net benefit of the annuity. But, because the annuity enjoys preferred tax treatment, the retiree will probably receive significantly more after-tax income than he could achieve through an equally safe, but much less tax-efficient investment as for example, in GICs.

The combination of an annuity and a parallel life-insurance policy is known as an ***Insured Annuity***.

Each of these options has benefits *and* costs. The funds may be locked in, and the fees high. The retiree must clearly understand each factor, before making a selection."

"Grandpa, I think this is one of those times when you really *should* hot-foot it to a reliable advisor," suggested Kevin.

"Consult an independent financial advisor and an accountant – not providers of these products – to help you make the appropriate decisions, tailored specifically to your situation."

> TIP #104..... Do not succumb to sales pitches in advertisements, or by sales representatives for retirement-income products, without first obtaining truly independent analysis and advice on all available options.

INSURANCE NEEDS

"In most cases, life insurance for a retiree is very expensive and very unnecessary.

A few exceptions are worth mentioning:

• The *insured-annuity*, which we've just discussed;

• *'Last-to-die' term insurance* products for very-high-net-worth retirees, whose estates may be subject to major tax obligations after their death.

  Such a policy will pay out the sum required for taxes, upon the death of the last insured member.

Other than annuities, other *insurance-based* products also exist, which guarantee a tax-efficient income-stream from a major capital investment."

....

"You know, Grandpa, I can see where having an annuity or one of the other guaranteed income products would appeal to a lot of seniors," observed Jenny. "It would give them peace-of-mind to know exactly how much they'll receive every month for the rest of their life. But then, this wouldn't really protect them from inflation, would it?"

"Some of these products *may* include some inflation protection, Jenny. All are worth exploring. However, the prudent retiree will consult with an *independent financial advisor* and an *accountant* before making any decision."

WILLS AND ESTATE PLANNING

"Ideally, every Canadian adult should have a *Will* in which his wishes regarding an executor, a trustee, and the disposition of assets are clearly detailed. As one travels through life, from the various stages of wealth accumulation and family formation, to retirement, a Will's importance increases.

On death, failure to leave a Will means that legal distribution rules will be followed by the *public trustee* – regardless of any contrary wishes of the deceased.

A simple *Will* can be drawn up economically, using the services of either a notary or a lawyer."

....

"Remember, as with a financial plan, a Will must be regularly reviewed and, when necessary, updated.

For the retiree, it may be advisable to supplement an up-to-date Will with *estate planning* appropriate to both the size of the estate, and the individual's family circumstances."

....

"See, Jenny," quipped Kevin. "I told you Grandpa would have you drawing up your Will before we finished!"

"No surprise there," agreed Jenny. "But I'm confused, Grandpa. How is *estate planning* different from the wealth management we've been talking about all these weeks?"

"Wealth management, Jenny, is what we actively pursue while we're alive and kicking. Estate planning on the other hand, seeks to optimize the after-tax value of our estate for our designated heirs, after we die.

You can relax about this for now, Jenny. Neither of you has to worry yet about estate planning. As you *approach* your retirement years and amass significant net-worth, it will be soon enough then to think about this complex subject."

....

"Grandpa, I have another question about seniors and their money. What are all those Reverse Mortgage ads about, encouraging seniors to take a big chunk of money from the equity in their home, without having to make any payments?" asked Kevin. "What's the deal?"

"I'm glad you asked, Kevin."

A REVERSE MORTGAGE is a type of mortgage loan whereby a Canadian homeowner over age 60 borrows against the equity value in his home. Neither principal nor interest payments are required until the homeowner sells his home or dies, whichever occurs first. At that time, the entire loan, along with accrued and compounded interest, becomes payable in full.

"In my *strong* opinion, reverse mortgages are *not* a good deal. I believe they are probably one of the worst enticements to which any senior can succumb."

"What's wrong with it, Grandpa?" asked Kevin. "When you listen to the ads, it seems like a good idea, especially for seniors who need a bit more available cash."

"Remember, Kevin, how amazed you were at the incredible power of time and compounding in growing your wealth? Well, a *Reverse Mortgage* uses the same principle, but to the exact opposite effect. It's an arrangement which can quickly erode, or even destroy, the wealth you have accumulated through your home ownership.

In the case of a reverse mortgage, that same incredible power of compounding, at a high rate of interest, is working *against* you, rather than *for* you.

The reason I'm so negative about *reverse mortgages* is that they can destroy wealth and shatter the dream of leaving a meaningful estate for one's family. The accumulating, and worse, *compounding* interest rate is set significantly higher than for a normal mortgage. Substantial set-up costs are also charged to the homeowner."

....

"Let's look at an example. We'll ignore the set-up fees which *can* run into several thousand dollars.

Mr. R.E. Morse, a 60-year old homeowner and widower, decides to take out the maximum-allowable 40% of his home's equity, by means of a Reverse Mortgage. He has $600,000 of confirmed equity value in his home. This yields Mr. Morse $240,000 cash, less the significant set-up fees. The interest rate is set at 6%. It accumulates and compounds for twenty years, until at age 80, Mr. Morse decides to move into an assisted-living facility. He sells his home. Luckily, home values have increased over the twenty years and his home sells for $1.2 million.

From the proceeds of his home sale, Mr. Morse is required to pay the mortgage lender $794,000. This leaves Mr. Morse with less than $406,000!"

....

"If by chance, the proceeds of the sale had been less than the mortgage debt, the lender would have been obliged to absorb the shortfall. Mr. Morse however, would have received zero from the sale.

The only hope Mr. Morse would have had of preserving the full $600,000 equity he had accumulated by age 60, would have been for home prices to have increased annually by the same 6% compounded rate that the mortgage was costing him over the twenty years.

Mr. Morse and his late wife had worked most of their life to pay off their home mortgage. In return for that one-time advance of $240,000, little did he realize that twenty years later, he may have lost a significant percentage of his home equity.

This loss of wealth may seriously have impacted the quality of care Mr. Morse could afford when he moved at age 80. Moreover, it would have severely eroded the value of any estate he had hoped to leave to his family."

"Now I understand why you're so opposed to reverse mortgages, Grandpa!" exclaimed Jenny. "When you really delve into the potential consequences, it's a terrible deal."

> TIP #105..... A Reverse Mortgage should be considered by seniors only as an absolute *last* resort for raising capital. An independent financial advisor, an accountant, and a lawyer, should all be consulted, and the consequences carefully evaluated *before* any contract is signed.

....

"A reminder...for those wishing to be more informed and better prepared for their retirement, a good resource to check out is the Ontario Securities Commission site, *Investor Education Fund*, at www.investored.ca.is."

....

"Grandpa, in all the tons of stuff we've discussed about smart strategies for wealth creation, you haven't mentioned how owning your own business can factor in," commented Kevin. "Isn't being a business owner another road to wealth-creation?"

"That's a great observation, Kevin. I had planned to cover that topic next week during our last session, but since you've raised it, let's tackle it now."

"Oh, groan," muttered Jenny. "But actually, it's a topic I'm very interested in – I'd love to be my own boss."

THE ENTREPRENEUR

· ·

CHAPTER TWENTY-EIGHT

OWNING YOUR OWN BUSINESS

"As you observed, Kevin, being your own boss is indeed another unique and challenging pathway to wealth-creation.

And as you've mentioned, Jenny, virtually every Canadian will dream at some stage in his life, of being his own boss and owning a business. Indeed, many have turned that dream into a reality.

Here are a few 2009 facts on *small business* in Canada:

- Small and medium-size businesses account for over 58% of total employment.

- Of Canada's 1.04 million businesses with employees, approximately 78% employ less than 5 people. About 97% employ fewer than 50.

- One in six Canadians, approximately 2.5 million, count themselves as 'self-employed'.

- More than half of Canada's self-employed operate their business from home.

- 'Self-employment' creates 75% of all new jobs in Canada.

- Approximately 130,000 new small businesses are created each year.

Clearly, *small business* is a very important and growing sector of Canada's overall economy."

· ·

"As appealing as this route may be, there are however, downsides to be considered. More Canadians than ever are choosing to start their own business, despite the challenges and risks involved. The risks are significant. Consider this:

- 25% of new businesses fail in their first year.

- Only about 35% of new businesses survive beyond their fifth year.

Clearly, in the minds of Canadians, the potential rewards of *entrepreneurship* far outweigh its daunting challenges. Canada's economic vibrancy and overall welfare are in fact, very reliant on the optimistic spirit and energy of its small-business owners.

The lure for the entrepreneur of course, is not only to create a comfortable living doing something he loves, but also the dream that he may become one of the few whose business develops into a renowned conglomerate.

Canada has produced its share of business superstars.

*Can there be a more dramatic example of spectacular success than that of British Columbia's **Jimmy Pattison**? A self-made Canadian multi-billionaire, he was by 2009, the sole owner of some one hundred individual enterprises, employing about 31,000 people in 431 locations. By 2014, aggregate annual sales revenues of the Jim Pattison Group were approaching $10 billion.*

Jimmy Pattison began his career in the 1960's as a small-business owner."

BENEFITS OF SMALL-BUSINESS OWNERSHIP

"The benefits of owning your own business are many. Key among them are:

- ***Being your own boss*** – You can set your own hours; work as hard as you wish; answer only to your customers, and perhaps your bankers. You are in control of your own destiny – your success or failure.

- *Enhanced learning* - As a business owner you never cease learning. Your brain is stimulated and tested. Your business demands keep your creativity flowing.

- *Challenges galore* - If challenge makes you thrive, starting your own business is something to consider. No matter how successful your business, it can always improve. You are in control of how well it takes advantage of new opportunities.

- *Financial rewards* - Your personal income is limited only by the success of your enterprise, and by the amount *you* choose to draw from it.

- *Tax advantages* - In recognition of the contribution of small business to the economic welfare of Canada, federal and provincial governments have created a tax regime for this sector that encourages entry and success. With the assistance of a good accountant, the business owner will generally find himself subject to much more favorable taxes, than he would as an employee of someone else's enterprise."

THE RISKS

"The risks of business ownership are also many. Among the primary ones are:

- *High business-mortality rate* - As mentioned earlier, a majority of new businesses do not survive long enough to see their fifth year completed. Franchise structures, with their training and support systems, have proven effective in reducing failure rates. They are worth considering.

- *Capital investment requirements* - The risk of failure increases proportionately with both the degree of debt with which your business starts, and which it carries into the future. For many new entrepreneurs, the only option in starting their own business is to borrow heavily for its start-up or acquisition. Franchises, while more likely to succeed, also usually require a substantial entry cost.

- **High Stress** - While many entrepreneurs will thrive on the challenges, others will find the role of business owner extremely stressful. As an owner, *you* are in large part, the business. The buck stops with you. Countless hours of personal effort may be necessary, while putting strains on family life and often, particularly in early years, family finances."

> **TIP #106.....** The risks and rewards of business ownership are worth careful consideration. For those who take up the challenge and succeed, the personal and financial rewards can be immense.

TIMING OF BUSINESS START-UP OR ACQUISITION

"There is no prescribed right time for easy entry into your own business. It will depend greatly on your *personal* circumstances.

Some general suggestions are worth keeping in mind:

- The younger you are, the less experienced you will be. On the other hand you will be full of energy and enthusiasm, and more able to roll with one or two setbacks. After all, when you are young, you generally have little to lose, and much to gain. Many ultimately successful entrepreneurs say they've learned far more from their failures than from their successes.

- The more years you spend climbing the career and salary ladder in someone else's employ, the more difficult it may become to break away from those golden handcuffs that being an employee can represent.

- Early retirement from salaried employment has proven to be an important entry point for the aspiring entrepreneur. By this time he is likely to have a pension or substantial investment safety-net as back-up. He should have easier access to required capital. And, perhaps too young and energetic for only golf and travel, he welcomes the challenge of a new career.

Often too, the early retiree has acquired over many years, a comprehensive set of business skills upon which he can rely. These skills can serve to dramatically improve the chances of success of his new business."

TIP #107..... **For those who, before jumping in, are meticulous in researching all aspects of the proposed enterprise, their chance of success with a small business increases dramatically. Be prudent. Do your homework first!**

....

"Don't kid yourself about your own abilities *and* shortcomings in terms of running a business. If you can't tell a balance sheet from an income statement, have few management skills, and know little about sales and marketing, you *may* be better off spending a few years acquiring relevant knowledge and skill, *before* charging out on your own with no safety-net.

Yes, you can hire an accountant and a skilled manager. But that requires even more start-up cash, *and* sufficient knowledge to properly manage their roles. It's best to take it one step at a time."

"So the motto should be 'Dream big – Think attainable – Take baby steps'?" asked Jenny.

"More or less, Jenny. And keep in mind that the first *real* challenge for the budding entrepreneur is whether he can put together for his dream, a *business plan* which can pass muster with his banker or other financial backers."

> **TIP #108.....** **A comprehensive and sound business plan is critical to the successful launch of a new business enterprise.**

....

"So, Grandpa, if I were to come up with an idea for my 'dream-come-true' business," mused Jenny, "how do I know if it's worth pursuing? I would sure hate to borrow a lot of money, only to see it go straight down the drain."

"Don't give up a dream of starting or acquiring your own business. But be smart. Do your homework, hone your skills, pick your timing, save and don't rely overly on borrowed capital.

Who knows? You may have it in you to become another *Jimmy Pattison* or *Bill Gates*. One thing is certain. You'll never know if you don't try."

....

"Enough said. Let's finish our discussions for today. Next Saturday, I'll plan to tie off a few remaining loose ends, and respond to any issues you think we may have missed. Soon after that, we'll probably come to the end of our marathon sessions."

"That's really good news, Grandpa," replied Jenny. "It's hard to believe that we could possibly have left anything out! And I want you working on that book fast, so *you* don't forget all the details we've covered – more than half of which we've already blanked out!"

"I have to admit," added Kevin, "much as it's been a blast, Grandpa, it'll be nice to call Saturdays my own again!"

MISCELLANY

MORE MONEY
MANAGEMENT

CHAPTER TWENTY-NINE

INSURANCE DECISIONS

"I'm impressed, Jenny and Kevin! Nine Saturdays, and you're still keen to show up. It must be either the free lunch, or the fact that today is our final session!"

"I think it's a bit of both, Grandpa," quipped Jenny. "And thanks for lunch. We're definitely going to miss that part of our Saturday sessions."

"Let's go to the upper deck and enjoy the fresh air while we strain our brains once again."

....

"So far the subject of *insurance* has come up only in the very limited context of retirement strategies.

Yet, having an understanding of the various insurance products, and their pros and cons is extremely important. Insurance decisions are a key element of any Financial Plan.

The insurance decisions you make throughout your working life will have a material effect on:

- The financial risk to which you and/or your family are exposed in the event of a major illness, disability, or death;

- The cost that you incur for various insurance products.

Many of us give too little thought to the importance of insurance. As a result we often go through life either accepting an imprudent level of risk, or paying too much for the insurance products we do buy, *or* perhaps both."

....

"What comes to mind when you think of insurance?"

"Well, we can't drive without auto insurance," replied Jenny. "And I know our house is insured for all sorts of things like break-ins and fire damage, and other things I'm not sure about."

"And," added Kevin, "I know that on our family holidays, you always insisted on travel medical insurance. Oh, and Mom pays a ton of insurance on her daycare business."

"Good thinking, Kevin and Jenny. You've hit on a few important areas of insurance that no one should ignore. A few others as well, are worth investigating.

To examine why insurance plays such an important role in our lives, we need to:

- Understand the range of insurance products available;

- Reduce our various risks to acceptable levels;

- Obtain best-value from the insurance products we choose."

....

"There are several important *categories of insurance*. It's best to deal with each individually:

- Life Insurance
- Mortgage Insurance
- Disability Insurance
- Accidental Death Insurance
- Travel Medical Insurance
- Home Insurance"

1. LIFE INSURANCE

LIFE INSURANCE is purchased for the primary purpose of paying out a specified sum of money to a beneficiary, upon the death of the insured individual.

"Our most important considerations when purchasing life insurance are:

- Why, and when, do we need it?
- How much coverage do we need?
- What type should we buy?"

Why and When?

"For young, *single* persons like you two, it makes little sense to buy life insurance while you are still students, or just beginning your careers.

Many employers do in fact, provide some *basic* life insurance coverage for their permanent employees. If not, paying for life insurance at this stage of your life, is truly discretionary. In most cases it is unnecessary.

However, once we acquire a personal partner and begin to form a family unit, insurance is no longer an option. It is a *responsibility*. To ensure, in the event of our death, that our family can continue to meet its needs in comfort, each adult wage-earner in the family should carry an appropriate amount of life insurance.

As the years pass, children grow up, mortgages are paid off, and hopefully, investment portfolios grow to meaningful levels. The pressure to carry large life insurance policies gradually diminishes, but may not disappear entirely.

By the time retirement arrives, life insurance becomes very expensive. To hold it, once again becomes truly discretionary. One may *perhaps* choose insurance to provide cash to build estate value, or to pay taxes which may become due on death.

Insurance may become necessary in special circumstances, such as our being the sole provider for a disabled family member. Few of us however, *require* life insurance by the time we retire."

How Much Insurance is Enough?

"During the years when we're in the process of family formation and growth – usually our early 30's to perhaps mid-50's, we require the *maximum* life insurance coverage. Precisely how much of course, will vary with each family's specific situation.

You become a home owner, with a large mortgage and other debts. The very *least* life insurance coverage you ought to carry is a sum sufficient to liquidate *all* debts. *If* you have no children, if your partner has a good job, and is likely to carry on working after your death, then this debt-liquidation amount may suffice.

Children enter the picture. A larger vehicle is required. Child-care, education, and extra-curricular costs mount up. Clearly, more than basic debt-liquidation insurance is advisable. To fully replace your financial contribution to the family's welfare, it may be appropriate to have life insurance approximating fifteen times your annual salary.

For instance, you earn $40,000 annually, and you have a growing family. You might purchase a $600,000 life insurance policy. Although you hope it will never be collected, this sum, carefully invested by your family, should over the long-term, generate 6 to 7% annual return. This would effectively replace your lost income."

"I think I caught you, Grandpa!" exclaimed Kevin. "Shouldn't you first use the insurance proceeds to pay off all debts including the mortgage, *before* investing the balance?"

"Thanks for catching that, Kevin. What I was attempting to show, is that if invested, the $600,000 should replace the lost income, leaving the surviving spouse no worse off *financially*, than before the partner's death. But you're right – in most cases, paying off all debts should be a priority. By doing so you avoid all those compounding interest payments, and life is made somewhat easier going forward."

....

"As I mentioned moments ago, your employer *may* provide life insurance as an employee benefit. You would then purchase only the additional coverage necessary to reach your goal of, in this case, $600,000."

> TIP #109..... Each partner in a relationship, particularly when children are a consideration, should carry an appropriate life insurance policy, which on the death of either partner, will adequately protect the lifestyle of the family.

"All insurance payouts are *tax-exempt* in Canada. Once invested however, the proceeds of an insurance policy will, unless they are in an RRSP or TFSA account, attract tax on future earnings or growth.

This further emphasizes the point you made, Kevin. It is a key reason why the *first application of any insurance proceeds should tend to be debt-reduction.*"

What Type of Policy is Best?

"Most life-insurance policies fall into one of two broad categories:

· Term Life Insurance

· Permanent Life Insurance

a) Term Life Insurance

TERM LIFE INSURANCE provides a specified dollar amount payable upon the death of the holder. It is purchased for specific renewable time periods, or terms.

A *term life policy* is the cheapest form of life insurance for any age bracket.

A term policy expires, usually after a ten or twenty-year period. To renew a policy near the end of its term, the insured individual is generally required to re-qualify health-wise.

As we discussed earlier however, most life insurance needs decline as mortgages and debts are paid off, and children leave home. Although costs of these policies go up with age, the decline in coverage requirements can balance age-related price increases."

"How do you decide whether to purchase a ten or twenty-year policy, Grandpa?" asked Jenny.

"The twenty-year policy may cost you a little more, Jenny. That's because the insurance company must cover you for the full twenty years regardless of any changes in your health. So although it's a bit more costly, you are protected for a longer period. The decision becomes a judgement call for each individual – again dependent upon the specifics of the family situation, and the period over which coverage will be needed."

b) Permanent Life Insurance

PERMANENT LIFE INSURANCE combines a specified monetary death benefit with a tax-sheltered saving arrangement. The policy is designed to be purchased on an installment basis, throughout the holder's life. Often, the policy can be borrowed against, or even cashed in, but with specified penalties in early years.

"Due to the high commission paid for this type of product, the initial set-up fee and maintenance costs which are included in the premiums are very high.

Returns on the *savings* portion of this insurance product are difficult to calculate and can actually be negative *if* the policy is terminated in the first ten years. Even if held for most of your life, returns are usually much lower than can be achieved over the same extended time period, by your own investment portfolio."

....

"Why on earth would anyone buy this type of policy with all its costs and penalties?" asked Jenny.

"That's a good question, Jenny. Almost 50% of those who purchase a permanent life policy terminate it within ten years. Early termination often results in the policy-holder being charged more in penalties, than his total policy earnings up to that date."

"That makes it even stranger that they would buy into such a policy," added Jenny.

"So why, Grandpa, would they cash in their policy, and risk wasting those years of accumulated earnings?" asked Kevin.

"It could be for any number of reasons, Kevin, including the following:

- Changing financial circumstances of the policy-holder;

- Realization that the ongoing cost is very high, compared to term-life coverage;

- The lure of a significant cash payout, even after penalty deductions."

....

"Because a savings component is included in the premiums of this type of permanent life policy, the annual cost of the death benefit will be many times that of simple term insurance.

Given the policy-holder's other options for saving, such as through his RRSP or TFSA accounts, the much-promoted tax-free investment-growth feature of these insurance policies is of questionable value."

TIP #110..... When life insurance is required, a *term life insurance policy* will usually provide best value, at lowest cost. Because of the high cost of *permanent life policy* coverage, and the modest potential returns on its savings component, it is best to avoid combining a savings feature with a death-benefit policy.

"To be fair, permanent life insurance policies do have one key advantage. Regardless of future health issues of the insured, the insurance carrier cannot deny continuing coverage once the policy is purchased.

However, since *term policies* can be bought for ten or twenty-year terms, they should provide an adequate protection period for most of us.

A healthy 30-year-old, non-smoking Canadian can purchase a $600,000 term policy for a fixed 20-year term, for less than $500 a year.

The same coverage with a permanent life policy would likely cost several thousand dollars."

TIP #111..... Life insurance companies and their agents would much prefer to sell one of their permanent life products than a term policy. The permanent life policy generates both greater profit for the insurance company, and far higher commissions for the selling agent.

2. MORTGAGE INSURANCE

"If a Bank issues your mortgage, it will routinely offer you, the borrower, *mortgage life insurance.*

This may appear to make sense and be a great convenience. But this kind of insurance is almost always a poor deal for the borrower:

- As you make regular mortgage payments, the insured benefit decreases. However, your insurance premiums remain unchanged.

- The actual cost of the insurance is amortized over the life of your mortgage. Compounding over the amortization period greatly inflates the cost.

- Upon death of the insured, the insurance proceeds are paid directly to the Bank to liquidate the mortgage, rather than to the policy-holder.

- Should you wish to change mortgage providers at the end of the current mortgage term, your ability to make that change may be restricted. If your health has deteriorated, you may no longer be insurable."

TIP #112..... **The most economical and flexible means of providing necessary mortgage-insurance coverage, is to purchase a term-insurance policy large enough to cover mortgage debt as well as other financial needs of the beneficiary.**

"One caution is in order:

*In following this TIP, be sure you have adequate term insurance in place **prior to taking out a mortgage**. Tragic examples have occurred in which a well-intentioned* *mortgage-holder secured the mortgage first, and then died suddenly, before securing the necessary term-insurance coverage."*

3. DISABILITY INSURANCE

"A disturbing statistic offered by the **Canadian Life and Health Insurance Association** indicates that a 20-year-old Canadian is about three times more likely to suffer a disability lasting more than 90 days, than he is to die before age 65.

Furthermore, the study continues, once that disability occurs, it's likely to last for an average of three years."

"That would be terrible for anyone, regardless of age," exclaimed Jenny. "How would a person manage financially?"

"You're right, Jenny. In that dreadful situation, the last thing one needs is the added stress of financial issues.

If a disabled individual were to meet the federal government's very strict *permanent disability* definition, he may become eligible for a maximum disability payment of approximately $1,200 per month – not very much if that's all he has to replace lost income."

"$1,200 a month wouldn't go far toward his rent or mortgage payments, not to mention basics like groceries," observed Kevin.

"Unless at the time the disability occurs, the individual is working for an employer with an adequate employee-disability program, an extended period of disability is an area of major vulnerability for the average Canadian and his family."

TIP #113..... **During years of family formation and growth, Canadians should weigh the risk of disability against the cost of adequate disability insurance.**

"Because the risk of disability is greater than the risk of death, the cost of disability insurance is significant. However, for those without coverage through their employer, it should be seriously considered."

4. ACCIDENTAL-DEATH INSURANCE

"Because of the relatively low risk of accidental death, insurance coverage for this eventuality is relatively inexpensive. Despite the low cost, accidental-death insurance generally represents poor value.

Death of a loved one, whether sudden or due to prolonged illness, is traumatic for survivors. Regardless of cause, survivors suffer *no greater financial impact* from a sudden, accidental death, than they do from a health-related one. The greater economic cost to a family is likely in fact, to be from a debilitating illness leading to death."

TIP #114..... **The individual who feels that he requires accidental-death insurance probably has inadequate term life insurance. Sufficient life insurance should exist, to cover *any* cause of death.**

"So I guess you'd tell us to ignore those tempting, low-cost mailers offering accidental death insurance," mused Jenny. "You'd say to spend our money on term life and disability insurance. Do I have Grandpa pegged, Kevin?"

"Yeah, that's Grandpa. But what about the insurance we always buy when we travel?" asked Kevin. "What's that for?"

5. TRAVEL-MEDICAL INSURANCE

"I'm glad you reminded me about travel insurance, Kevin. It's a very important topic. My concern isn't accidental death while travelling, but sudden illness or injury.

Compared to the huge risk of out-of-country medical costs, especially for travel in the United States, the *low* cost of travel-medical insurance is by any measure, an absolute bargain – *and* an absolute necessity."

TIP #115..... For travel outside one's country, the travel budget should *always* include an allowance for travel-medical insurance.

"NO one expects a medical emergency to arise when they travel, but it can.

Frightening examples exist of needless financial disasters related to health emergencies. Even at home, many U.S. citizens have been forced to declare personal bankruptcy due to the high cost of their uninsured medical services.

For foreigners visiting the U.S., costs skyrocket for those who need sudden medical care while visiting. Bills for hundreds of thousands of dollars for a several-week hospital stay are not uncommon.

Never take the chance – *always* insure yourself and everyone in your family against this risk *every* time you leave Canada, even for a day-trip."

"I remember," recalled Jenny, "when Grandma took us across the border for a day of shopping. You helped us buy medical insurance, and you didn't even complain about having to pay for the minimum three-day coverage."

"Now you know why, Jenny. Taking the risk is simply not worth the very few dollars invested to insure against it."

....

Here's an example of the very real benefits that can result if you should be unfortunate enough to have to draw on such insurance coverage.

*Friends Lorne and Lori purchased an **RBC Travel Medical** policy prior to their visit to the Dominican Republic.*

One week into their holiday, Lori experienced severe pains in her right side. She needed emergency surgery to remove her appendix.

After advising the insurance company of the situation, our friends received full reimbursement of the ambulance cost, the operation, and the hospital stay. Additionally, the insurance paid for a one-week extension of their hotel stay. Once Lori was fit to travel, the policy provided two first-class tickets back to Canada.

The medical insurance cost them less than $150. It saved them over $30,000 in costs."

"You've convinced us, Grandpa," assured Kevin. "We won't leave the country without medical insurance! Right, Jenny?"

6. HOME INSURANCE

"Your home is probably the most valuable asset you will ever own. Given that fact, it makes sense for you, a prudent homeowner, to accept home insurance as a mandatory, budgeted expense.

Insuring a $300,000 asset against most risks, usually for much less than $1,000 annually, provides very important protection – *and* peace-of-mind."

....

"Insurance costs can be drastically reduced by keeping your *deductible* at a high level, perhaps $1,000.

With a lower $500 deductible, I would think twice before making an insurance claim, even were my home to suffer an unexpected loss of around $1,000 in value. If for example, a policy holder registers two or three small claims within a five-year period, many insurance companies will either increase your rates dramatically, or even be reluctant to renew the policy.

It's wise to avoid making relatively minor claims. It's best to hold home insurance as a reserve for *major* losses that you hope will never arise. With this logic in mind, it is generally to your advantage to opt for a higher-deductible, pay less for the policy, and save money."

....

TIP #116..... **Regardless of the insurance product you decide to purchase, do so only after researching all options. Consider the cost of prudent levels of insurance coverage to be part of a sound financial plan.**

"And *that* is the essence of my advice on the subject of insurance."

"Grandpa, I notice you haven't discussed regular health insurance. Why?" inquired Kevin.

"You're right, Kevin. I purposely didn't talk about it because in Canada, we're extremely fortunate. Regardless of the province in which we live, we're covered automatically by a universal health-care program.

Premium costs are extremely modest, and are waived for those with a lower income. Many employers in fact may pay part, or even all of the annual premium.

Essentially, health-care insurance is a non-issue for Canadians. In the U.S. on the other hand, premium costs are very high. Despite recent efforts by "Obama Care", millions of Americans still lack *any* health insurance coverage."

"That would be scary," commented Jenny.

....

"Let's take a break and stretch out the kinks. Here we are talking about health, and my back is seizing up from all this sitting.

Then we'll talk briefly about the **Registered Disability Savings Plan (RDSP)**, recently made available by the federal government."

CHAPTER THIRTY

REGISTERED DISABILITY SAVINGS PLAN (RDSP)

"Since disability is such a significant risk factor for Canadians, the Canadian government established in late 2008, a Registered Disability Savings Plan (RDSP), designed specifically to assist those with serious disabilities.

Like both the RRSP and RESP, the RDSP is another tax-deferred savings vehicle. It is however, designed specifically to assist families planning for the long-term financial security of a seriously-disabled person.

Relatives or friends can contribute to an RDSP on behalf of a disabled individual, defined as anyone who is eligible for the federal *Disability Tax Credit*.

There are no annual limits on contributions. However, a $200,000 lifetime contribution limit does exist.

Depending on the contributor's net income, the government will contribute from $1 to $3, for every dollar of the first $1,000 contributed annually.

Like an RRSP or an RESP, funds may be placed in most investment products.

Also like an RRSP and an RESP, the RDSP permits funds to be invested tax-free until withdrawn.

The specific rules governing an RDSP are complex. They can be downloaded from the government website by googling ***Registered Disability Savings Plan***.

Canada has some 500,000 seriously-disabled residents. The RDSP provides not only a huge potential safeguard for them, but also relief for their family and friends' peace of mind, with respect to their long-term care and comfort."

"That's an incredible number of disabled people in Canada," commented Jenny. "I can now appreciate how both disability insurance *and* an RDSP can be very helpful."

"You're right, Jenny. And now, let's turn briefly to a happier challenge – how to best manage an inheritance."

. . . .

CHAPTER THIRTY-ONE

MAKING THE MOST OF AN INHERITANCE

"Canada's seniors population is *increasing* at a rapid rate. As a result, the next several decades will see a huge transfer of wealth from this aging sector of our population to the next generation. Many Canadians will suddenly become recipients of significant sums of tax-free funds or other assets, during this period.

Regardless of its value, an inheritance if handled wisely, represents a significant opportunity for the recipient to accelerate his net-worth growth.

So, what should the grateful, but prudent beneficiary do with his windfall?"

"Keep going, Grandpa," responded Kevin. "We know by now, that you don't ask a question without also having an answer."

"You think you know me well, don't you? Well, as it happens, I do have some suggestions."

1. Pay Off Miscellaneous Debts

"Remember in our early discussions, we agreed that the best guaranteed return is achieved by paying off debts and eliminating interest charges, particularly on charge cards of any kind? Starting with your highest-interest debt, paying off all outstanding balances should be a first priority."

2. Indulge Yourself – A Little

"Other than perhaps your mortgage, once your debts are cleared there's nothing wrong with spoiling yourself. Go for it – take that long-dreamed-of vacation; sell the rust-bucket and finally buy a new car.

As you indulge yourself however, keep in the back of your mind, an awareness of how difficult it normally is to accumulate the sum of money you are planning to spend on spoiling yourself. Make sure there is not a more urgent *need* or use for those funds."

3. Assist Family

"If the inheritance is large enough, nothing makes one feel better than helping members of the family toward for instance, a down payment on a home, or education costs. Remember however, whatever you do for one, be prepared to do for all. Depending on family size, and the amount of your inheritance, you may have to settle for giving each family member a sum of money, to spend as each sees fit."

4. Pay-Off or Pay-Down Your Mortgage

"Because mortgage-loan repayment stretches over many years, the total interest payments, even at relatively low rates, amount to a huge sum. Perhaps you will be able to pay off the entire mortgage. If not, paying it down as much as you can, will greatly shorten the amortization period, thereby saving you many thousands of dollars in future interest costs.

Some will argue that they might be better off to *not* pay down the mortgage. They would suggest instead that they invest the remainder of the inheritance, to take advantage of the proven power of *compounding*."

"What would *you* do, Grandpa?" asked Kevin.

"Without hesitation, I would pay off the mortgage. I would *then* divert the same monthly amount I had been paying on the mortgage to my long-term investment account. By adding for example, $1,000 a month to my regular *Pay Yourself First* wealth-building account, my portfolio value would rapidly skyrocket.

That way, I would get the best of both worlds – avoiding the negative effect of compounding interest charges on my mortgage debt, while accelerating my wealth-building plan, with its positive compounding benefits.

Remember also, investing on a regular *monthly* basis averages your purchase-price over the long term. On the other hand, were you to suddenly invest a single large sum, you would be buying in at whatever price level the market happened to be, on the day of purchase."

5. Invest The Balance

"Your inheritance may have been large enough to allow you to pay off debt, treat yourself and family, become mortgage-free, and *still* leave you with a substantial sum.

Topping up to the maximum limits of your RRSP and TFSA, regardless of specific investments within those vehicles, seems an obvious priority.

Consider consulting an *independent* financial advisor, *before* the actual investment of that balance. With the advisor's input, your first task should be to update your financial plan.

The advisor will help you refine your goals and your strategy for achieving them. He will assist you in making sound investment decisions in the most tax-efficient manner, in a way that appropriately complements and balances your current portfolio."

> TIP #117..... A substantial inheritance represents a golden opportunity to propel net worth upward – if it is allocated prudently. Avoid snap decisions. Seek independent advice. Carefully assess and select options which achieve the greatest possible, long-term benefit.

....

"Having to make the right decisions about *any* windfall, let alone a substantial one, would be a sweet problem to have, wouldn't it, Grandpa?" asked Jenny.

"You're right, Jenny. It *could* be a marvelous gift. Sadly though, more than a few of us really mishandle the opportunity presented by an inheritance. Too often, we end up with little long-term benefit from our windfall. It's a similar situation for lottery winners. Some handle it well; others, very poorly.

I have no doubt however, that with your and Kevin's new insight and interest in everything we've discussed, you would both handle the challenge very well."

"The mere thought of you haunting us in our sleep would keep us on track, Grandpa," assured Kevin. "That's a given."

CHAPTER THIRTY-TWO

....

THE LATE-STARTER INVESTOR

"I'm sure you both know individuals or families who, for one reason or another, have not yet managed to take full advantage of the investment magic of time-and-compounding. Because their financial road up to now has been bumpy, it does *not* mean they should give up on building their retirement nest-egg.

Age 40 is still a reasonable time to start our *Pay Yourself First* saving and investment strategy. Obviously, with less time for the benefits of compounding, either the final portfolio value will be less, or regular contributions to invested savings will have to be much higher than those of a 25-year old – *if* one wishes to achieve a similar end result.

Even at age 50, it is *not* too late to begin a retirement savings program. Consider this. By age 50, one's children are usually grown and for the most part, self-sufficient. Many 55-year olds have paid off their mortgage, or are close to doing so. Incomes are reaching peak earning levels. The combination of some or all of these factors should allow the *determined* individual or couple in this age bracket to fast-track the process, contributing very significant monthly amounts to their portfolio.

Starting an investment portfolio later in life however, will probably entail a lifestyle change. Success will be dependent on:

- Less spending and more saving;
- Less self-indulgence;
- Strong willpower.

Regardless of age however, the critical first step, is to develop a *personal financial plan*."

"I'll finish your thought, Grandpa," added Jenny, "...with both a specific objective, and a road map detailing how to achieve it!"

....

Let's revisit the **Banks** family whom we met early in our sessions. They're the couple who were deeply in credit card debt. It took them almost six years to pay it off, but they learned their lesson well.

Now, as they near their 50's, the Banks have finally paid off their mortgage, and are substantially debt-free.

- *They have a combined annual income of $80,000.*

- *Their recently-liquidated mortgage payments amounted to $1,500 per month.*

- *Having focused, after their early hard lessons, solely on debt liquidation, together they currently have only a modest $50,000 in their RRSPs to supplement their future CPP and OAS pensions.*

- *They each have accumulated over $50,000 of unused capacity in their RRSPs.*

- *They each have at least $10,000 of available contribution allowance in their TFSAs.*

- *Neither of them belongs to an employer-sponsored pension plan.*

- *Their net-worth is $600,000; however, $550,000 of that is the equity in their paid-off home.*

*The Banks' retirement plans are now becoming a compelling priority. They realize they **must** add substantially to their savings, if they are to have a comfortable retirement."*

....

"What can they do?" queried Kevin. "With only about 15 years to save and invest, how much might they reasonably accumulate by age 65?"

"Realistically, Kevin, you're correct to use 15 years as the Banks' saving and investment horizon. Their likelihood of an earlier retirement is slim.

Without crimping their current lifestyle, they can clearly divert to their savings and investment accounts, the $1,500 that they had been paying monthly on their mortgage. If they can afford a few hundred dollars more, even better. But for now, let's assume that only $1,500 will be saved and invested monthly.

Because of their age, the Banks' simple investment portfolio should probably be more conservative than that of 30-year olds.

A 65% equity and 35% fixed-income split, with an anticipated average annual return of 6%, might be prudent for their initial investment and planning purposes. This of course, is dependent on their personal levels of risk-tolerance.

Since neither partner has an employer-sponsored pension, their RRSP entitlement is significant. This allows them to hold all investments in their RRSPs. Their combined annual tax refund, estimated at $6,000, can be ploughed back as more RRSP contributions or, as we'll assume, will be invested in their respective tax-free TFSAs.

....

Fifteen years later, when the Banks reach age 65, their strategy should have produced a combined portfolio value approximating:

- In their RRSPs - $491,000

- In their TFSAs - $126,000

Total savings accumulated: $617,000

Even if their home value has not increased over that 15-year period, these investment values, when added to their previous home equity of $550,000, indicate that their net-worth at age 65 should be around $1.17 million – perhaps more, depending on the amount home values would have actually increased.

Without adjusting for inflation, the $617,000 in their investment accounts, assuming a more conservative 5% return during their retirement years, would allow the Banks at age 65, to begin withdrawing approximately $3,300 per month, every month for the next 30 years.

When this investment income is *added* to the inflation-adjusted $2,800 per month they expect to draw from their combined CPP and OAS, their total monthly income of $6,100 will be close to their current gross income.

An added bonus will be that all income from their TFSAs will be tax-free. Also, as seniors, they will enjoy many tax breaks that will enhance their disposable income – perhaps by enough to counter the effect of inflation.

Despite waiting until age 50 to seriously begin building a retirement fund, the Banks *should* in fact be able to enjoy a very comfortable retirement."

TIP #118..... While it is best to become a saver/investor early in life, it is never too late to start building an investment portfolio.

"Wow, Grandpa. That's amazing!" exclaimed Jenny. "I would *never* have guessed you could accumulate so much in just fifteen years."

"And remember, Jenny, because the Banks achieved this *exclusively* by diverting their previous mortgage payments to savings and investments, it was all accomplished with *no* change in their lifestyle.

The Banks' success was due to the combined effect of determination, commitment, and a hefty monthly investment. They learned their lesson well. They invested their tax refunds instead of spending them, and they let the power of time and compounding work its magic."

. . . .

"Wow! That's so unbelievably impressive," exclaimed Kevin. "I don't get why *everyone* doesn't do something like this. What am I missing?"

"Well, Kevin, the answer is usually a combination of factors:

- The ever-present lure of spending on instant gratification, rather than planning for the future;

- Lack of discipline in adopting and sticking to a **Pay Yourself First** savings plan;

- Taking foolish investment risks, or entrusting investment portfolios to those who charge high fees, often despite achieving inferior results;

- Not comprehending the tremendous boost to portfolio growth that flows from the combined effect of time and compounding."

. . . .

"Grandpa, something's been on my mind all these weeks. How are we supposed to enjoy ourselves without feeling guilty, if our focus always has to be on saving money?" asked Jenny.

"Jenny, you don't have to *focus* on saving at all. With our **Pay Yourself First** plan, saving becomes an automatic process. Remember too, even when you're saving 10% of your income, you still have another 90% to live on.

I would *never* want anyone to deprive himself of a comfortable lifestyle. But I firmly believe that most Canadians can live very well on 90% of their income.

I also believe that if carefully applied, the TIPS I've shared with you will save an average family much more than the 10% we've talked about regularly saving and investing."

TIP #119..... While living for today, we cannot afford to forget about tomorrow. Our retirement years may well be more than one-third of our life. It's well-worth planning for, to make sure those years are golden.

....

"Aside from addressing any final questions or topics you might want me to touch on, I have only one subject left to cover before we finish our marathon sessions."

"One last subject, Kevin! Is that music to your ears or what?" exulted Jenny.

"Because of the extensive downward slide which took place in the world's equity markets between mid-2008 and Spring, 2009, some investors and even some advisors have begun to question the previously proven *Buy and Hold* investing strategy, which we discussed a great deal during our sessions.

It's important to examine whether, in light of these events of 2008 and 2009, the *Buy and Hold* strategy remains valid."

"Good idea, Grandpa," replied Jenny. "I had actually meant to ask you that when we were talking about investments, but I forgot."

CHAPTER THIRTY-THREE

....

BUY AND HOLD STRATEGY – A RETHINK?

"As you couldn't have failed to notice throughout our discussions, I've actively promoted the **BUY and HOLD** strategy for **long-term** equity capital appreciation. This strategy has proven itself to be extremely effective over many decades.

As we discussed in our very first session, stock markets world-wide dropped precipitously during the nine-month period from mid-2008 to Spring, 2009 – many by well over 50%. Canada's stock market did not escape. It too nose-dived approximately 50% in value over this short period.

At the same time, real-estate markets plummeted around the world. In the U.S., the results were catastrophic – on average, well over 25%. In Canada luckily, our lending practices were much more stringent. Declines in house prices also occurred, but for the most part, were much more modest, averaging less than 10% nationally. Furthermore, by the end of 2009, Canadian residential real estate had on average, recovered to previous levels.

The combined short-term effect of these two simultaneous events caused the net-worth of Canadians to decline *drastically*. In interviews and in publications, some financial analysts and advisors began to question whether the traditional *buy and hold* strategies were still valid."

....

"Without a doubt, many investors suffered a major setback. Those approaching retirement, with a large proportion of their investments in equities, were seriously impacted. A good number of those investors may well have had to delay their planned retirement date."

"But, Grandpa, I thought you told us for this very reason, that if you're approaching retirement you should have no more than about 50% of your total investments in equities. Wouldn't that have been enough protection?" inquired Jenny.

"You're right, Jenny. Certainly for those fortunate to have a good employer-sponsored pension plan, it probably *is* enough protection. With such a solid pension-income safety-net, there is no immediate pressure to draw on investments. Equity markets always recover. It's only a matter of *how quickly*."

....

"Even in Canadian stock markets, strong signs of financial recovery began in fact, to emerge by March, 2009. The S&P TSX Index began rising, and within two months, had increased by some 30% from its lows."

"Hey, Grandpa," interjected Kevin, "did you bring this up as an example of how trying to *time* the equities market can cause an investor to lose out?"

"I sure did, Kevin."

*Meet **Bert**, a keen but impatient investor. Frustrated and frightened by falling market values, he felt the need to act. Thinking he could shrewdly buy back in when the market had turned up again, Bert sold his high-quality equity portfolio in February, 2009 – just **before** the market upturn began!*

The market turn, when it happened, was very rapid with no assurance that it was to be long-lasting. Many investors like Bert would have remained on the sidelines, waiting until the trend became more definite.

By the time it was crystal clear that the upswing really *was* the beginning of a major recovery, Bert had not only incurred losses when he sold, but had also missed out on very substantial gains."

"I know exactly where you're heading with this, Grandpa," exclaimed Kevin.

"And where would that be, Kevin?"

"Except for rebalancing his portfolio, Bert should have stayed put. He was in for the long-term, but instead decided to try to outguess the market," replied Kevin.

"Exactly, Kevin. Trying to time the market is rarely successful. By rebalancing his portfolio, Bert would have cashed in some rising bond values and used the proceeds to buy more bargain-basement equities. Remember our *sell-high, buy-low* rule which is an automatic by-product of rebalancing?"

"Well," added Jenny, "he probably didn't have a grandfather with tons of free advice."

....

"So, Grandpa, as a result of this 2008/09 market-meltdown, would you advise us to change any of our earlier investment strategies?" asked Kevin. "What about *Buy-and-Hold*? Would you change any of it at all?"

"Thanks for bringing me back, Kevin, to the very question I wanted to answer in the first place.

Rather than suggesting a *change* in strategy, I think recent events emphasize several of the strategies we have previously embraced:

- Within ten years of planned retirement, one is wise to ensure that he moves to a much more *conservative balance* in his investment portfolio. Even a 50/50 investment split between equities and fixed-income products *may* be too aggressive, *if* the individual plans to start drawing significant income from investments immediately upon retirement.

*Some advisors recommend that the percentage of bonds or bond funds in your total portfolio should **equal** your age.*

- If reassessment of risk results in a decision to rebalance the portfolio toward a smaller percentage in equities, it should be done gradually, perhaps over the entire 10-year period leading to retirement. This will, in effect, average-out over ten years, the equity selling price. It will avoid the risk of selling during a major market downturn, such as that of 2008/2009.

- Particularly critical as one approaches retirement, is to have one's equity investments in primarily high-quality, *dividend-paying* products. In good times, annual dividends add greatly to the portfolio's growth. During market downturns, they have a major moderating effect on portfolio declines."

....

"Many **Canadian Dividend ETFs** are available. They offer an annual dividend stream, often payable monthly. The annual *MER* is typically less than *0.6*.

If set up as a **Dividend Reinvestment Plan (DRIP)**, this results in automatic reinvestment of all dividends, resulting in the accumulation of even more units in the fund. This in turn leads to even more dividends being paid."

"Cool! A great dividend, happily multiplying like rabbits over many years, would sure help the portfolio value a lot," enthused Kevin. "I could go for that."

"I'm thinking that you've probably taken your own advice and bought ETFs like these, Grandpa," observed Jenny. "Did you buy some for our investment accounts?"

"You're on the ball, Jenny. Not only did I buy such ETFs for you and Kevin, but I also bought them for Great-Grandma, Grandma, and myself!"

"Wow, *that's* putting your money where your mouth is!" observed Kevin.

"I simply couldn't resist the opportunity to be invested in so many of the best companies in Canada, while earning a good dividend. By doing so, I've achieved:

· Broad diversification,
· High quality,
· High yield,
· Excellent growth potential.

All this in one low-cost investment product."

....

"Does that mean, Grandpa," asked Jenny, "that if an investor buys such ETFs today, he'll always get the same dividend, *plus* any increase in the market value of the ETF itself?"

"Not exactly, Jenny. Remember, an ETF will hold investments in many individual companies. Periodically, each reviews its dividend-payout capability. Most will maintain the status quo. Others will increase dividends; some will decrease them. Although it's highly unlikely that the *average* dividend payment would change drastically, it definitely will not remain precisely the same.

While there is *no guarantee* that these dividends will not change in the future, it's exactly this kind of highly-diversified, index-based, income-producing investment, that goes a long way toward *moderating* an equity investor's risk.

And now.... My very last TIP:"

TIP #120..... In making investment decisions, every investor must always consider his personal time horizon and level of risk-tolerance. In full recognition that a major equity-market correction *will* occur some time in the future, his ultimate investment decisions should err on the conservative side of his comfort level.

....

"So, to repeat myself, I remain a firm supporter of the '**Buy and Hold**' strategy for equity investments."

"So if the investor puts as much thought and research into his *original* investment and asset allocation decisions, as he does his hockey pool, he'd be a lot better off," clarified Kevin.

"You're right, Kevin, the soundness of a *'Buy and Hold'* strategy is very much dependent on *what you have bought and what you are holding*."

"Sticking to your original strategy is such a relief, Grandpa!" exclaimed Jenny. "I was afraid we'd have to become familiar with a totally new approach. So what you're saying, is that by being really careful in initial investment decisions and using rebalancing, we can really moderate the risks, and ride out the market fluctuations."

"That's how I hear it too, Jenny. But I think Grandpa's also saying that the investor can't lose track of his investment *time-frame*. As he closes in on retirement, he needs to gradually shift from more volatile equity products, into more boring but more predictable, fixed-income products," added Kevin.

"These Saturday sessions have really paid off. I can tell you've both been listening. You've summarized my advice as well as I could! – and you're speaking a whole new language!"

....

"The very last thing to do is to ask if there are any major questions or ambiguities to clear up. Anything at all?"

"Well, Grandpa, one thing still confuses me. If I *do* want to use the famous '*Couch Potato*' investment strategy, I haven't much clue how stock markets work, or how I would actually go about buying various ETFs, Index Funds, Bonds, GICs, or other products. Could you quickly clarify that for me?"

"Sure, Kevin, I'll be glad to. What about you, Jenny? Any lingering questions or concerns?"

"Just one, Grandpa. I know we spent some time talking about the importance of using a truly *independent* financial planner or advisor. And I accept the logic. What I don't understand is exactly how would I go about finding such an individual. Where would I look? I can't find any listings in the yellow pages, or on the web for that matter, which would point me in the right direction."

"That's a really good question, Jenny. Why don't I cover off Kevin's question first? Then I'll handle yours, before we wrap up."

"Sounds good, Grandpa," responded Jenny.

CHAPTER THIRTY-FOUR

PURCHASE and/or SALE of INVESTMENT PRODUCTS

"Kevin, let's start to answer your questions by gaining some insight into Canadian stock market exchanges.

The TMX group is an umbrella company that owns and operates both the **Toronto Stock Exchange (TSX)** and the **TSX Venture Exchange**. If you are purchasing or selling Canadian stocks, the transaction will occur on one of these two exchanges.

The TORONTO STOCK EXCHANGE (TSX) is a world-class capital market which provides mature Canadian companies access to new capital, as well as providing an efficient mechanism for investors to buy and sell equities.

The TSX VENTURE EXCHANGE provides access to capital for early-stage Canadian companies, as well as a well-regulated mechanism for the purchase or sale of shares in such companies."

"So, Grandpa, am I right in thinking those risky *penny stocks*, which we briefly discussed, will be on the Venture Exchange?"

"Yes, Kevin. That's where most will be listed."

STOCK TRADING

"When an individual wishes to buy or sell equities, he himself **cannot** access one of these exchanges to execute the transaction.

Securities legislation requires that such trades be handled only by legally-licensed **brokerage firms** and their licensed **brokers**.

These firms and their brokers charge a *commission* for their services. Part of the commission cost will go to the exchange handling the transaction.

Whether you buy or sell an ETF or a stock on an exchange, you will be assessed a commission by the **broker** who made the trade for you. That commission cost can be relatively insignificant, *or* quite substantial, depending on which brokerage service you are using.

If you choose to use a *full-service* broker at a major, bank-owned brokerage house for example, your commission can amount to several hundred dollars on a $10,000 transaction.

On the other hand, you may opt to set up an *online* trading account with a *discount broker*, also often owned by the bank. The same trade executed on your behalf, could cost you as little as $4.95.

The difference, aside from the dramatic commission cost, is that with the discount brokerage service you will receive no personal advice or input. *You* are the researcher and the decision-maker."

"Wow, that's quite a cost difference!" exclaimed Jenny.

"It is, Jenny, but remember, if you are a novice, the extra human input and advice may be worth the one-time higher commission cost. Furthermore if you recall, the wise investor invests for the long-term. He's not flipping in and out of investments trying to outguess the market in the short term. So the higher, very infrequent trading cost may not be that significant. For some, the extra service is worthwhile.

If however, you are working with an independent financial advisor to assist you in making the right investment decisions, the online discount-brokerage arrangement should be all that you require."

....

"Is it the same, Grandpa, for buying or selling bonds or bond funds? Do we use the same brokerage system?" inquired Kevin.

BOND TRADING

"When we wish to buy or sell an individual bond, the process is not as straightforward as it is with stocks, where we can access a real-time *quote* on a stock exchange.

There is no such thing as a bond exchange, accessible by the retail market. Bonds are traded at the wholesale level through **brokerage houses** acting as buyers and sellers. They will obtain a quote for you and handle the transaction, with no *visible* cost to the retail customer.

As a buyer or seller of individual bonds you are charged a fee; you just don't see it. The broker retains a portion of the transaction value as his fee. In absolute terms the charge may be relatively small, but it is not insignificant.

An excellent *online* site to assist you in making a bond selection, and for checking your broker's quotation against latest wholesale prices, is **www.canadianfixedincome.ca**. By making your broker aware that you are tuned in to the wholesale price, you may receive a sharper price quote."

....

"Would buying an *ETF bond fund* on the stock exchange, using an online discount broker, not avoid this hidden cost, Grandpa?" asked Jenny.

"Yes it would, Jenny. You're on the ball. But remember there are pros and cons to holding bonds compared to bond funds, all of which we discussed. Before selecting one or the other, you would have to be sure that the decision is compatible with your financial plan and your risk profile."

MUTUAL FUND MARKET

"As we discussed, in Canada alone, hundreds of companies offer mutual fund products, both actively and passively-managed.

In each of these two categories several thousand fund options are available to Canadians.

Actively-managed funds are easily identifiable through online inquiry for any investment sector you wish to specify. Many fund managers will sell their product to you directly through their own sales force, or through the same full-service broker we talked about earlier.

Remember my big red flag – investigate thoroughly, the *high costs of these funds relative to their performance.*"

....

"If, as is *my* preference, you select only *passively-managed funds* through *index funds* or *ETFs*, your choice is straightforward, and your costs very low.

Index funds will generally be available through, and managed by, banks. ETFs, as we discussed, can be bought and sold like a stock, on the stock exchange."

GICs and T-BILLS

"Along with setting up basic or high-interest savings accounts, GICs and T-Bills can be bought directly at most major financial institutions in a very straightforward manner."

....

"I hope this answers your broad question, Kevin, on how and where you as an individual can access these various investment products. Are you left with any remaining questions on this topic?"

"I think I understand it better now, Grandpa." replied Kevin. "But I do have one last question. What in the world are a *'Bull Market'* and a *'Bear Market'* that I hear about quite often?"

"A really good question, Kevin! I should have defined these terms earlier.

A BULL MARKET is a prolonged period in which investment values on a major stock exchange – like the TSX – rise faster than their historical average.

A BEAR MARKET is a prolonged period in which investment values fall, accompanied by widespread pessimism.

If the period of falling stock prices is short and follows closely after a longer period of rising stock values, it is instead called a **market correction**.

Bear markets usually occur when the economy is in a recession and unemployment is high, or when inflation seems out of control.

The most dramatic bear market was the world-wide Great Depression of the 1930's which lasted a full decade, until World War II sparked an economic recovery."

"Thanks, Grandpa. That helps a lot. Now I understand what you mean when you say you're feeling *'bullish'* about a particular investment."

CHAPTER THIRTY-FIVE

SELECTING A FINANCIAL PLANNER / ADVISOR

"Now to your question, Jenny. How to find and select that independent financial planner or advisor.

Remember what we previously discussed? A truly *independent* financial advisor receives compensation only from the fee that you pay for his advice.

He does not sell investment products, nor does he receive commissions as a result of your purchase of any investment product that he has recommended.

Your ultimate test therefore, of a potential advisor, is to receive assurance that he really does meet this criterion of true independence."

WHERE TO LOOK

"As is usually the case, personal recommendations from friends or acquaintances who have successfully used the services of an independent, fee-for-service planner, will be your best starting point.

"Unfortunately, very few of us insist that this *independence* test be met. Therefore few of us retain the services of an advisor who meets this stiff truly-independent criterion. This lack of consumer demand also helps explain why relatively few independent advisors are to be found. But they do exist.

The web may yield some results. You may however have to dig beyond the advertisement. A few advisors do indeed highlight their total independence. Most of the ads you will encounter will feature so called '*Full-Service*' firms and advisors. Because of the inherent conflict-of-interest under which most usually operate, I have avoided starting out with a full-service advisor.

I use the word *generally*, because exceptions do exist.

One 'Wealth Manager' whom I encountered works with a major, national brokerage firm. He offers all his clients a straight 1% 'fee-for-service' arrangement. His fee covers all planning assistance, portfolio structuring and management, and all trading commissions on products he purchases on a client's behalf.

This approach is most often available to higher-net-worth individuals with large investment accounts. What surprised me, was that this individual offered the same structure to even fairly modest-value account holders. Furthermore, he shared my antipathy for actively-managed mutual funds. Instead, he preferred to invest his clients primarily in a basket of low-cost ETFs.

I also met some of his clients – all of whom seemed very happy with his service.

While I was pleasantly surprised to encounter such an individual, he is definitely an exception, not often encountered within a major brokerage firm."

....

"A possible advisor option attractive to some investors is **Edward Jones** or **Raymond James**. Their offices are found in virtually every community. Although head-office-supported with excellent research, these are boutique, *'one person'* offices. As such they present the investor with the opportunity to receive very personalized, well-researched service, *always* from the same advisor who has a significant vested interest in the long-term success of *his* office.

Those who opt to use such a firm's services will be charged a 'full-service' level of trading commission. However, if one follows the 'couch potato' strategy, such commission costs will be infrequent and generally very minor in the total scheme of things.

I suspect in this case, that it will be the personal characteristics of the individual advisor, which will determine whether or not he meets *your* expectation of independence."

THE RIGHT FIT

"A prospective advisor has been recommended to you. You've checked his references, and found them to be more than satisfactory.

You now meet with the advisor for *the* interview. Aside from the obvious – professionalism, smarts, discipline, and effective communication – what do you look for?"

"Well, wouldn't you want to explore whether or not the advisor fits in with *your* planning and investment needs and philosophy?" asked Jenny.

"Exactly, Jenny. If you're looking to be *an equal partner* in the process of planning and investment, you certainly don't want an advisor who is less than open-minded to that approach.

Also, you want to make sure that you are comfortable with the individual on a personal level. Do you *click* – are you speaking the same language? Does he really listen to your concerns and needs? Does he respond to them appropriately?

. . . .

The prospective advisor passes these tests. But I have two final hurdles I like to apply:

- A review of the ***performance reports*** you can expect to receive on *your* portfolio – will these reports provide you with a good insight into how *your* portfolio is performing, relative to *meaningful* benchmarks?

- How available, and how attentive can you expect the advisor to be? Will you be one of hundreds of clients vying for his attention; or will you be able to drop in or call whenever you feel the need? Will you be able to thoroughly discuss your issues or concerns?

Over the years I have encountered numerous investors who have felt neglected by a 'name' brokerage house. In their opinion, the lack of attention was due to their modest-value portfolio which clearly did not merit the attention of the higher-net-worth clients."

....

"If any of these tests applied to a prospective advisor are not met – keep looking!

You must be totally comfortable with the individual you select to advise you on the achievement of your financial goals. He must meet all your needs and expectations.

If your financial advisor fails to meet your reasonable expectations, even after you have clearly communicated your concerns – look for a new advisor."

"I would guess, Grandpa," suggested Kevin, "that if you retain a totally independent 'fee-for-service' advisor, *and* you do your own plan-implementation, then you're less likely to be uncomfortable with your advisor. Is this right?"

"Yes it is, Kevin, at least in the sense that you are receiving independent advice that you can take or leave, *and* you control the implementation and future management process. This means you are not locked-in to a long-term advisory relationship, unless you *choose* to be."

"I still think *my* solution is best, Grandpa," crowed Jenny. "I've already selected my advisor – a wise old goat – you! The advice is sound; the availability is excellent; and you can't beat the price!"

"Can't beat that strategy!" added Kevin.

FINAL WISDOM

. . . .

CHAPTER THIRTY-SIX

KEY STEPS TO WEALTH-CREATION – A SUMMARY

"Well, Jenny and Kevin, we've climbed a virtual mountain in only nine Saturdays. Along the way, I've tried to share with you some key concepts associated with successful wealth-creation."

"Please don't tell us there's a test, Grandpa," begged Jenny.

"It won't be that bad, Jenny," reassured Kevin. "Knowing Grandpa, I bet he's going to remind us again of the main points. Right, Grandpa?"

"You know me too well!"

. . . .

"If we cast our minds back over our discussions, you'll find we've identified many useful TIPS. However, the *foundation* of successful wealth-creation can be summed up even more briefly."

"If we'd known *that*, Grandpa," quipped Kevin, "we might have shown up just for today!"

"That's why I kept it to myself till now, Kevin. In fact, all **120 TIPS** can be boiled down to the following **fifteen** *overall strategies*:

1. Always strive for *best-value* from your disposable income.

2. Except for mortgage and education loans, avoid interest-bearing debt.

3. Reduce debt-drag on wealth-creation by paying off all debt as quickly as possible.

4. As early in life as possible, create a lifelong habit of saving.

5. Automate the process of saving through the *Pay Yourself First* approach – preferably at 10% of salary. Once you have a partner, encourage a similar habit.

6. Develop a financial plan early; update it as often as your circumstances change.

7. For financial planning and investment advice, consult an accountant, and *only* financial advisors who are totally *independent*.

8. Minimize tax on investments by investing through TFSAs and RRSPs, RESPs for children's education, and RDSPs for disabled family members.

9. Other than for shorter-term saving targets through TFSAs, invest for the *long-term*. Be an investor, not a trader.

10. *Diversify* investments within a product class, between classes, and internationally.

11. Minimize initial and ongoing costs, by investing primarily through Index Funds and Exchange-Traded Funds.

12. Buy sufficient insurance to cover potential catastrophic events – *do not* mix insurance with investment.

13. Moderate investment-mix proportions, and hence risk, as retirement years approach.

14. Integrate investment strategies with CPP and OAS benefit entitlements.

15. For retirement years, develop, and regularly update, a tax-effective *income-withdrawal plan*, which complements the post-retirement *financial plan*."

....

"Unreal! You've just boiled the next seventy years of my life down into fifteen key points!" exclaimed Jenny. "But when you summarize it like that, Grandpa, it all sure makes sense. With what we've learned about each concept, they *should* be relatively easy to follow."

"You sure know how to put it all in a nutshell, Grandpa," added Kevin. "For me, the superstars are still the **Pay Yourself First** saving concept, and the **Couch Potato** investing strategy. I'm convinced that these will result in really incredible long-term benefits.

It's a given that I'll do my best to follow these principles. I definitely plan to become an *inflation-adjusted* millionaire," added Kevin. "Top of my list too, is to be *able* to retire early, if that's what I end up wanting!"

"No doubt about it. You're both smart enough to put these strategies and all the related TIPS to work, *and* to be able to retire wealthy – and early, if you wish!"

....

"Now it's time for me to honor the commitment I made before we started our Saturday sessions. As I'm *sure* you recall, I promised that if you were to sit through this entire learning process, you would each receive $1,000, to add to your investment account.

How to invest it would be your decision.

You are both now knowledgeable enough to make that decision. Here are your cheques."

"Thanks, Grandpa!" exclaimed Jenny, "I actually thought you were kidding when you made that offer. I like this – no exam, free lunches, and $1,000 to boot. How can you beat that for a deal? You won't mind if I go out and buy a new wardrobe? *Just kidding!*

After what you told us about available Dividend ETFs, with their solid dividends and DRIP features, that's how I'm investing my $1,000."

"Likewise, Grandpa. Thanks a lot! I'm with Jenny on those ETFs. They sound like a great long-term investment," added Kevin. "But *please* don't forget to put all our chats in that book you promised. I know we'll need to refresh our memory – over and over again!"

"I'll get started on it right away, Kevin, before it all fades away. I imagine a lot of your friends might appreciate the same wealth-creation insight that you now enjoy."

"Speaking of appreciation, Grandpa," invited Jenny, "and to butter up our *ongoing*, cheap independent advisor, Kevin and I pooled our resources to buy *you* lunch next Saturday. You're our guest, but it'll have to be something really inexpensive. You'd have our heads on a platter if we had to break into the $1,000 just for lunch."

"Once our investments really pay off, Grandpa," added Kevin, "we'll take you out again, and *you'll* be able to name the place!"

"Thanks to both of you for your thoughtfulness! I'll be happy to join you for a burger, and *no lesson*, next Saturday.

I've really enjoyed our get-togethers. Holler anytime you have questions as you navigate through life, building your wealth and financial independence."

"Thanks again, Grandpa!" echoed both Jenny and Kevin.

POSTSCRIPT
. . . .

Writing this book was prompted by the obvious interest of two of our grandchildren, in saving and investment with their own modest, but growing investment portfolios.

I enjoyed sharing my knowledge, often acquired the hard way, over some 40 years of experiences.

It is my hope that other Canadians, of all ages, will benefit from the key principles underlying this book, and from the individual **TIPS** highlighted throughout.

It is important that every reader view my advice as only one key source of information, as they make their own strategic saving and investment decisions.

Although I believe very strongly in the outlined principles, I recognize that every individual is different, with unique needs, aspirations, and levels of risk-tolerance.

Only by carefully considering your own combination of factors – age, family size, income level, and retirement expectations, can you arrive at the ***best strategies for you***.

Never be shy about retaining the services of an *independent financial planner, advisor, or accountant*. Test my advice, as well as the advisor's, as you develop *your* personal approach. A good advisor may help you arrive at a low-risk plan which you can then implement and manage yourself.

As a rule, Canadians are living longer. Many spend almost as many years in retirement as they did in the workforce. Retirees tend to live reasonably well, thanks largely to our first-rate social support systems and favorable seniors' tax laws.

It is my hope that the contents of this book will help readers enhance their net-worth, and eventual retirement income.

But why be merely comfortable for all those retirement years when, with a little knowledge and effort, we can become *very* comfortable?

Here's to your becoming a successful and *Smart Canadian Wealth-Builder*.

One last *TIP*:

SPEND SMART!

SAVE SMART!

INVEST SMART!

....

Your comments are welcome. I can be reached by e-mail at **pdolezal@smartcanadianwealthbuilder.ca**

My website: **www.dolezalconsultants.ca**